D1603521

Brent Scowcroft

Biographies
IN AMERICAN FOREIGN POLICY
Joseph A. Fry, University of Nevada, Las Vegas
Series Editor

The Biographies in American Foreign Policy Series employs the enduring medium of biography to examine the major episodes and themes in the history of U.S. foreign relations. By viewing policy formation and implementation from the perspective of influential participants, the series humanizes and makes more accessible those decisions and events that sometimes appear abstract or distant. Particular attention is devoted to those aspects of the subject's background, personality, and intellect that most influenced his or her approach to U.S. foreign policy, and each individual's role is placed in a context that takes into account domestic affairs, national interests and policies, and international and strategic considerations.

Volumes Published

Lawrence S. Kaplan, *Thomas Jefferson: Westward the Course of Empire*

Richard H. Immerman, *John Foster Dulles: Piety, Pragmatism, and Power in U.S. Foreign Policy*

Thomas W. Zeiler, *Dean Rusk: Defending the American Mission Abroad*

Edward P. Crapol, *James G. Blaine: Architect of Empire*

David F. Schmitz, *Henry L. Stimson: The First Wise Man*

Thomas M. Leonard, *James K. Polk: A Clear and Unquestionable Destiny*

James E. Lewis, Jr., *John Quincy Adams: Policymaker for the Union*

Catherine Forslund, *Anna Chennault: Informal Diplomacy and Asian Relations*

Lawrence S. Kaplan, *Alexander Hamilton: Ambivalent Anglophile*

Andrew J. DeRoche, *Andrew Young: Civil Rights Ambassador*

Jeffrey J. Matthews, *Alanson B. Houghton: Ambassador of the New Era*

Clarence E. Wunderlin, Jr., *Robert A. Taft: Ideas, Tradition, and Party in U.S. Foreign Policy*

Howard Jablon, *David M. Shoup: A Warrior against War*

Jeff Woods, *Richard B. Russell: Southern Nationalism and American Foreign Policy*

Russell D. Buhite, *Douglas MacArthur: Statecraft and Stagecraft in America's East Asian Policy*

Christopher D. O'Sullivan, *Colin Powell: American Power and Intervention from Vietnam to Iraq*

David F. Schmitz, *Brent Scowcroft: Internationalism and Post–Vietnam War American Foreign Policy*

Brent Scowcroft

Internationalism and Post–Vietnam War American Foreign Policy

David F. Schmitz

ROWMAN & LITTLEFIELD PUBLISHERS, INC.
Lanham • Boulder • New York • Toronto • Plymouth, UK

Published by Rowman & Littlefield Publishers, Inc.
A wholly owned subsidiary of The Rowman & Littlefield Publishing Group, Inc.
4501 Forbes Boulevard, Suite 200, Lanham, Maryland 20706
http://www.rowmanlittlefield.com

Estover Road, Plymouth PL6 7PY, United Kingdom

British Library Cataloguing in Publication Information Available

Library of Congress Cataloging-in-Publication Data

Schmitz, David F.
  Brent Scowcroft : internationalism and post-Vietnam war American foreign
policy / David F. Schmitz.
      p. cm. — (Biographies in American foreign policy)
  Includes bibliographical references and index.
  ISBN 978-0-7425-7040-5 (cloth : alk. paper) — ISBN 978-0-7425-7042-9
(electronic)
  1. Scowcroft, Brent. 2. National Security Council (U.S.)—Biography. 3. Cabinet
officers—United States—Biography. 4. Internationalists—United States—
Biography. 5. United States—Foreign relations—1989- 6. United States—
Foreign relations—1974-1977. 7. United States—Foreign relations—1981–1989. I.
Title.
  E840.8.S38S36 2011
  353.1'224092—dc22
  [B]   2010039017

Printed in the United States of America

To Polly

Contents

Acknowledgments

This book is dedicated to my wife Polly. From her positive response the first time I mentioned that I was thinking of writing about Brent Scowcroft to the editing of the final paragraph, she has provided the consistent support, understanding, and love necessary to finish this project.

It was my great pleasure and fortune to work again with Andy Fry, the series editor. He helped me shape the scope of the book, sharpen my analysis, and clarify my conclusions with his probing questions and sharp editorial pen. He is an ideal editor, and his support and input have made this a much better work. I thank Niels Aaboe for including my book in this series, and Michelle Cassidy, Sarah David, and Melissa McNitt for all of their assistance during the publication process. It has been a pleasure to work with each of them.

The archivists at the Gerald R. Ford and George H. W. Bush presidential libraries were unfailingly professional and helpful in my research. In particular, Geir Gunderson at the Ford Library and Elizabeth Meyers at the Bush Library went out of their way in providing assistance and expert advice.

Whitman College provided generous support that allowed me to travel to the various archives to conduct research and provided release time for writing. Former provost and dean of the faculty Lori Bettison-Varga enthusiastically encouraged my work, and I thank her for the support she provided. The college also provided funds through the Lewis B. Perry Summer Research Scholarship Program, which allowed me to hire Destiny Cowdin-Lynch for two summers. Destiny was an exemplary research

assistant who helped me during my research at the Ford and Bush libraries; in collecting and analyzing Scowcroft's op-ed pieces; in locating documents in the public record, particularly online; and in conducting specific
research on the Helsinki Accords and Scowcroft's views on détente. She
also read early drafts of the introduction and first chapter and helped
me to clarify my thoughts throughout. Lee Keene, head of reference and
information literacy at Whitman's Penrose Library, provided enormous
assistance in locating some difficult-to-obtain documents. Eleanor Zais
Schroeder helped with the final research on the chronology and in identi-
fying photographs for the book, and Kathy Guizar of Image Management
in Walla Walla again provided me with her expertise in preparing the
photographs for the book. Keith Farrington lent me his recording ma-
chine to conduct interviews and assisted me with the process of moving
them to my computer.

Lloyd Gardner helped me work out some of my interpretations in two
long conversations on Scowcroft. He also invited me to participate in a
conference on the fiftieth anniversary of the publication of William Appleman Williams's *The Tragedy of American Diplomacy* at Rutgers University
in April 2009, where I first presented some of my research on Scowcroft.
I am grateful to him for sharing his vast knowledge on American foreign
policy with me over the past thirty years, as well as for his mentoring
and his friendship. Bartholomew H. Sparrow generously shared some of
his insights and knowledge on Scowcroft in a conversation at the 2009
conference of the Society for Historians of American Foreign Relations,
and he provided me with copies of documents from the Jimmy Carter
Presidential Library.

Ambassador Ryan Crocker assisted me in setting up an interview with
Brent Scowcroft and shared his insights and knowledge about the Middle
East and American foreign policy, which have helped shape my understanding of the Gulf War and the War in Iraq. I also thank my former
student Danielle Garbe of the State Department for helping to arrange my
interview with Condoleezza Rice.

To return to where I started, I want to thank my family for the consistent support they provide for my work. Going to Washington, D.C., to
conduct research has greater value now that my daughter Nicole lives
there. During the writing of this book, we also welcomed James Ward into
the family as our son-in-law. His required reading list just grew. My son
Kincaid has always understood my having to miss some of his games or
other events due to research travel. His growing questions about American history have provided me with new opportunities to think through
the issues in this book. Polly enhances it all.

Chronology

1925   March 19: Brent Scowcroft is born in Ogden, Utah.
1941   January 6: Roosevelt delivers his "Four Freedoms" speech.
       February 7: Henry Luce's editorial "The American Century" is published in *Life* magazine.
       December 7: Japan attacks Pearl Harbor.
1946   February 22: The Long Telegram, written by U.S. ambassador to the Soviet Union George Kennan, arrives in Washington.
1947   March 12: President Truman delivers his "Truman Doctrine" speech.
       June 5: Scowcroft graduates from the U.S. Military Academy at West Point.
       July 25: Congress passes the National Security Act, which establishes the National Security Council, the Air Force, the Central Intelligence Agency, and the Department of Defense.
1948   October: Scowcroft graduates from pilot training.
1949   April 4: The North Atlantic Treaty Organization (NATO) is formed.
1953   June: Scowcroft earns his Master of Arts degree from Columbia University.
       July: Scowcroft is appointed assistant professor and teaches Russian history in the Department of Social Sciences at West Point.
1957   August: Scowcroft enrolls in the Strategic Intelligence School in Washington, D.C.
1959   June: Scowcroft begins a two-year tour as assistant air attaché at the American embassy in Belgrade, Yugoslavia.

1961   January 20: President John F. Kennedy appoints McGeorge Bundy to serve as the first official national security advisor.

1962   February: Scowcroft is appointed associate professor and acting head of the Political Science Department at the U.S. Air Force Academy.

1964   September: Scowcroft joins Headquarters, U.S. Air Force, in the Office of the Deputy Chief of Staff, Plans and Operations and serves in the Long Range Planning Division, Directorate of Doctrine, Concepts and Objectives.

1965   March 8: The first U.S. ground troops enter Vietnam.

1967   June: Scowcroft earns his doctorate in international relations from Columbia University.
        September: Scowcroft enrolls as a student at the National War College.

1968   July: Scowcroft is assigned to the Office of the Assistant Secretary of Defense for International Security Affairs and serves in the Western Hemisphere Region.
        November 5: Richard Nixon is elected president.

1969   July 25: Nixon announces the Nixon Doctrine.
        September: Scowcroft is reassigned to Headquarters, U.S. Air Force, in the Directorate of Plans as deputy assistant for National Security Council matters.

1970   March: Scowcroft is appointed special assistant to the director of the Joint Chiefs of Staff.

1972   February: Scowcroft is appointed military assistant to the president.
        May 26: The Strategic Arms Limitation Treaty I (SALT I) is signed.

1973   January 27: The Paris Peace Agreement is signed ending U.S. military involvement in the Vietnam War.
        April 6: Scowcroft is appointed deputy assistant to the president for national security affairs.
        September 11: A U.S.-supported coup ousts Chilean president Salvador Allende.
        October 17: The Organization of Petroleum Exporting Countries (OPEC) imposes an oil embargo on the United States.

1974   August 8: Nixon resigns and Gerald R. Ford succeeds to the presidency.
        August 16: Scowcroft is promoted to lieutenant general.

1975   April 30: Saigon falls, bringing an end to the Vietnam War.
        May 12–15: The *Mayaguez* affair occurs.
        August 1: The Helsinki Accords are signed.
        November 4: Ford names Scowcroft as his national security advisor.

December 1: Scowcroft retires from the U.S. Air Force with the rank of lieutenant general.

1976 March 22: The so-called Sonnenfeldt Doctrine is published in the *Washington Post.*

November 3: James "Jimmy" Carter is elected president.

1977 May 22: Carter gives a commencement address at Notre Dame University emphasizing his commitment to a foreign policy based on human rights.

1979 June 18: SALT II is signed.

July 17: Saddam Hussein declares himself president of Iraq.

December 27: The Soviet Union invades Afghanistan.

1980 January 23: Carter announces the Carter Doctrine for the Persian Gulf.

September 22: Iraq invades Iran, beginning the Iran-Iraq War.

November 4: Ronald Reagan is elected president.

1983 January 3: Reagan appoints Scowcroft the chairman of the President's Commission on Strategic Forces (the Scowcroft Commission).

March 8: Reagan labels the Soviet Union the "evil empire."

October 23: Terrorists bomb the U.S. marine barracks in Beirut, Lebanon.

1985 February 6: Reagan announces the Reagan Doctrine.

July 15: Reagan appoints Scowcroft to the President's Blue Ribbon Commission on Defense Management.

1986 November 26: The Iran-Contra scandal breaks.

December 1: Scowcroft is appointed a member of the President's Special Review Board (the Tower Commission) in the investigation of the Iran-Contra affair.

1988 November 8: George H. W. Bush is elected president.

1989 January 20: Scowcroft is appointed national security advisor.

May 12: Bush announces his "Beyond Containment" strategy.

June 3: Protests in Tiananmen Square climax when thousands of student demonstrators are wounded and killed by armed units of the People's Liberation Army.

July 2: Scowcroft departs with Deputy Secretary of State Lawrence Eagleburger for secret meetings in Beijing.

November 9: The Berlin Wall falls.

December 9: Scowcroft and Eagleburger return to Beijing to begin the process of restoring U.S.-China relations.

1990 February 13: "Two-plus-Four" is agreed upon by the United States, the Soviet Union, Great Britain, and France.

August 2: Iraq invades Kuwait.

August 8: Operation Desert Shield commences.

October 3: Germany is reunified and is accepted into the NATO alliance.

November 29: The United Nations adopts UN Security Council (UNSC) Resolution 678.

1991 January 12: Congress passes a resolution authorizing the use of military force to liberate Kuwait.

January 15: The deadline set by UNSC Resolution 678 for Iraqi withdrawal from Kuwait.

January 16: Operation Desert Storm begins.

February 23: Bush orders the use of ground forces against Iraqi troops in Kuwait.

February 27: Bush announces the end of the ground phase of the Persian Gulf War. Kuwait is liberated.

July: Bush presents Scowcroft with the Presidential Medal of Freedom Award.

September 2: The United States recognizes the independence of Estonia, Latvia, and Lithuania.

December 21: The Declaration of Adherence to the Commonwealth of Independent States is signed.

December 25: Soviet President Mikhail Gorbachev resigns, and the Soviet Union ceases to exist.

1992 June 5: Scowcroft becomes the first recipient of the Eisenhower Leadership Prize.

November 3: Bill Clinton is elected president.

1994 February: Scowcroft founds his international advisory company, the Scowcroft Group.

1995 June 5: Scowcroft is awarded the Distinguished Graduate Award from West Point.

1998 September 7: The book *A World Transformed*, coauthored by George H. W. Bush and Scowcroft, is published.

2000 December 12: The U.S. Supreme Court declares George W. Bush the winner of the presidential election.

2001 September 11: Terrorists attack New York City and the Pentagon.

October 7: British and American forces attack Afghanistan.

2002 January 29: President Bush announces that Iraq, Iran, and North Korea are an "axis of evil."

June 1: President Bush delivers the commencement address at West Point.

August 15: Scowcroft's article "Don't Attack Saddam" is published in the *Wall Street Journal*.

September 17: President Bush's "National Security Strategy for the United States of America" is released, providing the foundation for what would come to be known as the Bush Doctrine.

2003   March 20: Operation Iraqi Freedom begins.
        May 1: Bush declares victory in Iraq.
        December 13: Saddam Hussein is captured.
2006   December 30: Saddam Hussein is executed.
2008   November 4: Barack Obama is elected president.

Introduction: Internationalism and Post–Vietnam War Foreign Policy

Since the end of World War II and the emergence of the Cold War, there have been two pivotal moments in American foreign policy: the Vietnam War and the end of the Cold War. Both brought forth sharp debates about what direction American foreign policy should take. The Vietnam War shattered the post–World War II consensus on containment. Questions were raised about the nature of American foreign policy and the efficacy of the containment policy that had led the nation into the war. By its end, the proper direction of American foreign policy was bitterly contested, and different approaches, such as détente and a foreign policy based on human rights, emerged as alternatives for how best to promote and protect American interests in the world. Similarly, the end of the Cold War brought new and different challenges as the central defining experience of the previous forty-five years came to an end. What direction should foreign policy take and what should be the nature and extent of America's role in the world? Answers ranged from neoisolationist prescriptions to hubristic calls for an American empire. Brent Scowcroft was at the center of all of these debates as the only person to serve twice as assistant to the president for national security affairs, more commonly called the national security advisor, under President Gerald Ford from 1975 to 1977 and under President George H. W. Bush from 1989 to 1993, and as an advisor, writer, and commentator on foreign policy.

Scowcroft's long career provides a unique framework for analyzing American foreign policy from the final days of the Vietnam War to the end of the Cold War and into the twenty-first century. A West Point graduate

and career military officer, Scowcroft earned a Ph.D. in international relations at Columbia University before joining the National Security Council
as President Richard Nixon's senior military advisor in 1972. He became
the deputy assistant to the president for national security affairs in January 1973. On the basis of his extensive service as a military theorist, defense intellectual, and national security expert, Scowcroft was promoted
to lieutenant general in August 1974, the rank he held when he retired
from the military on December 1, 1975, shortly after being named President Ford's national security advisor. In his first tenure in this position,
Scowcroft played a central role in U.S. foreign policy debates following
the Vietnam War and in efforts to sustain an internationalist perspective.
He played a critical role in bringing about the Helsinki Accords of 1975
and the continuation of détente during the turmoil of the post-Vietnam
period. Scowcroft consistently provided a voice of restraint and caution
about the use of American power, seeking arms control agreements and
limitations where possible and prudent, a position he maintained under
President Jimmy Carter, who named him as a member of the President's
General Advisory Committee on Arms Control from 1978 to 1981. In
1983, President Ronald Reagan appointed him chairman of the President's Commission on Strategic Forces (the Scowcroft Commission), and
in 1986–1987, he served as a member of the President's Special Review
Board (the Tower Commission) that investigated the Iran-Contra scandal.

Scowcroft again became assistant to the president for national security affairs at the start of the first Bush administration in 1989, where
he shaped the U.S. response to the collapse of communism in Europe,
the demise of the Soviet Union, and the end of the Cold War; where he
orchestrated Washington's handling of China after the crackdown in
Tiananmen Square; and where he was the key advisor to the president
during the Gulf War. In addition, Scowcroft has been a prolific writer
on foreign policy, and he was a leading Republican critic of the war in
Iraq and of neoconservative foreign policy views. His involvement in the
development of American foreign policy over the past thirty-five years,
therefore, allows for an examination of the main events, concerns, and
debates on policy, and an analysis of both the changes and continuity in
America's relations with the rest of the world.

The National Security Council was created in 1947 to coordinate all
aspects of American foreign policy, diplomacy, defense planning, intelligence, and international economic policy. Under the direction of the
president, it brings together the secretaries of State, Defense, and Trea-
sury, along with the head of the Central Intelligence Agency (CIA), the
vice president, National Security Council staff, and others for discussion
and planning of American foreign policy. The legislation that created the
National Security Council also established the Air Force and the CIA and

formed the Department of Defense out of the departments of War and the Navy. The position of national security advisor was formally established by President John F. Kennedy to allow McGeorge Bundy to manage the growing National Security Council staff and apparatus. By the time Henry Kissinger became national security advisor under Richard Nixon, the National Security Council was the primary source of information for decision making in foreign policy, and the daily briefing by the national security advisor most mornings marked the beginning of the president's workday.

As the chief foreign policy assistant to the president, the national security advisor wields a great deal of power and influence within the executive branch. The National Security Council has its own staff that studies major foreign policy issues, defense needs and programs, and policy development; prepares special studies as requested by the president; and produces reports and recommendations on various foreign policy issues. In addition, it is designed to respond to crises by coordinating the nation's response and by providing necessary information to senior policy makers. Responsible for coordinating the often competing, and sometimes opposing, views of the State Department, the Pentagon, the CIA, and other agencies, the national security advisor controls the flow of information to the president, prepares the president's morning national security briefing, and meets with him a number of times during the course of a normal day.

Brent Scowcroft is commonly described as a protégé of Henry Kissinger and an advocate of realism in making foreign policy decisions.[1] This portrayal is misleading both in terms of what shaped General Scowcroft's thinking and in terms of his approach to policy making. While Kissinger was certainly influential in his career, Scowcroft became part of President Nixon's National Security Council staff before the two had ever worked together, and he arrived in the Nixon White House with well-defined views shaped by his military career, his study of history, and his experiences in the Cold War. While Scowcroft was well versed in the central tenets of realism, his understanding of America's role in the world and his fundamental ideas on policy making were based more on the lessons he drew from history, in particular the American experience in World War II and the development and implementation of the policy of containment, than from any adherence to a particular intellectual approach or from rigid consistency.

Scowcroft was heir to the Cold War internationalism that shaped American foreign policy after 1945, and he came to exemplify that position in the midst of debates over American foreign policy after the Vietnam War. The key tenets of his thinking, shaped by the Second World War, were that national security policy had to protect the nation from aggression, provide international stability, control arms while maintaining

President Ford confers with National Security Advisor Brent Scowcroft in the Oval Office and Secretary of State Henry Kissinger. Courtesy of the Gerald R. Ford Presidential Library.

preparedness, and shape an international environment that was conducive to America's goals and needs. He believed that the United States had to serve as a world leader, with its influence and power extended to all parts of the world. National defense was best maintained through collective security, by working with allies and with international organizations that promoted America's interests, institutions, and values. Moreover, the United States needed to retain a willingness to intervene militarily if necessary to protect its interests and to uphold U.S. policies. The bipartisan agreement on containment that marked the pre–Vietnam War years served as Scowcroft's guide for making policy and for promoting U.S. values and institutions globally. After World War II, the United States saw the Soviet Union as an aggressive and expansive power, hostile to U.S. interests and determined to spread communism around the globe. Similarly to World War II, the United States was faced with an enemy that threatened its security and freedom in the world. The lesson learned at Munich, that you cannot appease an aggressor, was adopted to guide postwar American policy in an ostensibly bipolar world where all international events were connected to the struggle against communism.

Like so many of his generation, Scowcroft believed that the United States was an exceptional nation, different from other great powers that had come before it and uniquely qualified to lead and solve world problems. American ideals and values were universal and were therefore welcomed by people in other lands. For this reason, Scowcroft asserted that "only the United States can exercise enlightened leadership," not through dictates, but by setting the correct direction for the world community to follow: "We're the only ones who can be the guiding light."[2] For Scowcroft, this meant leadership by example, multilateral cooperation, and pragmatic policies designed to achieve what was historically possible at the time. He was well aware, however, of the dangers inherent in this view and of how easily these ideas could become hubris and lead to disaster. Scowcroft saw this as a central dilemma that policy makers had to manage. Yet his belief in American exceptionalism also provided confidence that the United States could find the right balance for leading without being resented by others, could overcome any paradoxes in its policies, and could serve both its own national interests and the interests of others. His battles with those who opposed the foreign policy he recommended and implemented revolved around this problem.

While not always successful, Scowcroft provided a consistent internationalist voice in the midst of change. The end of the war in Southeast Asia elicited new challenges to the internationalist policy of containment from Congress, which sought more of a say and oversight in the making of policy. Advocates of giving human rights a more prominent role in policy making, and those who sought reduced American involvement in the Third World, also argued for moving beyond containment. Moreover, there were divisions among those who wanted to maintain the policy of containment. Some continued to hold to the verities of the Cold War containment policy as developed in the 1940s and 1950s, while others supported détente as the proper policy toward the Soviet Union. In navigating these debates, Scowcroft developed a reputation as an honest, deliberative, and open-minded advisor who listened to different arguments and represented divergent positions fairly, as a strategic thinker who took a broad view of events and policy, and as loyal to the president he served.

During his second tenure as national security advisor, Scowcroft's cautious attitude provided the right tone and approach to the rapidly changing events in Eastern Europe and the Soviet Union. He sought to work with like-minded Republicans and Democrats to construct a post–Cold War foreign policy that would provide consistency and stability in American policy making in the new international environment, that would defend the internationalist position from challenges and criticisms, and that would buffer the conduct of diplomacy from the turbulence of domestic politics. He continued to believe in the necessity of U.S. preeminence in the world, in the need to work with allies, and in the value of promoting stability to secure American interests. He saw all of this at stake after Iraq's invasion of Kuwait in 1990, and he persuaded President Bush that the United States had to mobilize the international community against Saddam Hussein to liberate Kuwait. In doing so, the administration drew parallels to World War II, Munich, and the need to confront aggression, and it sought to construct a foreign policy that would create what Scowcroft termed a "new world order" in the wake of the Cold War.

With the collapse of the Soviet Union and the end of the Cold War, Scowcroft worried that the public would no longer support an active and extensive role for the United States in world affairs. Simultaneously, he was concerned about the emerging Cold War triumphalism of the neo-conservatives and their hubristic visions of American power, a disagreement that would come to a head during the run-up to the second Iraq War. Scowcroft and his allies had been unable to reconstruct a foreign policy consensus in the wake of the Vietnam War, and the climate at the end of the Cold War proved no more amenable. Through it all, in achievements and failures, Scowcroft held to his convictions, and his career was an instructive reflection of the debates, crises, frustrations, and accomplishments of the time.

NOTES

1. Excellent recent examples include Jeffrey Goldberg, "Breaking Ranks: What Turned Brent Scowcroft against the Bush Administration," *New Yorker*, 31 October 2005; and Bartholomew H. Sparrow, "Realism's Practitioner: Brent Scowcroft and the Making of the New World Order, 1980–1993," *Diplomatic History*, January 2010, 141–75.

2. Zbigniew Brzezinski and Brent Scowcroft, *America and the World: Conversations on the Future of American Foreign Policy*, moderated by David Ignatius (New York: Basic Books, 2008), 35.

1

✦

Accidental Policy Maker

In early 1972, Brent Scowcroft became a member of the National Security Council, working as the military assistant to the president. That year, during a trip on Air Force One, he got into a confrontation with White House Chief of Staff H. R. Haldeman, who was admonishing Scowcroft about a procedural matter. National Security Advisor Henry Kissinger witnessed the exchange: "I saw Scowcroft disagreeing with Haldeman," Kissinger recalled, "and Haldeman very imperiously tried to insist on his point of view, but Scowcroft disagreed with him, and he was a terrier who had got hold of someone's leg and wouldn't let it go. In his polite and mild manner, he insisted on his view, which was correct . . . [and] he was challenging Haldeman at the height of Haldeman's power." At this time, Kissinger was looking for a deputy, a person of character, personal strength, and backbone. "I knew a lot of people with intelligence," Kissinger noted, "but I needed a strong person as my deputy, who would be willing to stand up to me if necessary—not every day—but to stand up for what he thought was right."[1] Soon after, Scowcroft was named the deputy assistant to the president for national security affairs.

This vignette is instructive for understanding Scowcroft's rise to the position of national security advisor. He had steadily moved up in the Air Force by consistently impressing his superiors with his intelligence, thoroughness in preparation, breadth of knowledge, straightforwardness of manner, and commitment to serve, all of which allowed him to earn his first general's star without having seen any combat or led any operations. Scowcroft held personal honor, duty, service, loyalty, and honesty as the highest values. As a military officer, he had a sense of obligation to serve the country and a clear code for the proper conduct of the nation's affairs. He was widely respected for his probity and his loyalty, as well as for his desire to foster discussion, his willingness to listen to opposing viewpoints, and his ability to build consensus around a policy.

Another key trait that led him to the National Security Council was his modesty. Scowcroft noted jokingly that his selection as Kissinger's deputy came about because he was a Mormon, and "Mormons were supposed to be loyal and faithful."[2] This self-effacing humor was telling, as Scowcroft did not seek public attention, was nonpartisan in his approach to issues and problems, and sought to build consensus on policies and decisions. What concerned him was the proper process, evaluating information, and achieving goals. Indeed, he epitomized the saying that a lot can be accomplished if you do not care who gets the credit.

Scowcroft never questioned his core belief in the need for U.S. leadership in the world for maintaining stability, peace, and prosperity, nor the central components of the internationalist approach to policy making, which emphasized collective security, cooperation with allies, military preparedness, the promotion of American interests and institutions abroad, and the need to prevent aggression. These ideas guided him at all times, and he remained convinced that enemies could be contained and defeated while the nation's influence spread. People of goodwill and

National Security Advisor Brent Scowcroft listens intently during a National Security Council meeting. Courtesy of the Gerald R. Ford Presidential Library.

peaceful intentions would understand that American leadership served their interests, as well as the interests of the United States, and that it would lead to a more peaceful and prosperous world.

Born March 19, 1925, Scowcroft was raised in a middle-class Mormon family in Ogden, Utah. His father owned a grocery business that provided food and other essentials to much of northern Utah. Scowcroft attended the city's public schools, and it was there at the age of twelve that he read about West Point and began planning to attend. He recalls that there was something about being a cadet that "just captured me." His father, who had not graduated from high school, encouraged his son's ambition, and the young Scowcroft received his appointment to the U.S. Military Academy in the middle of World War II, assuming "when I went in that I would fight." The war ended before he graduated, and he was left wondering what he would do. During the summer of 1945, he was in upstate New York training on mortars on V-J Day, and he found himself thinking, "What the hell am I doing here? The war is over. There aren't going to be any more wars." Scowcroft graduated in 1947 and joined the Army Air Corps because "all my friends were joining."[3] It was a fateful decision.

His career as a fighter pilot was brief. During training, Scowcroft was flying an F-51 Mustang while practicing dogfighting. The pilot he was training with gained an advantage immediately after takeoff. Scowcroft pushed the plane's speed, causing the propeller to overspin and the governor to break. As he lost power, he maneuvered for an emergency landing, searching for an opening as he flew low over the forest of New Hampshire. The last things he remembered were checking his airspeed, which was about ninety miles per hour, "the speed at which the F-51 Mustang stalls," and "looking under my wing at the tops of the last trees." He had broken his back and was told he could never fly again. "And when you suddenly can't do what you thought you were destined to, you simply have to find something else to do."[4] For Scowcroft, that became studying history and international politics, teaching, and becoming a defense intelligence expert, especially regarding arms and airpower. This alternative path led him to the National Security Council.

Scowcroft earned a master's degree in 1953 from Columbia University and went back to West Point to teach Russian History for four years. In 1957, he entered the Strategic Intelligence School in Washington, D.C. Starting in June 1959, Scowcroft served a two-year term as the assistant air attaché in the American embassy in Belgrade, Yugoslavia, an assignment that played a significant role in his thinking about the problems of Eastern Europe and issues of nationalism later in his career. In 1962, he transferred to the Air Force Academy as a professor and head of the Political Science Department.

Scowcroft's first policy-making assignment in Washington, D.C., came in September 1964 when he joined the headquarters of the U.S. Air Force in the Office of the Deputy Chief of Staff, Plans and Operations and served in the Long Range Planning Division, Directorate of Doctrine, Concepts and Objectives. He left the Air Force headquarters in June 1966 to complete his Ph.D. in international relations at Columbia University in 1967. In his dissertation, Scowcroft examined the role of Congress in making foreign policy by analyzing foreign aid programs to Spain and Yugoslavia. Not surprisingly, he found that "Congress can have a significant, even decisive, impact on the foreign policy behavior of the United States where the involvement of the appropriation process gives it the requisite power." More significantly, Scowcroft concluded that the attitude of Congress toward foreign policy was more conservative than that of the executive branch, and that the legislature "appears unwilling to subordinate ideological considerations to those of pragmatic national interest." Emotion and ideology, not a sophisticated grasp of issues and interests, drove congressional thinking and action.[5] This conclusion re-inforced Scowcroft's conviction that policy making had to be buffered against domestic politics or rash decisions made in the heat of the moment. A broader and longer view was necessary to effectively defend the nation's interests.

Scowcroft spent the 1967–1968 academic year as a student at the National War College, whose motto, "Trained in Theory, Crowned in Practice," he found compatible with his own thinking and approach. Upon completion of his year of study in Washington, D.C., in 1968 General Scowcroft was sent to the Office of the Assistant Secretary of Defense for International Security Affairs where he served in the Western Hemisphere Region. Scowcroft was reassigned to the headquarters of the U.S. Air Force in September 1969, this time in the Directorate of Plans as the deputy assistant for National Security Council matters, a position that put him inside the White House for the first time. In March 1970, he joined the Organization of the Joint Chiefs of Staff and became the special assistant to the director of the Joint Staff, a position he held until he became the military assistant to the president in 1972, at which point he came to the attention of National Security Advisor Henry Kissinger and was promoted to deputy assistant for national security.

A SOLDIER IN THE COLD WAR

Scowcroft's understanding of international affairs was shaped by his historical studies and knowledge of the twentieth century. While many others saw World War II and the emergence of the Cold War as a distinct break with the past, Scowcroft believed that the period from World War I through the Cold War was of a whole, and he would come to see the end of the Cold War as marking a sharp historical discontinuity. As Scowcroft noted in his joint memoir with President George H. W. Bush, the end of the Cold War "concluded nearly three quarters of a century of upheaval, the tides of totalitarianism, world wars, and nuclear standoff."[6] For the lieutenant general, the Great War was an epochal conflict. The period of the late nineteenth and early twentieth centuries, he believed, was one of great optimism and progress that seemed to promise scientific, economic, and social advancement. World War I, in contrast, was a barbaric struggle, one that shattered the confidence of Europe and gave rise to antiliberal thought and antidemocratic movements that claimed the liberal state was at its end. "World War I resulted in a whole series of consequences, among which were communism and fascism, those social movements to reorder society that racked the world. It also marked the end of the world's great empires. Two of them collapsed at the end of World War I: the Ottoman Empire and the Austro-Hungarian. And the last to go was the Soviet." Thus, it set in motion the main currents of unrest and conflict during the twentieth century—the Great Depression, World War II, the Cold War, and the rising aspirations of the Third World—that bred revolution and war and threatened American interests and national security. As Scowcroft noted in 2008, the "current axis of turmoil running from the Balkans up through central Asia is also the territory of the last of the world's empires."[7]

World War I also marked a break for the United States from the policy of nonentangling alliances and neutrality in Europe's disputes. Woodrow Wilson's effort to overcome this legacy was the first attempt to move the nation toward acceptance of an internationalist perspective on foreign policy. In particular, with his Fourteen Points and the establishment of the League of Nations, President Wilson sought to establish a new international order in which the United States played a crucial role in postwar Europe. Scowcroft agreed with much of the realist critique of Wilson's ambitions. He thought Wilson's vision was ill-conceived, as it set the United States out to transform other nations, and that Wilson's emphasis on pushing for democracy in the world was certain to fail and involve the United States in conflicts that did not serve the national interest. "When we say we are going to make the world democratic," Scowcroft opined, "that's too much."[8] At the same time, the Treaty of Versailles was a victor's peace that guaranteed resentment and instability in postwar Europe.

Scowcroft also believed, however, that Wilson correctly recognized the need for the United States to be actively involved in European settlements, and that his failure stemmed from overreaching and trying to transform Europe. A more modest goal, of creating a peaceful world order led by the United States in order to protect liberalism and secure support for international institutions, Scowcroft thought, could have succeeded. On this issue, he was more in line with thinkers such as Elihu Root, who sought to reshape the international system around rule of law, military preparedness, collective security, and a close alliance with Great Britain, an Atlanticist approach to national security that became central to the World War II internationalism of Franklin D. Roosevelt. Instead, Wilson's ill-fated effort to gain American participation in the League of Nations produced a political backlash against the Treaty of Versailles and against the United States assuming its proper role in the world.

When analyzing history or making policy recommendations and decisions, therefore, Scowcroft did not see himself as guided by realism or the specific prescriptions of a foreign policy school of thought. If the choice was only the dichotomy of idealist versus realist, then he was on the realist side, but he called himself an enlightened realist and was not bound by strict categories or ideological commitments. Indeed, Scowcroft agreed more with Henry Luce than he did with Wilson's realist critics that in 1919 the United States missed "a golden opportunity . . . to assume the leadership of the world,"[9] not as a result of misguided idealism but due to faulty policy making, an effort to impose democracy rather than support it, and the public's misunderstanding of the essential role of the United States in the world. The result was the rise of fascism, the Great Depression, and another world war. World War II, in Scowcroft's view, provided the United States with a second chance to achieve world leadership and foster an internationalist foreign policy that avoided Wilson's overreaching.

Moreover, Scowcroft rejected certain core elements of realist thought. He has noted that, "When I went to graduate school, Hans Morgenthau's *Politics among Nations* was the bible for students of international politics. At his purest, Morgenthau held that international politics is a struggle for power, and that power is the only thing that matters. States try to maximize their own power or that of their group against other groups."[10] Yet, conducting diplomacy is about much more than just a struggle for power, he acknowledged; nor is power the only or even the most important factor in making policy. Idealism is also essential, and the United States, he believed, should strive to promote its values and institutions in the world. The problem with idealism, from Scowcroft's perspective, was that it could lead policy makers to focus on the goal and neglect the means and the dangers of trying to achieve important objectives. It was essential not to cause more problems in the process of trying to achieve ideals that were out of reach. Instead, sights should be lowered to goals than can be realized at a reasonable cost while serving as an example to other nations and as a beacon for freedom. "Realism," Scowcroft believed, "is a recognition of the limits of what can be achieved. It's not what your goals are, but what can you realistically do." It was necessary, therefore, to "strike some balance between the extremes of realism and idealism."[11]

It was essential, Scowcroft was convinced, that the United States be "the focal point around which nations can gather." Only the United States "can serve as the galvanizer of the world on behalf of great ideas and great projects." Washington did not have all the answers, but the United States was "essential" for international cooperation, economic progress, and the promotion of freedom. For there to be peace, the fundamental values of liberalism and the liberal state had to take hold around the world. Scowcroft, therefore, deemed the "Atlantic community" to be vital in providing world leadership.[12] "American exceptionalism," in Scowcroft's view, "is really based on the idea of human dignity. . . . In that sense, everybody wants to be like us. They want a better life."[13] Only the United States could serve as the guiding force and inspiration for the maintenance of peace and prosperity. In this, he was building on the internationalist views of Franklin D. Roosevelt during World War II.

As part of his battles against isolationist thought, Roosevelt framed the internationalist definition of America's role in the world. During World War II, his beliefs that the United States had to be a world leader, working in consort with its allies and through the United Nations to protect the national interest through collective security and to promote American values, became the guiding principles upon which the postwar policy of containment was built. For Scowcroft, Roosevelt's vision of the four freedoms—freedom from want, freedom from fear, freedom of speech, and freedom of religion—and his efforts to continue the Grand Alliance through the United Nations Security Council, what FDR called the "four policemen," were the right ideas and approach. But they were a little premature given the Soviet Union's postwar totalitarian threat to the West. In particular, communism challenged the fundamental "notions that motivate Western Civilization, man and his relationship to the state." America's liberal values were not shared or understood by "much of the world."[14]

Thus the central paradox for American foreign policy, according to Scowcroft, was to reconcile the position that the United States and the liberal state were central to world peace and prosperity with the understanding that Washington did not have all the answers. The dilemma arose over how to extend American influence in the world without overstepping the limits of power and influence. Washington could not dictate what others should do, but instead should provide leadership and direction to the world community, because the United States was "exceptional in offering hope."[15]

After World War II, it was axiomatic to American internationalists that the United States should accept responsibility for the postwar world, should provide global leadership, and should ensure postwar peace and prosperity through the promotion of free trade, self-determination, and collective security. Only the United States could decide whether freedom would flourish and the world would progress materially. If the United States failed, economic depression, war, and revolution would return. For American leaders, political freedom and capitalism were interrelated, and American prosperity was dependent upon world trade, access to markets and raw materials, and European recovery. President Truman articulated this in 1947 when he announced that "peace, freedom, and world trade" were inseparable. The only thing Americans valued more than peace, he declared, was freedom: "freedom of worship—freedom of speech—freedom of enterprise."[16] These were inseparable and had to be protected.

The Soviet Union threatened this American vision of peace and prosperity. As postwar problems mounted, it appeared that Moscow was the source of all difficulties. George F. Kennan wrote from the Soviet capital that the United States was faced with "a political force committed fanatically to the belief that with US there can be no permanent *modus vivendi*, that it is desirable and necessary that the internal harmony of our society be disrupted, our traditional way of life destroyed, the international authority of our state destroyed."[17] He recommended a policy of opposition to Soviet postwar demands and containment of Soviet power.

The central theme of the Truman Doctrine, announced in March 1947, was that there was a global contest between the free world and totalitarian communism, and a broad consensus emerged in Washington that the containment of communism had to be the basis of American foreign policy. Policy makers agreed that the Soviet Union was an aggressive, expansive power, hostile to American interests, and a threat to the nation. Moreover, communism was seen as monolithic, emanating from Moscow to other parts of the world. It was, therefore, a bipolar world where any gain for the Soviet Union was a defeat for the United States. Similar to World War II, the United States faced an enemy that was the antithesis of its values and posed a threat to its security and international interests. The lesson of Munich, that an aggressor cannot be appeased, was quickly applied by American policy makers, and Scowcroft rarely wavered from his commitment to this cornerstone of American national security policy.

The most important postwar actions, in Scowcroft's estimation, were the Marshall Plan, for European economic recovery and stability, and the North Atlantic Treaty Organization, to ensure collective security and an American commitment to preparedness and European defense. "After World War II," the United States established a "new world order governed by open systems." The American commitment to postwar European reconstruction was intended to remedy the mistakes made after the Great War and embodied certain fundamental aims.[18] The main goals, Scowcroft believes, were an adequate defense of the nation's security, economic cooperation, and political stability. For Scowcroft, this meant a middle course between those who downplayed the Soviet threat to the United States, or who thought the nation could make common cause with communism, and others who believed that only the use of force could contain Moscow. Scowcroft always saw the Soviet danger as real and active, and he was a consistent advocate of sufficient arms and preparedness. Simultaneously, he thought it foolish to believe the Soviets could be forced to capitulate and dangerous to advocate preventive war. The goal had to be to contain the Soviet Union by whatever means available, while leaving room for negotiations.

For any policy to be successful, Scowcroft believed, it had to maintain the support of the American people and their willingness to meet the demands of world leadership. Scowcroft thought that the history of the first half of the twentieth century should have convinced the American public that the nation's prosperity was dependent on collective security and that the United States could never thrive or have peace if it failed to maintain its global commitments and responsibilities. These commitments had costs, but Scowcroft contended that a world without American leadership would be forever unstable and dangerous. Moreover, the wisdom of an internationalist approach and of shouldering global responsibilities existed independently of the Soviet challenge. The essential question remained—could the United States defend its national interests in freedom and prosperity, and shape an international order conducive to its institutions and values?

In forming his views, Scowcroft was part of what Thomas Paterson has termed the "containment generation," policy makers who came of age during World War II, who witnessed the triumphs of American postwar policies, and who learned well the lessons of the 1930s and the perils of appeasing an aggressor, totalitarian state. The Soviet challenge had to be met head-on, negotiations had to be conducted from strength, and the United States had to work with allies to stop communist gains in the Third World.[19] An active engagement by Washington with the rest of the world through multilateral cooperation and institutions was necessary to protect American interests and shape a world conducive to American values.

None of this would be easy or quickly achieved. The construction and maintenance of a stable, peaceful world was a difficult, ongoing, and elusive task, but one that was essential for Washington to undertake. Scowcroft was certain that it had to be done and that the future of the world depended on the resolve and the patience of the American people.

Politics had to be put aside and bipartisan agreements sought to shape the nation's diplomacy. For over two decades, the broad consensus in favor of containment, to which Scowcroft subscribed, held in Washington and guided American foreign policy. The main tenets of internationalism— American leadership of the world, collective security, and cooperation with allies through international organizations—became the hallmarks of U.S. policy. The Vietnam War shattered that consensus, engendering new and contentious debates about America's role in the world. It did not, however, change Scowcroft's view that international participation by the United States was indispensable for achieving a prosperous, peaceful world.

CONSENSUS CHALLENGED

The United States entered Vietnam committed to upholding the credibility of its containment policy and to demonstrating its resolve against its enemies. Americans were also optimistic about their ability to shape events in Southeast Asia. From the end of World War II until 1965, Washington took incremental steps that increased the American commitment and culminated in sending ground troops. At first, the Truman administration limited its efforts to providing supplies to France to assist in that country's efforts to reclaim control over its colony, but as the Cold War developed and intensified, Vietnam came to be seen as part of the communist world's efforts to undermine the free world. Ho Chi Minh's revolutionary nationalist movement was cast as part of the expansion of the international communist movement. In May 1950, the United States formally recognized the government of Bao Dai as an independent nation and part of the French Union. As the State Department noted in 1950, the choice was between supporting an anticommunist government established by France or a communist government led by Ho. There was "no other alternative."[20] Vietnam had to fit into the bipolar world of the Cold War.

The consensus on American containment policy was made clear by President Dwight D. Eisenhower during his first inaugural address. He declared that in the struggle with communism, "freedom is pitted against slavery; lightness against the dark," and that the United States' war in Korea was part of the same fight the French were waging in Vietnam.[21] He summarized the importance of Vietnam to the United States the next year when he outlined the "domino theory." Vietnam was vital to the free world for its raw materials, for the defense of freedom, and, most importantly, for the security of the free world. The loss of Vietnam to communism would lead to "the beginning of a disintegration" in all of Southeast Asia. As the president explained to the nation, "You have a row of dominoes set up, you knock over the first one, and what will happen to the last one is the certainty that it will go over very quickly." Thus the costs of the fall of Vietnam to communism were "just incalculable to the free world."[22]

When France was defeated at the battle of Dien Bien Phu in May 1954, the United States took over the effort to contain communism in Southeast Asia. What was needed, Washington believed, was a strong anticommunist leader who could defeat Ho's forces. After the Geneva Conference of 1954, the United States helped establish the State of South Vietnam under the leadership of Ngo Dinh Diem and embarked on an ambitious effort of nation building. Diem's stock rose throughout the decade as he established his authority and appeared to "save" South Vietnam from communism. By the end of the decade, American officials believed that containment had worked to create a pro-Western government in Vietnam that was stable and provided a model for other nations in Asia and Africa to follow as they gained independence and struggled to stay free of communist subversion.

By the time John F. Kennedy took office in January 1961, the American effort in Vietnam was experiencing problems. Fighting had returned in the fall of 1960 with the formation of the National Liberation Front (NLF), and the Diem government's inability to stop the insurgency exposed its corruption and lack of support. To stem the downward spiral, the Kennedy administration escalated the American commitment to Saigon to uphold containment and ensure that South Vietnam did not fall to communism. "The battle against Communism must be joined in Southeast Asia," Vice President Lyndon B. Johnson wrote the president from Saigon in 1961, "or the United States, inevitably, must surrender the Pacific and take up our defenses on our own shores."[23]

Following the advice of Johnson and other senior officials, Kennedy increased the American commitment. The number of American military advisors grew from five hundred in 1961 to over sixteen thousand by 1963 as part of an escalated counterinsurgency program that included strategic hamlets designed to protect villagers from the NLF, more sophisticated weaponry, and training in guerrilla warfare by the Green Berets. These new efforts proved insufficient to turn the tide of the fighting or provide political stability. By the summer of 1963, discontent with Diem's rule spilled out into to the streets of South Vietnam's cities as students and Buddhists protested his corrupt, repressive, and ineffective regime. Fearing a stunning military loss if it stayed with Diem, the Kennedy administration supported a military coup that ousted Diem on November 1, 1963, and replaced him with a series of generals at the head of the government.

Just three weeks after the coup in Saigon, Kennedy was assassinated in Dallas. President Johnson vowed to continue the American effort in

Vietnam and uphold American credibility and containment. However, the military government of South Vietnam was no more able than Diem to stabilize the worsening political situation or reverse the growing strength of the NLF, and Johnson soon found himself facing the question of further escalation or withdrawal. In January 1965, National Security Advisor McGeorge Bundy wrote Johnson that he and Secretary of Defense Robert McNamara were "convinced that our current policy can lead only to disastrous defeat." Johnson's advisors were not questioning the basic assumptions of American policy but the methods being employed to carry it out. Bundy argued that there was "no real hope of success . . . unless and until our own policy and priorities change," and that he and McNamara recommended the use of American "military power . . . to force a change of Communist policy."[24]

Johnson outlined the issues at stake and the need to uphold containment in Vietnam in a speech to the nation in April 1965. The United States was fighting in Vietnam, the president declared, "because we must fight if we are to live in a world where every country can shape its own destiny, and only in such a world will our own freedom be finally secure." South Vietnam, he stated, was a victim of aggression by international communism and was under attack from North Vietnam, which was supported by Red China. It was essential that the United States meet this challenge, that it demonstrate its credibility and willingness to uphold its containment policy and avoid another Munich. The policy he was following, Johnson reminded his audience, was the one set out in the Truman Doctrine and followed by every president since. "Let no one think for a moment that retreat from Viet-nam would bring an end to conflict. The battle would be renewed in one country and then another. The central lesson of our time is that the appetite of aggression is never satisfied."[25]

Facing the collapse of the government in Saigon and a defeat at the hands of communism, and certain of the necessity of containment and the support of the American people, Johnson decided in the summer of 1965 to send American forces to Vietnam. The United States would fight to uphold the policy of containment, deter aggression, and demonstrate its resolve. Communism was combative, expansive, and monolithic, with South Vietnam under attack by allies of the Soviet Union. Twenty years of Cold War consensus on containment and the bipolar worldview it was based on made the events in Vietnam a threat to the security and prosperity of the United States. Moreover, success seemed a given. The United States had successfully contained communism in Europe, held the line in Korea, and turned back communist forces in nations such as Greece, Iran, and the Philippines. The nation was confident in its values, institutions, and power, and Vietnam was proclaimed to be the front line of the Cold

War, with victory being vital for the protection of freedom and prosperity. It was these beliefs that would be called into question as the war in Vietnam became a stalemate and the consensus behind American policy dissolved between 1965 and 1968.

From July 1965 to January 1968, the United States steadily escalated the war in Vietnam, increasing the number of ground troops to over 500,000 while intensifying the bombing campaign in both the north and the south. It was a war of attrition as American forces sought to crush the enemy's capacity and will to fight with the application of U.S. firepower. To Washington's surprise, the NLF and North Vietnam did not succumb to American military pressure and instead met U.S. escalation with their own. The communist forces countered the American war with a strategy of fighting a long, protracted, and inconclusive battle that eroded the will of the American people to carry on the struggle. The continued escalation of troops and costs with no end in sight raised questions concerning the rationale for the war and led to a public debate in the United States about both the wisdom of the war in Vietnam and the efficacy of the policy of containment. By 1967, it appeared to many that the best the American forces could attain was a bloody stalemate.

Critics of the war argued that Vietnam did not pose any threat to the United States, and they challenged the logic and rationale of American policy. Dissenters rejected the argument that the war in Vietnam represented Soviet and Chinese expansion and aggression, contending that there was no such thing as monolithic communism and that the domino theory was not an accurate understanding of revolutions and social change in the Third World. Rather than serving as a pawn of China, Vietnam had a long history of conflict with its northern neighbor and feared Chinese domination; the war in Vietnam was better understood as a civil war and revolution that had indigenous roots in the struggle against French colonialism and the quest for independence and self-determination. The logic of containment, therefore, was flawed, and no fundamental American interests were at stake.

Moreover, protesters argued that U.S. policy and actions violated America's professed ideals and values of supporting democracy and freedom. They saw the war as immoral because Washington was backing a corrupt, ineffective, and unpopular military dictatorship in Saigon that lacked legitimacy and maintained its control by force alone. This made the policy self-defeating in the long run as it placed the United States in a position of propping up a government without any base and made American moral arguments against communist regimes appear hypocritical. By supporting the government of Saigon, the United States had placed itself on the wrong side of the changes sweeping the Third World, and this threatened the long-term interests of the United States and its relations with other nations. Thus, the war was not only unwinnable; it also led to a change in American Cold War policy.

By the fall of 1967, a plurality of Americans believed the Vietnam War was a mistake. The Johnson administration responded by assuring the nation that the war was being won and by reiterating the logic and rationale of containment and the necessity of maintaining American credibility. President Johnson called together the so-called Wise Men, the past architects of containment and American Cold War policy, who assured him that progress was being made and that the war was necessary to stop the spread of communism and protect American interests in the world. The problem was not American policy but the public's understanding of the war. As part of an all-out public relations blitz in November, President Johnson brought General William Westmoreland back from Vietnam to explain the progress and necessity of the war. Westmoreland called the stalemate thesis a fiction and declared that the United States was winning the war. American success in defeating the communists "will impact not only on South Vietnam, but on every emerging nation in the world."[26] For his part, the president assured the nation that the enemy was being defeated and that "aggression will never prevail."[27]

The Tet Offensive brought all the issues of the Vietnam debate to a head and forced a reevaluation of American policy that culminated in President Johnson's decision to cap the American escalation of the war and seek negotiations with Hanoi. Beginning on January 30, 1968, Tet was the largest set of battles in the war up to that date and the first to be waged in the cities. The enemy's ability to conduct such an extensive and well-coordinated attack appeared to disprove all of the administration's claims about progress and victory in the war. After Tet, the consensus on containment broke within the Johnson administration, and many senior officials changed their views. Vietnam was important to American officials due to the logic of the policy of containment. It was supposed to be a limited war to demonstrate the resolve and commitment of the United States to stand against communist aggression without leading to a direct superpower conflict. The second meeting of the Wise Men on March 26, 1968, showed the extent of the change. The majority of the Wise Men now concluded that Vietnam was not worth the cost and that American policy had to be reevaluated. The direction that American foreign policy would take after Vietnam became a contested issue.

POLICY DEBATES

When Richard Nixon became president in January 1969, the Vietnam War overshadowed all other foreign policy questions. The ever-increasing public disillusionment with the war led to a wider and more receptive audience for critics of containment and produced a crisis of legitimacy concerning American foreign policy. Nixon and National Security Advisor Henry Kissinger retained their belief in the verities of containment. Nonetheless, they knew that changes had to be made in how the policy was implemented and presented to the American public. The president's strategy was to find mechanisms for reducing the costs of the Cold War while continuing to uphold the primary axioms of American containment policy and postwar internationalism. This was to be achieved by the Nixon Doctrine, a new policy toward the Third World, and détente with the Soviet Union.

The Nixon Doctrine, a direct response to the public's disillusionment with the fighting in Vietnam and the president's desire to withdraw while maintaining credibility, upheld America's global commitment to containing communism, but it called for an end to the use of American combat forces in the Third World as the means of implementing and upholding that policy. Instead, the United States would provide weapons, intelligence, and material to nations threatened by subversion, but it would expect those countries to provide the ground forces for their own defense. The Nixon Doctrine, therefore, sought to prevent revolutions and the spread of communism by ensuring the ability of Third World governments to impose order in their societies. In addition, the United States sought to build up specific Third World nations as regional powers to help provide security and stability.

In President Nixon's mind, the way the Vietnam War ended was crucial to the maintenance of containment and American credibility. Simultaneously, he believed that adjustment had to be made in terms of the Cold War and America's global commitments. It was no longer politically or economically possible for the United States to continue to intervene in the Third World. Withdrawal from Vietnam had to be carefully orchestrated so that it was not seen by the Soviet Union as weakness or the abandonment of containment.

Nixon set out his thoughts in a 1967 article, "Asia after Viet Nam," published in *Foreign Affairs*. He began by reaffirming the need for containment, the threat posed by China, and the danger of communist expansion. The Vietnam War had deeply and bitterly divided the nation, and Nixon doubted whether "the American public or the American Congress would now support a unilateral American intervention" if another friendly nation were threatened by "an externally supported communist insurrection." Recognizing the end of the consensus on containment, he acknowledged the limits of American power and that the "role of the United States as world policeman" was coming to an end.[28]

This meant that other countries had to assume a greater share of their own defense, particularly in terms of providing ground troops. In order to implement his new strategic vision, President Nixon needed to buy time in an effort to control the withdrawal from Vietnam. Pursuing a policy called Vietnamization, Nixon sought to turn more of the fighting over to South Vietnamese forces while pulling out American troops. The United States would continue to provide arms, money, intelligence, and airpower, but it would reduce its role in fighting the ground war. For Nixon, this was not an exit strategy for Vietnam but a means of staying in Asia and continuing containment, as well as of getting reelected in 1972.

On July 25, 1969, the president outlined what would become known as the Nixon Doctrine. Expanding on Vietnamization, the Nixon Doctrine reaffirmed the American commitment to Asia and the policy of containment, but it stated that the goal of American policy was to avoid direct intervention and significant troop commitments abroad. The United States would keep its treaty commitments, provide a military shield for other nations in case of attack by a communist superpower, and furnish military and economic aid to countries facing subversion or guerrilla war. In turn, the threatened nation would be expected to provide the soldiers for its defense. The United States would only involve itself where there was local support for that role.

President Nixon also initiated the policy of détente toward the Soviet Union as an alternative strategy of containment. It was designed so that the United States would "stay in the world, not . . . get out of the world."[29] Thus, Nixon sought to soften East-West tensions, gain greater stability, and reduce the number of conflicts in the world while preserving America's role as world leader and lowering Cold War costs. The latter would be achieved by pursuing containment through negotiations rather than confrontation. Employing a traditional carrot-and-stick method, Nixon hoped to bind the Soviet Union to the status quo through a series of agreements on arms control, trade, and access to Western technology. Thus, Nixon worked to secure a Strategic Arms Limitation Treaty and limits on anti–ballistic missile systems with the Soviets, which provided greater control over the cost of weapons, granted the Soviet Union most-favored-nation trade status, made U.S. grain available for export to Russia, and allowed for limited transfers of more advanced technology from the West to Moscow and its Eastern European allies.

At the same time, the president moved toward the normalization of relations with China. This was one of the two main sticks to be used in the grand strategy Nixon pursued to maintain America's global dominance. While the opening to China had its own benefits in terms of stability in Asia and greater trade with the most populous nation in the world, and it brought to an end the fruitless U.S. policy of diplomatic nonrecognition of China, it also presented the potential threat of a U.S.-China alignment against Moscow if its policies were deemed dangerous or threatening to American interests. The other main deterrent to Soviet challenges was set out in the concept of linkage. Nixon and Kissinger were convinced that Moscow understood that it had much more to gain through a reduction of conflict in Europe and improved relations with Washington than by supporting revolutions in the Third World or challenging the United States in areas vital to its national security. The continuation of improved relations, availability of goods, and arms limitations would be dependent upon Soviet acceptance of the status quo in the Third World. If the Soviet Union's policies or actions were seen as threats, the benefits of détente could be withdrawn due to the linkage of East-West bilateral relations with actions in other parts of the world.

Scowcroft agreed with Nixon's and Kissinger's position and with the intention and goals of containment, and he sought to continue détente as national security advisor. He believed this approach was a necessary change in the way containment was implemented. First, it was useful for reducing tensions with the Soviet Union that caused unnecessary and dangerous competition and led to constant crises and policies based on worst-case scenarios. Second, it would help manage the costs of the Cold War and would provide a more realistic basis for understanding what the United States could expect to achieve in the world. Third, properly pursued, détente could help repair the damage that had been done to relations with allies in the wake of the Vietnam War. And, finally, it would base policy on the altered objective conditions in the world that the United States faced in the early 1970s and would recognize the limits to American power.

In his first significant publication, "Deterrence and Strategic Superiority," stemming from his time at the National War College, Scowcroft took on the questions of the arms race, the concept of strategic superiority, and deterrence. Appearing in *Orbis: A Journal of World Affairs* in 1969, a magazine on national security and defense issues published by the Foreign Policy Research Institute, the article brought Scowcroft to the attention of others outside the military and people inside the Nixon White House. Scowcroft noted that there was growing discussion of and support for the notion of the United States gaining strategic superiority over the Soviet Union in the form of a comparative advantage of American offensive and defensive forces over the Russians, which would provide deterrence against any attack. While this may have been the case in the years immediately following World War II when the United States held a nuclear monopoly, it was surely no longer a given when the Soviets had the capacity to inflict unacceptable damage on the United States. Scowcroft, therefore, questioned the assumption that strategic superiority in fact provided such a deterrent, as the war in Vietnam served to demonstrate, and he argued that the quest for such an advantage created both greater instability and the likelihood of war. "What meaning can strategic superiority have," Scowcroft asked, "in a situation where both the United States and the Soviet Union possess assured destruction capabilities?"[30]

Furthermore, Scowcroft queried, "is the concept of strategic superiority relevant to consideration of U.S.-Soviet strategic relationships at the present time? A thoughtful answer must be in the negative." There was "no innate requirement for superiority," and the quest to achieve what was unobtainable would only bring a greater risk of conflict at a higher cost than the nation could afford. It misjudged the nature of the Soviet strategic threat and challenge to the United States. Moscow's "aggressive ambitions can be expected to take the form of pressures and probes of various types requiring the United States to maintain a force posture that will make obvious and unmistakable its capacity for assured destruction." To try and go beyond this and create ballistic missile defense systems and larger stockpiles of weapons was self-defeating. Any effort to do so would add to international instability and spur on Moscow's attempts to spread its influence in the Third World to redress an imbalance in strategic weapons while hampering Washington's ability to respond to new Soviet initiatives.[31]

Finally, an effort to gain strategic superiority would play into Soviet hands by shifting a disproportionate amount of resources to the top of the escalation ladder and encouraging Soviet support for limited, regional wars. If the United States were not prepared to challenge Soviet aggression in means short of nuclear war, Moscow "could perceive this as a gap in force capability and undertake military action at that level. . . . On balance, making preparations for the possibility of limited strategic conflict would seem to be more in consonance with the principles of deterrence and to serve better the national interest."[32]

For Scowcroft, the central lesson of the Vietnam War was similar to his concerns about strategic superiority. Washington had made a strategic mistake in calculating the importance of the conflict in Vietnam and had overestimated the ability of the United States to manage world affairs unilaterally. The early successes of containment in the Cold War had led to the belief that with enough American guidance, money, and support, the United States could effectively change the course of events in almost any nation in a way that was favorable to American interests, and that Washington's leadership could lead the Third World to political maturity and support for U.S. policies and goals. Some saw the policy of trying to manage Third World nationalism via "nation building" as unrealistic and as creating false hopes in ever-expanding commitments of American prestige and credibility. These distorted beliefs had led to the quagmire in Vietnam, which had harmed rather than advanced American interests. It was wise, therefore, to disengage from the fighting as part of an overall strategic reassessment.

The goal of détente and the Nixon Doctrine was not to pull back from the world but to find ways to maintain the policy of containment in the new political climate at home and amid changed conditions abroad. As damaging as the hubris was that had led the United States into South Vietnam, Scowcroft thought it was just as dangerous for America to withdraw from the world in the wake of its defeat and to underestimate or misjudge the Soviet and Chinese threats to American national security. Rather, it was necessary to return to the core values of internationalism, particularly multilateral cooperation with allies and collective security, and to intervene in the Third World only where there was clear support from the local people. If Washington hoped to continue to provide global leadership and ensure postwar peace and prosperity through the promotion of American values and institutions, it needed to understand these revised guidelines.

There were, however, problems with Nixon's policy of détente. From Scowcroft's point of view, the Nixon White House had relied too much on secrecy in negotiations with Russia and China and had left key allies out of the process. The European allies and Japan did not understand American goals in Vietnam, finding the war a misplaced application of American power; moreover, they could not perceive why the Nixon administration continued the war while at the same time trying to improve relations with the communist superpowers. This had led to a deterioration in relations as a result of détente.

More importantly, Scowcroft thought that détente had been oversold domestically as a policy that was bringing peace between the United States and the Soviet Union. This left the administration vulnerable to charges that it was weakening the United States and failing to maintain its vigilance over Soviet machinations and threats. Combined, these two problems led simultaneously to a backlash from the political right, which asserted that the United States had abandoned containment and the need to confront Moscow around the world, and to criticism from the left, which held that détente was a cynical, Machiavellian policy that served to undercut American values and the need to promote democracy and human rights in the world.

Thus, when Scowcroft was promoted to national security advisor, the policy of détente was under attack from three different perspectives. First, there were the strict adherents to the verities of containment who saw any negotiations with Moscow as weakness, the Vietnam War as a correct policy, and the world as a bipolar, zero-sum contest that demanded increased arms spending, confrontation with Russia and China, intervention in the

Third World, and support for all nations that aligned themselves with Washington no matter what their internal political conditions. A variant of this was the emergence of the neoconservative critics of détente, who were anti-Soviet proponents of human rights, who supported unilateral American action in the world, and who advocated for the aggressive promotion of democracy and regime change in enemy states. Neoconservatives rejected what they saw as the fundamental assumptions of détente, the notion that there were common interests with the Soviet Union and the idea that there could be peaceful coexistence with a repressive form of government. For them, the call for human rights was a weapon to be used against the Soviet bloc and not a basis for critiquing U.S. policies in the world or rethinking the fundamental premises of the Cold War.

Yet, at the same time, a coherent alternative policy to containment in the form of human rights and nonintervention emerged that challenged the Cold War paradigm. The failure of the United States in Vietnam called into question for many the logic and rationale of containment that had led to the war and to the policies that supported it. Many saw the failure in Vietnam as a symptom of larger problems in U.S. policy, including its acceptance of right-wing dictators, its willingness to intervene in the Third World, its overreliance on military power, and its violation of the nation's avowed values and political beliefs. Proponents of this alternative view sought to overcome what they saw as the contradictions, and sometimes hypocrisy, of U.S. actions in the world.

President Gerald R. Ford and National Security Advisor Brent Scowcroft point to a map during a National Security Council meeting on Lebanon. Courtesy of the Gerald R. Ford Presidential Library.

The making of American foreign policy in the 1970s was a divisive issue in a way that it had not been since the 1930s, a contested component of domestic politics that divided the nation over the best way to engage the world and protect American interests. The various critiques of détente challenged the Ford administration's efforts to conduct diplomacy in the post–Vietnam War world. President Ford turned to Brent Scowcroft to navigate these debates and provide a steady vision that protected the internationalist position of the administration and guided the policy of détente. Due to the Vietnam War and the fractured Cold War consensus, the containment generation was forced to confront the central dilemma of its policy: on the one hand, seeing American ideals and values as universal and the United States as an exceptional nation uniquely qualified to lead the world, yet, on the other hand, recognizing the limits to power and the difference between aspirations and ideals and what was historically possible and within the power of the United States to control.

Scowcroft had to confront this dilemma head-on and navigate these divisions. His primary objective of upholding the central tenets of internationalism and maintaining American world leadership guided Scowcroft during the tumultuous two and a half years of President Ford's tenure. He remained convinced that the "ideal of America: the hope that we can make ourselves better, and make the world better," was still relevant and should inform decision making. It was essential that the country maintain its "optimism to go out and do good." The United States, he believed, remained a beacon to others, and the faith in an exceptional America was "why we've accomplished so much."[33] Still, the nation had to know its limits, understand what was historically possible, and distinguish essential needs from ideological desires.

NOTES

1. Jeffrey Goldberg, "Breaking Ranks: What Turned Brent Scowcroft against the Bush Administration," *New Yorker*, 31 October 2005.

2. Goldberg, "Breaking Ranks."

3. Goldberg, "Breaking Ranks."

4. Mark Warren, "Brent Scowcroft: What I've Learned," *Esquire*, 17 December 2008.

5. Brent Scowcroft, "Congress and Foreign Policy: An Examination of Congressional Attitudes toward the Foreign Aid Programs to Spain and Yugoslavia" (Ph.D. dissertation, Columbia University, 1967), 328, 343.

6. George Bush and Brent Scowcroft, *A World Transformed* (New York: Vintage, 1998), xiii.

7. Zbigniew Brzezinski and Brent Scowcroft, *America and the World: Conversations on the Future of American Foreign Policy*, moderated by David Ignatius (New York: Basic Books, 2008), 8.

8. Brzezinski and Scowcroft, *America and the World*, 243.

9. Henry Luce, "The American Century," in *America in Vietnam: A Documentary History*, ed. William Appleman Williams, Thomas McCormick, Lloyd C. Gardner, and Walter LaFeber (Garden City, NY: Doubleday, 1985), 22–23.

10. Brzezinski and Scowcroft, *America and the World*, 243.

11. Brzezinski and Scowcroft, *America and the World*, 243.

12. Brzezinski and Scowcroft, *America and the World*, 243.

13. Brzezinski and Scowcroft, *America and the World*, 248.

14. Brzezinski and Scowcroft, *America and the World*, 248.

15. Brzezinski and Scowcroft, *America and the World*, 251.

16. *Public Papers of the Presidents: Harry S. Truman, 1947* (Washington, DC: Government Printing Office, 1963), 167–70.

17. Department of State, *Foreign Relations of the United States: 1946* (Washington, DC: Government Printing Office), 6:699–701 (hereafter *FRUS* followed by year and volume).

18. Brzezinski and Scowcroft, *America and the World*, 115.

19. Thomas Paterson, *Meeting the Communist Threat* (New York: Oxford University Press, 1988), 194–95.

20. *FRUS: 1950*, 6:711–15.

21. *Public Papers of the Presidents: Dwight D. Eisenhower, 1953* (Washington, DC: Government Printing Office, 1960), 4.

22. *Public Papers of the Presidents: Eisenhower, 1954* (Washington, DC: Government Printing Office, 1960), 382–83.

23. Johnson to Kennedy, 23 May 1961, NSF: Bundy Files, Boxes 18 and 19, Lyndon B. Johnson Presidential Library, Austin, Texas (hereafter LBJL).

24. Bundy to Johnson, "Basic Policy in Vietnam," 27 January 1965, NSF: Memos to the President, Bundy, Box 2, LBJL.

25. *Public Papers of the Presidents: Lyndon B. Johnson, 1965* (Washington, DC: Government Printing Office, 1966), 1:394–98.

26. William Westmoreland, "Vietnam War Progress Report," 21 November 1963, Westmoreland Papers, Box 14, LBJL.

27. *Public Papers of the Presidents: Johnson, 1968–1969* (Washington, DC: Government Printing Office, 1966), 1:25.

28. Richard Nixon, "Asia after Viet Nam," *Foreign Affairs* 46 (October 1967): 111–25.

29. *FRUS: 1969–1976*, 1:191.

30. Brent Scowcroft, "Deterrence and Strategic Superiority," *Orbis* 13 (1969): 435–54.

31. Scowcroft, "Deterrence and Strategic Superiority," 435–54.

32. Scowcroft, "Deterrence and Strategic Superiority," 435–54.

33. Brzezinski and Scowcroft, *America and the World*, 240–41.

2

⁓

Constructing a Post–Vietnam War Foreign Policy

The Vietnam War forced a reassessment, by many, of America's position in the world and how best to manage the Cold War. Thus, when Gerald Ford became president in August 1974, he faced a number of foreign policy challenges, most prominently the ongoing war in Vietnam, debates surrounding détente, relations with China, and public questions concerning American intervention in the Third World. Conducting diplomacy was complicated by the Watergate scandal and Ford's pardon of Richard Nixon, by the economic stagflation of the time, and by the emerging congressional challenges to executive power and the direction of American foreign policy. Finally, given that he was not elected to be president or vice president but was appointed to the vice presidency to replace the disgraced Spiro Agnew and was then elevated to the presidency when Nixon resigned, Ford had to establish his legitimacy as president and demonstrate his ability to conduct the affairs of the nation.

Toward these ends, Ford sought to provide continuity by keeping Henry Kissinger as his secretary of state and national security advisor and by making détente central to his foreign policy. He strove to maintain the better relations with the Soviet Union begun under Nixon, to reduce tensions with the communist rival, and to secure further agreements on arms control. Simultaneously, the Ford administration was committed to maintaining America's image abroad as a great power and influence in the world after the devastating loss in Vietnam. The new president understood that American relations with much of the world had become strained during the Vietnam War, and he set out to rebuild relations with U.S. allies, particularly in Europe; to reestablish American credibility in the world; to contain the spread of communism; and to promote international stability.

Scowcroft supported these positions and sought to provide a coherent framework for them that reflected his internationalist thinking, his historical understanding of the changes in the international system, and the challenges facing the nation. He believed that the United States had become overconfident after World War II and had politically and materially overextended its commitments. The nation's defeat in Vietnam was a manifestation of a larger problem, a result of America's hubristic approach to the world that overestimated its ability to shape events. Still, he did not want the United States to cease acting as a great power. Thus, the central problem that confronted American policy making remained and would not be easy to resolve.

Washington needed to recalibrate its approach to the world in order to balance its resources and goals, Scowcroft argued, and manage its commitments in a way that sustained a high level of involvement in the world. Détente represented a necessary strategic adjustment given the changing international realities and domestic responses to the Vietnam War. For Scowcroft, the United States had to have more limited objectives in seeking to obtain the same goals of containing communism and promoting international stability, peace, and prosperity. The best means for doing this would be to draw the Soviet Union into a relationship that placed constraints on its actions in return for an easing of Cold War tensions, increased trade, and arms control. In essence, he sought a different form of containment that was sustainable, that reduced the threat of war, and that promoted greater stability.

Achieving these goals would not be easy since the Cold War consensus had been fractured. The sharp debates over the meaning of the Vietnam War, the nature of American foreign policy, and the direction of the nation's relations with the world brought criticisms from the right and the left. Committed to maintaining executive control over foreign policy, to the policy of containment through détente, and to diplomacy based on credibility that supported covert actions and the Nixon Doctrine, the Ford administration found itself forced to confront domestic critics on both sides of the political aisle. On the right, vocal critics of détente objected to arms control and accommodations with the Soviet Union, viewing any agreements as misguided and weakening the nation, and continued to support a confrontational approach to the Soviet Union as the only effective form of containment.

The most immediate challenge, however, came from opponents on the left. They questioned the central tenets of Cold War policy making, saw the end of the Vietnam War as an opportune time to reassess American foreign policy and the nation's role in the world, and called for the United

States to reorient its moral compass to promote human rights rather than rely on force, clandestine actions, and support for dictators to protect American interests.

In dealing with these multiple problems, the new president came to rely on Brent Scowcroft's advice. He found Scowcroft's cautious approach and personal modesty more in line with his temperament and outlook than the mercurial and egotistical Kissinger. Scowcroft's historical perspective, his "first-rate intellect," and his ability to manage the National Security Council were attractive to Ford.[1] In addition, the president was impressed with Scowcroft's long-range thinking, his commitment to the principles of internationalism, his belief in diplomacy rather than conflict, and his broad knowledge of arms control. In a time of deep divisions and uncertainty, Scowcroft provided Ford with a top advisor who sought consensus and had the respect of members of both parties. General Scowcroft's deliberate method and his commitment to the tenets of internationalism provided consistency amid the turmoil of the mid-1970s.

In a meeting with students from Georgetown University's School of Foreign Service at the beginning of the Ford administration, Scowcroft outlined the ideas that would inform his advice to the president and his policy recommendations. He began by putting the issues that confronted the nation into historical perspective. The United States had emerged from World War II victorious over its enemies, self-confident, militarily dominant, and ready to take up the responsibilities of world power. It quickly found itself in a struggle with "the communist monolith opposition [that] divided the world into a black and white problem." In response to this challenge, "since World War II the United States had a continuous and, by and large, successful foreign policy" of containment that had served the nation well. America's allies counted on Washington for leadership and assistance, and Third World countries looked "to the United States and the ideals upon which it stands to help them emerge into a community of independent states."[2]

While the nation's foreign policy remained consistent, the world changed. The key problem that confronted the United States was the need to "bring American foreign policy in tune" with current objective realities. "The Communist nations no longer were a monolithic opposition," the nuclear monopoly and strategic superiority the United States had enjoyed after the war had given way to "a functional parity in strategic forces," allies had recovered from the war and were in many ways competitors with the United States, and their former colonial holdings had largely achieved independence. Adjusting to these changed circumstances meant that the United States "had to disengage . . . from a long and difficult war—the Vietnam War," which "had brought fundamental attacks at home on American foreign policy." The United States would now pursue a different approach to containment in the Third World built on self-reliance and the view that those nations had "the primary stake in their own survival." Through the Nixon Doctrine, the United States was "determined to help when necessary and in areas where [it] could assist them, but the first efforts must be their efforts."[3]

In terms of relations with the Soviet Union, these changes necessitated that Washington reopen the dialogue with Moscow and Beijing that had been shut off in the 1940s. "There is still no fundamental change between the United States and Soviet Union," Scowcroft noted, "but now we are trying to find areas in which we can talk, to define our mutual interests." Détente was a strategy for managing the Cold War so that "we don't try to make every point of difference a major issue, or score debating points," and we were able to "build where we can and treat disputes through communications enhanced by the contact we've had." With China, it was necessary to reopen contacts that had been closed for a generation. With the end of the Vietnam War, "there were no fundamental points of antagonism with the Chinese" to block improved relations.[4] The outlines of his internationalist approach were clear: the United States had to continue to serve as world leader, pursuing containment through negotiation and seeking to create a great power consortium to provide stability and protect American interests.

CONGRESSIONAL CHALLENGES

As opposition to the Vietnam War grew during the late 1960s and early 1970s, the nature of the criticisms of the war expanded from seeing the war as a mistaken application of the policy of containment to viewing it as a symptom of a larger flaw in the nation's foreign policy. In the process, many critics raised fundamental questions about the nature of the Cold War, the basic assumptions of containment, and the conduct of American foreign policy, and they differed with Scowcroft on the proper direction for American foreign policy. The end of the Vietnam War, critics believed, provided the perfect moment for a reevaluation and reassessment of the policies that had led the nation into war. For the first year and half of the Ford administration, congressional proponents of change challenged the administration's policies toward the Third World, particularly what they saw as an exaggeration of the Soviet threat that rationalized American support of brutal dictators, covert operations, and military interventions.

In Scowcroft's estimation, this critique combined the two biggest challenges that immediately faced the Ford administration in terms of making foreign policy: the disillusionment within the United States regarding its role in the world and the negative effect of the Vietnam War on the credibility and international position of the United States. Concerning what he saw as the malaise of the nation, he thought it was natural that there would be questioning and doubt in the wake of the failure of Vietnam, and this was reflected in the congressional hearings on American policy toward the Third World.

The "Vietnam War and Watergate were terribly destructive" to the nation's unity, Scowcroft believed, and the bitterness persisted and grew with time, creating an "increasing gulf between the executive and the legislative branches." Presidents had previously met with congressional leaders just to talk, and to "bring the opposition into the cabinet room for discussions." This was critical for creating national policy and cooperation, but it became more difficult to achieve as partisanship grew over foreign policy after Vietnam and distrust mounted against the presidency in the wake of Watergate. Foreign policy became a political issue rather than an area of consensus, and this, Scowcroft worried, was undermining policy making.[5] He therefore sought to ameliorate the problem the best he could by seeking consensus and following cautious policies around the globe.

Scowcroft agreed with critics of the Vietnam War that the United States had made a mistake in sending troops to Vietnam. It had overestimated its ability to shape the course of events in Southeast Asia and around the world. Success in the period after World War II had led to the belief that, with enough money and effort, the United States could determine the outcome of events, modernize Third World nations, and establish governments that would support American policies. In the process, Washington overreached in Vietnam, with serious consequences at home and abroad.

Where he disagreed with opponents of the war was over the source of this failure. Critics questioned the logic and assumptions of containment and sought a broader definition of national security. As Senator Frank Church, a leader of the congressional opposition, saw it, the problem was that "the United States expended its major energies on the foreign military and political aspects of national security" and lost sight of the promotion of American values and human rights. Church demanded a return to democratic values as the basis of American policy. For Scowcroft, containment remained a correct policy, just one that was misapplied in the case of Vietnam due to overconfidence, previous successes, and misplaced priorities.

The first clash between the Ford administration and congressional critics was over the ultimate conclusion of the Vietnam War. President Ford sought to maintain American support to the Saigon government as a central component of containment in Asia. He believed that American credibility and prestige in the world demanded that the United States continue to provide assistance to the regime of General Nguyen Van Thieu. In the fall of 1974, the administration requested $1.5 billion in military aid for South Vietnam, arguing that a failure to sustain the Thieu government would undermine the position of the United States in the region and raise questions among American allies about future support.

Demonstrating the change in the domestic political environment and doubts about further assistance to Saigon, Congress approved only $700 million, less than half the amount requested. A pattern was set for the next half year as Congress repeatedly authorized less money than the administration requested. In early 1975, President Ford and Secretary of State Kissinger sought to build public pressure for aid to South Vietnam to force congressional approval of more funds. In speeches to the nation, they stressed the importance of keeping America's commitments to an ally, the necessity of preserving U.S. credibility, and the ongoing validity of the domino theory as a justification for continued military support of Saigon. Kissinger warned that a final defeat in South Vietnam would have a devastating impact on American prestige and would lead to further reversals, and he told reporters that it was crucial that other nations be able "to rely on the word of the United States." If they could not, there would be "serious consequences. I know it is fashionable to sneer at the word 'domino theory,'" he asserted, but that was the danger the nation faced in Southeast Asia.[6]

The administration made it clear that it had no intention of changing the two fundamental premises of American foreign policy, containment and credibility. The nation could not abandon Saigon without placing U.S. security and the safety of its allies in jeopardy. The concerns of nations such as the Philippines and Thailand, Ford stated, "tend to validate the so-called domino theory." It might be the case that the loss of South Vietnam itself would not cause great harm. The danger was that, "if we have one country after another—allies of the United States—losing faith in our word . . . I think the first one to go could vitally affect the national security of the United States." Therefore, the domino theory retained "a great deal of credibility."[7]

These arguments, which had once served as the rationale for American intervention in Vietnam and had routinely produced the full support of Congress, no longer evoked the same responses or the desired money. The administration's requests were either defeated or scaled back, and in April 1975, in response to the last request for emergency military aid, Congress only approved funds for the evacuation of Americans and for humanitarian use. Opponents had no desire to continue the U.S. involvement in South Vietnam. The issue to them was not credibility. It was ending what they saw as an incorrect and immoral war and changing American policy that led to the support of dictators in Third World nations.

With the fall of Saigon on April 30, Ford indicated that there would be no reevaluation of the policy of containment and that he would resist efforts to use the end of the war to change the fundamental assumptions of American foreign policy. He told the public that the final defeat closed that chapter of the nation's history, and he asked "all Americans to close ranks, to avoid recrimination about the past, to look ahead to the many goals we share, and to work together on the great tasks that remain to be accomplished."[8] A week later, he was even more adamant, stating that "we are going to maintain our leadership on a world-wide basis, and we want our friends to know that we will stand by them, and we want our potential adversaries to know that we will stand up to them."[9] The key, as Scowcroft saw it, was to make it clear that the United States was leaving Vietnam, but it was not leaving Asia. The withdrawal from Vietnam did not change the strategic significance of Asia or the role of the United States there.

It was, therefore, critical to restore the confidence of America's allies and demonstrate that the withdrawal from Saigon was a tactical move that did not reflect a policy change or abandonment of containment. "A lot of it is in the approach," Scowcroft told America's ambassador to

President Gerald R. Ford discusses the evacuation of Saigon with Secretary of State Henry Kissinger and Deputy Assistant for National Security Affairs Brent Scowcroft on April 28, 1975. Courtesy of the Gerald R. Ford Presidential Library.

Thailand. "The problem is not to create the impression that we are pull-ing out. The impression we should create is that we want to reaffirm, in whatever language, that we are not interested in cutting and running."[10] Some means had to be found to demonstrate American resolve to remain credible while withdrawing from Vietnam.

This was the main reason for what Scowcroft termed the "severe re-sponse" to Cambodia's seizure of an American containership, the S.S. *Mayaguez*, on May 12. Coming less than two weeks after the fall of Phnom Penh and Saigon to communism, the administration was quick to see the event as a test of American will and an opportunity to demonstrate its resolve. A week prior to Cambodia's action, Ford told the nation that the United States was going to maintain its "leadership on a world-wide basis," and that it would stand by its allies and stand up to potential ad-versaries.[11] The president thought that, "in the wake of our humiliating retreat from Cambodia and South Vietnam . . . our allies around the world began to question our resolve."[12] It was necessary, Scowcroft believed, for the United States to demonstrate that it would still have a presence in Asia. A swift and strong response was necessary to reassure allies in Asia and put the nation's adversaries on notice that Asia remained a strategi-cally significant area to the United States.

The discussions in the National Security Council focused on the broad ramifications of the incident, on credibility, and on the perceptions of America's determination to protect its interests. It was seen as necessary to draw the line, to take quick and firm military action. After the first NSC meeting, the military was readied for action, and when the necessary ships and personnel were in place on May 15, they were ordered into ac-tion. Marines landed on local islands where the crew had originally been taken, airstrikes were launched against the Cambodian mainland, and navy ships secured the *Mayaguez*. Bombings continued after the crew was safe, as it was seen to be necessary to punish Cambodia to demonstrate that the United States, in Ford's words, "meant business."[13]

One of the key allies the United States sought to reassure with its re-sponse to the *Mayaguez* affair, the shah of Iran, arrived in Washington the same day as the military assault. He was followed soon after by President Mohammed Suharto of Indonesia, another dictator who was seen as cru-cial to the success of the Nixon Doctrine and the maintenance of stability and containment in a key area of the world. It was considered vital to reassure such leaders that the administration was committed to playing an active role in the world despite the setback in Vietnam. Furthermore, as Kissinger wrote to Ford, given the "difficulties the Administration has had in relations with Congress as well as a fear that Congress and the American people may be moving toward isolationism," it was imperative

Deputy Assistant for National Security Affairs Lt. Gen. Brent Scowcroft and Secretary of State Henry A. Kissinger work into the night of May 14, 1975, to monitor developments in the retaking of the S.S. Mayaguez. *Courtesy of the Gerald R. Ford Presidential Library.*

that allies understand that the United States would continue to meet its commitments around the world.[14]

   In addition to providing assurances to friends of the firm determination of the administration to remain engaged in the world, it was also deemed necessary to deter potential adversaries, most notably China. According to Scowcroft, the same tension concerning the maintenance of American credibility while withdrawing from Vietnam was foremost on the minds of administration officials addressing U.S.-China policy. The United States was in the process of an evolving relationship with the People's Republic of China toward one of closer accommodation, especially with respect to both nations' mutual interest in containing the Soviet Union. The biggest problem and source of difficulty between the two nations had been the Vietnam War. The American withdrawal from Vietnam thus solved a major problem in relations with China, but it was essential to make it clear to the Chinese that it was a tactical move, not a strategic change in U.S. policy. The United States was not pulling back from world affairs, it could still use its power, and it was determined to continue to play a central role in Asia.

   The second area of disagreement between the administration and its congressional critics on the left concerned the broader question of

American relations with the Third World. A series of startling revelations in the fall of 1974 concerning CIA covert operations and assassination attempts against foreign leaders, as well as efforts by American multinational corporations to destabilize foreign governments and bribe officials, led to the establishment of the Senate Select Committee on Intelligence, chaired by Senator Church and commonly referred to as the Church Committee. Rather than conduct an exhaustive investigation into every covert operation, Church decided to make American involvement in the recent coup in Chile the centerpiece of the hearings. There were several reasons for this. First, the American effort to block the election of Salvador Allende in 1970 and the subsequent role of the United States in his overthrow by the Chilean military on September 11, 1973, contained all of the key elements of diverse U.S. covert operations. Second, it involved American multinationals as well as the CIA. Third, it was the most recent case of the United States working to overthrow a government and replace it with a right-wing dictatorship. Finally, the charge that CIA Director Richard Helms had previously lied to Congress concerning American covert operations in Chile was one of the sensational stories that led to the formation of the Church Committee.

American intervention in Chile dated back to the 1964 Chilean presidential election, when the United States spent over $3 million to defeat Allende. As a socialist, Allende was seen as a threat to extensive American economic interests in Chilean mines and communications. Moreover, Washington feared that an Allende victory would lead to the establishment of another communist state in the Western Hemisphere. Following traditional Cold War logic, the United States again set out in 1970 to ensure Allende's defeat. On September 4, however, he won a plurality of the vote in a three-way race, and the Nixon administration saw the outcome as a threat to U.S. national security. Kissinger cast the vote in Chile as "a challenge to our national interest," making it difficult to "reconcile ourselves to a second communist state in the Western hemisphere." Chile under Allende, he claimed, would provide the Soviet Union with a base to attack the United States and threatened to set off a domino effect in South America, where radical movements operated in Argentina, Peru, and Bolivia.[15]

Nixon gave orders to prevent Allende from taking office, and the United States worked, unsuccessfully at that time, to promote a military coup. Once the Chilean Congress had ratified Allende's election, the Nixon administration implemented a series of policies designed to undermine the Chilean economy, destabilize the government, and encourage a military takeover. Nixon wanted a policy that made it clear that the United States opposed Allende and that there were consequences to adopting policies of which Washington disapproved. In November in an

NSC meeting, Nixon emphasized the importance of deposing Allende. "If we let potential leaders in South America think they can move like Chile . . . we will be in trouble." He was adamant that "no impression should be permitted in Latin America that they can get away with this, that it's safe to go this way. All over the world it's too much the fashion to kick us around." He would tolerate no illusions about Allende and his plan to make Chile communist. It was imperative, therefore, that "if there is any way we can hurt him, whether by government or private business—I want them to know our policy is negative."[16]

Over the next three years, more than $8 million was spent on covert operations. At the same time, the United States cut its nonmilitary aid to Chile and pressured international lenders and institutions such as the World Bank to do the same. The issue at stake, for the Nixon White House, was American credibility. As the NSC put it, the inability to defeat Allende would represent "a failure of our capacity and responsibility as a great power." If the United States could not control Latin America, it could not expect "to achieve a successful order elsewhere in the world."[17]

The military overthrow of Allende was welcomed in Washington, which moved quickly to provide support for the new government of General Augusto Pinochet. Aid was promptly restored in record amounts, to over $116 million, and Chile was able to secure loans from the World Bank and the Inter-American Development Bank for over $100 million. Kissinger made it clear that it was the intention of the United States to support the new regime "in every appropriate way," including the sale of military weapons, despite the brutal crackdown, executions, mass arrests, and martial law inside of Chile.[18]

The Ford administration continued the support given to Pinochet by Nixon, as Washington considered his rule necessary to block communism in South America, protect American interests, and maintain American credibility. But, in the wake of the withdrawal of American forces from Vietnam, as well as Nixon's resignation and the evidence of U.S. complicity in the Chilean coup, Ford faced congressional efforts to block arms sales and demands that Pinochet respect human rights as a condition for further U.S. assistance. Congressional inquiries on the situation in Chile exposed the widespread use of torture, arrests without charges, and executions of American citizens by Pinochet's regime. In December 1974, Congress suspended military aid to Chile for six months while it further investigated the role of the United States in the coup.

The contrast in positions could not have been starker. Kissinger, invoking all of the verities of the Cold War, was determined to aid Pinochet. He told the American ambassador to Santiago, David Popper, in July 1975 that "there can be no doubt about my policy. I want to strengthen Chile."[19] Furthermore, he assured the Chileans that he was doing everything he

could to overcome congressional opposition, and he asked for only cos-
metic improvements in human rights to allow aid to continue without
interruption. In his only meeting with Pinochet, Secretary of State Kissinger assured the general that he welcomed the overthrow of the Allende
government, but that he faced "massive domestic problems" over the
issue of human rights that were leading to restrictions on aid. Kissinger
explained that any public statements on human rights were necessary to
keep the opposition at bay, and that if he did not appear to be applying
some pressure, there would be "a reaction in the U.S. which would lead
to legislative restrictions."[20]

Scowcroft concurred with the overall approach to Chile, although he
did worry about its impact on America's image in the world. He feared
that Allende was moving Chile to embrace communism, which would
have threatened American interests in South America. While Washington
would "naturally . . . like to see solid democratic regimes brought to the
world," that should not be a primary goal of foreign policy. The priority
had to be a nation's actions and "whether they are a threat to the United
States' self-interest and security." The covert operations were justified,
he believed, because of the threat posed by Allende's socialist economic
changes. Still, he acknowledged that "certain activities . . . are in the
interest of the United States but become self-defeating if they become
publicized." That would negate the purpose. It was a dilemma for which
Scowcroft had no easy answer, and he saw it as one of the unfortunate
costs of the Cold War and of being a great power.[21]

Church saw the situation in dramatically different terms. He told
Kissinger that American policy toward Chile was "appalling," "utterly
unprincipled," and contradictory to American values and traditions,
"leaving a hollow ring when we begin to apply them to other aspects
of American foreign policy." The United States had helped overthrow
a democratically elected government and was now supporting a regime
that ruled through terror and force, a military government that conducted a "blood bath" and eliminated all opposition. The senator could
not see how this was justified or served the national interest. Moreover,
when the United States criticized the Soviet Union and its allies, "we
have all kinds of references to moral principles here that distinguishes
this country and what it stands for" in the world. Yet, the United States
denied the right of self-determination to Chile and flouted its most basic
political beliefs in the name of anticommunism. The contradiction demanded a rethinking of the premises and assumptions on which American policy was based.[22]

The Church Committee hearings revealed a series of unsavory U.S.
actions conducted in the name of containment and the protection of freedom. It discovered assassination attempts against such foreign leaders as

Fidel Castro of Cuba, Patrice Lumumba of the Congo, and Rafael Trujillo of the Dominican Republic, as well as Allende, and U.S.-sponsored coups in Iran, Guatemala, Vietnam, Congo, Brazil, and Indonesia. Speaking for the committee, Church argued that the United States had to acknowledge the "wrongdoing of the CIA" and change its assumptions and policies to prevent similar covert operations in the future. Regarding the issue of credibility, Church thought the question put the emphasis in the wrong area, on American willingness to use force. Rather, he thought the greatest strength of the nation, and what people abroad most respected, was the country's values. It was, therefore, vital that they be upheld.[23]

The Church Committee found the claim that Chile presented a threat to the United States groundless. What concerned the members of Congress was that American leaders had deliberately engaged in covert operations that destroyed a democratically elected government and violated the announced principles and stated ideals of the nation. The central flaw in American foreign policy was its use of force and its support of right-wing dictatorships in the Third World. These actions came at a high cost. The credibility and legitimate concerns of the United States were called into question as the country was perceived to be hypocritical, contradicting its own claims about the proper behavior and institutions of nations and acting in violation of its stated commitments.

In response to the committee's findings, both the Senate and the House established new intelligence committees to provide oversight of covert operations. In 1975, Congress passed the Harkin Amendment, which banned economic aid to nations that consistently violated internationally recognized standards of human rights. It called upon the executive branch to provide written reports to Congress on an annual basis on human rights so that Congress could decide whether to continue, restrict, or stop assistance. The next year, the International Security Assistance and Arms Export Control Act was passed. It established in the State Department the position of coordinator for human rights and humanitarian affairs, it required a full report to Congress on human rights practices in all nations receiving military assistance from the United States, and it established a provision for withholding such support if a country were found to consistently violate the human rights of its citizens.

The combination of the Vietnam War, disclosures of covert operations, and American support for brutal dictatorships served to legitimize an alternative approach to foreign policy that placed an emphasis on human rights, nonintervention, and American democratic values. Opponents of the logic and rationale of containment sought to decenter the Cold War and the contest with the Soviet Union as the organizing principles of U.S. policy and replace them with an emphasis on morality, nonintervention, and a commitment to freedom.

The tension between Congress and the Ford administration stemmed from these issues of priorities and what posed the greatest threat to the nation. Scowcroft saw this as one of the central paradoxes that confronted the United States. He thought the congressional hearings and reports were "irresponsible"[24] and that critics underestimated the Soviet threat, the need to preserve strong presidential leadership in foreign policy, the importance of credibility and American strength, and the necessity of maintaining stability in the world even if it sometimes meant supporting authoritarian regimes and using covert measures to protect national security. American leadership was the only way to promote peace and prosperity in the world.

Yet Scowcroft did not think the United States had all of the answers or that Washington was without fault. He agreed that the United States had overreached in Vietnam, an area that was not vital to American security, and that it was necessary to be cautious in the use of power. Moreover, he believed it was important to include a sense of moral purpose in foreign policy, as was sought by the American public and which had been lacking when making policy toward the Third World. For Scowcroft, as always, the need was for balancing the tension between the goal of placing a premium on morality and human rights and the caution required in protecting other interests and making progress in the world. Finding this balance and a means for promoting freedom became one of Scowcroft's key objectives in formulating policy toward the Soviet Union.

BATTLES OVER DÉTENTE

At the same time that the administration was fighting with Congress over human rights in U.S. policy toward the Third World, it found itself under attack from conservatives regarding the policy of détente. Scowcroft understood that the effort to achieve a peaceful coexistence between the United States and the Soviet Union represented a shift in America's containment policy. Rather than being a new approach, he saw it as a return to the vision of cooperation between great powers sought by Franklin D. Roosevelt at the end of World War II and, therefore, in line with his basic internationalist approach. In place of confrontation and open hostility, Scowcroft favored a policy that relied on diplomacy, compromise, and superpower collaboration in order to avoid direct conflict and the possibility of war. This vision would better provide world order and international stability while easing East-West tensions and the threat of nuclear attack. Concurrently, it would help reestablish America's credibility and position as the dominant world power in the wake of the defeat in Vietnam, and it would be a reassertion of America's moral leadership. In the process,

Scowcroft believed that détente could blunt Congress's and the left's criticisms of American policy and their efforts to curtail American power and commitments in the world.

Scowcroft also worried about the challenges emerging on the right, particularly with regard to arms control and improved relations with Moscow, and he encouraged Ford to push ahead quickly in talks with Moscow while at the same time working to improve relations with allies to create stability and order in the post–Vietnam War world. Less than four months after taking office, Ford traveled to the Siberian port city of Vladivostok to meet with Soviet Premier Leonid Brezhnev as the last stop on a trip to East Asia that had included visits to Japan and South Korea. The president sought to reassure America's regional allies of America's commitment to the area as it was disengaging from Vietnam, and to assure them that his administration planned to keep them informed about negotiations with China and the Soviet Union. Nixon had kept the Japanese in the dark concerning his talks with China and had surprised Tokyo with the announcement of his 1972 trip. In conjunction with economic issues, specifically the U.S. devaluation of the dollar and protectionist calls against Japanese imports, this lack of communication had strained U.S.-Japanese relations. The trip to Japan was a signal that it remained America's most important Asian ally.

Ford also wanted to demonstrate to the Soviets his commitment to détente, to improved relations between the superpowers, and to arms control. Central to these efforts was putting a cap on the arms race. The 1972 Strategic Arms Limitation Treaty (SALT I) was due to expire in October 1977, and Ford wished to reach a final and more permanent agreement on arms limitation prior to the presidential election of 1976. The essence of the SALT I agreement was a freeze on new land- and sea-based ballistic missiles at 2,360 for the Soviet Union and 1,710 for the United States. There were no limitations on the number of heavy bombers or multiple warhead missiles (MIRVs) either side could have, and these were key issues for a second treaty.

After a recent Kissinger trip to Moscow, the president was optimistic about what could be accomplished in balancing the U.S. and Soviet missile capabilities, and he gained the concessions he sought from Brezhnev on the issue of the overall number of missiles regardless of size. While the technical details still had to be worked out and there remained issues to be resolved concerning American cruise missiles and the Soviet Backfire bomber, Ford secured an agreement that each side would have 2,400 ballistic missiles and that the maximum number of allowable MIRVed warheads was 1,320. As the president recalled in his memoirs, he "was euphoric" over the negotiations that accomplished much more than he expected, and he believed the agreements reached would be popular at home. "Vladivostok had been an appropriate ending [to the trip] designed to strengthen ties with old friends and expand areas of agreement with potential adversaries. The results of the trip had exceeded my expectations."[25] He looked forward to finalizing the treaty the next year and to a continued thawing of the Cold War.

Yet, as the fighting in Vietnam was reaching its end and the last of American personnel were leaving, conservative criticism of détente, and arms control in particular, intensified. Opponents of détente believed the United States gained nothing from SALT II. A new agreement would allow the Soviets to obtain at the bargaining table what they had failed to achieve on the production line. Parity with or even superiority over the United States would inhibit the innovation and implementation of new generations of weapons; would restrain the development of a more flexible missile system—the nuclear triad of land-, sea-, and air-based weapons—to counter the Soviet strength in large, land-based missiles; and would create a false sense of confidence and comfort instead of alarm and concern.

Moreover, critics on the right believed that the Soviets were taking advantage of the West in other areas, particularly with regard to the Third World. In the continuing unrest in newly independent states still struggling to gain independence, conservatives argued that the Soviets were becoming more adventurous in providing support to insurgents and radical movements that threatened America's allies and interests. From the Middle East to the Horn of Africa, from South America to South Africa and Southern Asia, critics of détente saw Moscow's hand in the political upheavals and urged greater American involvement and support for those groups friendly to the United States. As the United States focused on negotiations, those who held to the traditional understanding of containment were convinced that the Soviets did not really believe in peaceful coexistence, were using the talks as a diversion, and were continuing their aggression in the Third World. Confrontation rather than accommodation with Soviet tyranny was the goal of the critics of détente. The proposed Helsinki Accords represented all that they feared.

In July 1975, Scowcroft traveled with Ford and Kissinger to attend the thirty-five-nation Conference on Security and Cooperation in Europe (CSCE) in Helsinki, Finland. The purpose of the summit was to have the nations of Europe reach agreements on security, borders, economic cooperation, and human rights. Long sought by Moscow as a substitute for a final peace agreement in Europe, the CSCE meeting was controversial in the United States and within the Ford administration. Many believed that the Helsinki Accords gave the Soviet Union greater access to Western trade and technology, more involvement in all European issues, and ratification of the post–World War II borders and political order with nothing in return for the West. Kissinger in particular did not like the idea of a CSCE meeting or the Helsinki Accords, calling them a "bunch of crappy ideas."[26] He told Ford that the Soviet Union's "purpose was to present a substitute for a peace treaty and to create the mood that NATO was no longer necessary."[27]

The CIA concurred that Moscow sought to use the proposed Helsinki agreements "as a divisive tool, splitting the US from its Allies."[28] As laid out by the CIA in a special report on the CSCE, the Soviet Union wanted to use the meeting to improve its position and influence in Europe. Moscow saw the security conference "as a useful device to secure more forward-looking objectives," and the Soviets hoped that a successful meeting "would facilitate their access to Western technological and financial resources." In addition, they sought "some kind of permanent body that would enable them to play a role in all European affairs."[29] In brief, the Soviet Union hoped to use the CSCE to further its access to Western technology, gain greater influence in the West, and erode the Western alliance while cementing its hold on Eastern Europe. Ford's briefing book for the trip summarized the prevailing view that Moscow saw the CSCE as "a vehicle by which the Soviet Union hoped first to freeze the political map of Europe and then extend its political influence westward."[30]

Conservatives who held to the verities of the Cold War as established in the 1940s and 1950s, and who opposed détente and arms control, rejected any notion of a thaw in the Cold War or of improved relations with the Soviet Union. The only route to success, they believed, lay in maintaining constant pressure on the Soviet Union and challenging its power wherever and whenever possible. Hard-liners, therefore, saw détente in general and Helsinki in particular as a sellout of Eastern Europe by ratifying the borders of the Cold War. They claimed that it was a second Yalta, referring to the Big Three meeting in the Crimea in February 1945, where critics believed that Franklin D. Roosevelt had sold out Eastern Europe to Joseph Stalin. Senator Henry "Scoop" Jackson of Washington, the leading congressional critic of arms control, claimed that SALT II was taking the nation "backward, not forward, in the search for a genuine peace," and California governor Ronald Reagan, preparing to challenge Ford for the Republican presidential nomination, declared that he was against the Helsinki meeting and that "all Americans should be against it."[31]

The administration's response to a request by the most prominent Soviet dissident, Aleksandr Solzhenitsyn—author of *The Gulag Archipelago* and other terrifying exposés of the Soviet system—for a meeting with the president confirmed for the conservatives their fears of the consequences of seeking to negotiate with Moscow. Solzhenitsyn, having been deported to West Germany, arrived in the United States in early 1975 to extensive media coverage. The Russian writer's trenchant critiques of the Soviet

Union were matched by his disdain for détente and for any efforts by Washington to reach agreement with Moscow, much less pursue a policy of peaceful coexistence. Rather, he called for actions against the Soviet Union, he characterized American policy as appeasement, and he rejected any compromise. Conservative senator Jesse Helms of North Carolina requested that President Ford meet with the Soviet dissident and hear his views prior to going to Helsinki.

The president found himself in a difficult situation. Scowcroft told Ford that he would be ill-advised to see Solzhenitsyn so close to the summit meeting, as it ran the risk of sabotaging the meeting before it began. The Soviets would take it as a slight and an indication that the president was backing away from détente and aligning himself with the conservative critics. Such a meeting would be greeted favorably by conservatives and would help Ford politically, but it would jeopardize the SALT II agreement and all the benefits that came with controlling the arms race. As Ford recalled, "I decided to subordinate political gains to foreign policy considerations."[32] Ford's decision enraged his critics on the right and served to cement their opposition to détente as an immoral and dangerous policy.

Scowcroft was the biggest advocate within the administration of full American participation at Helsinki. He noted that the CSCE was very important to the Europeans and that it was necessary to work more closely with NATO allies in the wake of disputes over the Vietnam War and the secretive process the United States had employed in pursuing détente. Handled properly, the CSCE meeting could be used to forge more cohesion in the Western alliance while easing tension between the East and West and furthering the goals of détente. Finally, it provided an opportunity for the United States to show that it cared about the issue of human rights. It was necessary for the administration to take up human rights to demonstrate that détente did not preclude concern with issues of morality and thus counter the administration's critics in Congress. Because the Soviets were so concerned with having the final accords reached at a summit-level meeting and obtaining an agreement on postwar borders, the United States was able to introduce the issue of human rights, which also served as a means for allowing the allies to participate in the détente process.

Ford agreed. For the president, it offered him the chance to reinforce the American commitment to Europe, hold talks with other Western leaders, and travel to Poland, Romania, and Yugoslavia to encourage an independent course from the Soviet Union in those Eastern European nations, as well as for personal talks on SALT II with Brezhnev to overcome the remaining hurdles to an arms agreement. A final treaty would be an enormous achievement and would boost Ford's stature in the world and, he hoped, his political standing at home. All of this provided a chance for the United States to advance its goals by going to the Finnish capital and signing the Helsinki Accords.

In order to counter his critics' points and assuage their fears about the Helsinki agreements, Ford met with seven congressmen and with representatives of Americans of Eastern European background to constructively engage the opposition's views and provide a clear explanation of the objectives anticipated from the CSCE meeting. Ford acknowledged that there were some "who fear the Conference will put a seal of approval on the political division of Europe that has existed since the Soviet Union incorporated the Baltic nations and set new boundaries elsewhere in Europe by military action in World War II. These critics contend that participation by the United States in the Helsinki understandings amounts to tacit recognition of a status quo which favors the Soviet Union and perpetuates its control over countries allied with it." Conversely, others said "the meeting is a meaningless exercise because the Helsinki declarations are merely statements of principles and good intentions" that were neither binding nor enforceable, yet they would lead the West to become more trusting of the Soviets and to the dropping of NATO's guard and defenses. "If I seriously shared these reservations I would not be going, but I certainly understand the historical reasons for them" and the concern that many Americans have for the fate of Eastern Europe.[33]

The purpose of the Helsinki Accords was, Ford explained, the "lessening of tensions and opening further the lines of communication between the peoples of East and West." Most importantly, Ford argued, "we are getting a public commitment by the leaders of the more closed and controlled countries to a greater measure of freedom and movement for individuals, information and ideas than has existed in the past, and establishing a yardstick by which the world can measure how well they live up to these stated intentions." There was no doubt, the president said, that this was in "the best interest of the United States and of peace in the world." Helsinki, therefore, "is linked with our overall policy of working to reduce East-West tensions and pursuing peace."[34]

Yet there was another obstacle to achieving the goals Scowcroft sought at Helsinki. Since Ford had taken office, there was a division within the White House between the people he brought with him from Capitol Hill and his congressional office and the national security staff he inherited from the Nixon administration. The political advisors around Ford remained more concerned about the conservative criticisms of détente than the policy issues at stake and worried that no explanations by the president would prevent him from losing the support of Eastern European ethnic groups in the United States. These groups were convinced that the Helsinki Accords were a ratification of the Cold War borders and Soviet domination of Eastern Europe, and they would hold the agreements against Ford in the next election. There was a deep division in the White House over whether Ford should go to Helsinki or not. Even after it was decided that he would go, the efforts to distance Ford from the Helsinki summit continued as the president's political advisors sought to sabotage Helsinki all the way up to the writing of the president's departure speech.

Ford was scheduled to make comments at Andrews Air Force Base before boarding Air Force One for Europe. Scowcroft was to write it in conjunction with Robert Hartmann, Ford's former chief of staff when he was in the House of Representatives, his speech writer and close advisor. The drafting of the speech did not go well and was unfinished the day before Ford was due to leave. Scowcroft called Hartmann that afternoon only to find out, to his surprise, that Hartmann had already submitted a speech to Ford that sought to distance the administration from the agreements. Hartmann's speech was the polar opposite of what Scowcroft sought, grudgingly acknowledging that the president would attend the summit even though he disagreed with the objectives. Such a speech would have undercut the whole meeting. Scowcroft proceeded to write his own speech and delivered it that night to Ford in the presidential residence with a note explaining why there were two speeches and that his speech set out the positive reasons for going to Finland and what was at stake for the United States.

Scowcroft's speech was in line with the president's own thoughts on the summit, and it was the one Ford delivered. It called the trip "a mission of peace and progress" designed to assure American allies of the continued commitment of the United States to their defense, and to convince the people of Eastern Europe of Washington's desire to "seek additional improvements in our relations" as the nation pursued "increased cooperation and stability between the East as well as the West." It was part of the administration's overall efforts "to achieve a more stable and productive East-West relationship" through increased contact and better understanding, and to bring more security to all of Europe. In particular, the Helsinki Accords were in line with U.S. support for the "aspirations for freedom and national independence of peoples everywhere" and were "a forward step for freedom."[35]

Once in Helsinki, Ford failed to make any progress in his negotiations with Brezhnev on SALT concerning cruise missiles and the Backfire bomber, and the American delegation was disappointed that it was no closer to a new treaty than when they arrived. Still, Ford believed the summit was "a great success."[36] Scowcroft concurred. He saw the Helsinki Accords as demonstrating the benefits of engagement with the Soviet Union and the value of a process based on mutual restraint and practical agreements. The CSCE agreements were the result of lessons learned in the years after World War II that peace was a process that required great power consultation and reciprocal arrangements to avoid unnecessary conflicts. Helsinki was part of a larger policy to ease tensions, solve problems, and promote stability.

To the surprise of the administration, the American public did not see it that way, and Ford's approval ratings dropped after Helsinki. Ethnic groups that Ford had courted before leaving still saw, as predicted, the accords as a sellout that recognized Soviet domination of Eastern Europe and as an acceptance of the political status quo. The administration found this outcome paradoxical. Eastern European nations supported the CSCE as a way to lessen Soviet influence and provide for political openings and the movement of people and ideas, and they took very seriously the parts of the agreements that pledged all signers to respect basic human rights, self-determination, and the peaceful change of borders. In addition, the crowds that greeted the president in Eastern Europe were genuinely enthusiastic. Given this, why did their relatives in the United States oppose the arrangements? How, Scowcroft wondered, did they expect there could be any progress toward liberalization and peace if the United States continually attacked the Soviet Union and offered no incentives? It was easy to be a hawk and a strident cold warrior, Scowcroft thought, but that did not always advance American interests or the cause of freedom.

This was the irony of Helsinki. Ford was criticized for recognizing boundaries that had actually been established in the 1940s, for ratifying the borders of the Cold War, and for seemingly agreeing to a permanent division of Europe. According to Scowcroft, the critics were off base because they did not understand the changes occurring in Europe and how to best approach the Soviet Union. There was a new era emerging in Europe and a growing ferment in the Soviet Union and its Eastern European satellites that Washington needed to encourage in a careful manner. Rather than Helsinki cementing the Cold War, it was the critics who treated relations with the Soviet Union as static and unchanging. Détente was a different form of containment that was a response to the new realities of American power and the changing manifestations of the Cold War. It was not based on continuous confrontation; rather, it was a good tactical move to force changes in Soviet behavior. It was to the United States' advantage to reach agreements that set the parameters for relations. It was clear, Scowcroft believed, that unremitting hostility was not in the long-term interests of the United States. In this case, belligerency would play into the hands of Soviet hard-liners and provide an excuse for a continued tight grip on the nations of Eastern Europe and a crackdown on dissent.

Events a decade and a half later would demonstrate the correctness of this view. The much maligned Helsinki Accords had the exact impact that Scowcroft claimed at the time, creating political and cultural contact between East and West, thus challenging Soviet domination. The agreements reached at the CSCE summit provided encouragement and opportunity for dissenters in Eastern Europe to challenge their governments and the Soviet Union. The "great achievement" of Helsinki, Scowcroft opined, was that it started the process that undermined Moscow's ability to dominate its neighbors.[37] It helped set in motion the forces that would eventually lead to the end of the Cold War.

INTERNATIONALISM IN THE CROSS FIRE

As he looked toward the 1976 presidential election, Ford named Scowcroft his national security advisor in November 1975. Believing he had to establish that he was fully in charge, and looking to reduce Kissinger's dominance over foreign policy and the appearance that the secretary of state set the foreign policy agenda, as well as to put an end to the internal disagreements between Kissinger and Secretary of Defense James Schlesinger, the president made the move as part of a larger shake-up of his foreign policy team. Ford fired Schlesinger and asked William Colby to resign as the director of the Central Intelligence Agency. He named White House Chief of Staff Donald Rumsfeld to be the new secretary of defense, George H. W. Bush to head the CIA, and Dick Cheney to be chief of staff.

Kissinger did not take the move well. He claimed, correctly, that the press would report it as a demotion and a signal that the president was not happy with his policies. More than that, as Ford noted, Kissinger's ego was bruised at the same time as his power was reduced. Taking away the position of national security advisor stripped the secretary of state of his base in the White House and his control over the interagency committees that produced key information, reports, and recommendations. While Kissinger and Scowcroft got along well and saw many issues in a similar manner, the change at the top of the National Security Council was significant because it opened up the discussion on foreign policy and allowed for a greater variety of opinions to be heard by the president.

Whereas Kissinger consistently presented his personal views, Scowcroft sought to provide the president with a variety of opinions and dissenting viewpoints prior to giving his own advice. The key to success, according to Scowcroft, was that the national security advisor had to make sure the chief executive received the information and material he sought and needed, and had "to be able to speak with the authority of the president." He believed a centralized system was necessary to efficiently provide the studies and information necessary for decision making, and that the advantage of the National Security Council over the other agencies was that "the NSC can operate very quickly" in times of emergency. "It's important to preserve that capacity for instant response to the president."[38]

Scowcroft saw his role as that of a facilitator of this system, making sure that the president heard the various views of the members of the National Security Council, as well as different opinions from other sources, and to offer his own summaries of the issues and recommendations. His goal was to take the national view, rather than the perspective of a particular department, and explain to the president how that fit with his policy goals, including any political impact that a decision might have. If there was a meeting, Scowcroft would not provide Ford with a decision memorandum in advance. Rather, he would wait to see if the president reached a decision and then prepare a memo that reflected what he had set forth during the discussion. At the same time, Scowcroft kept his opinions private and did not show his memos and recommendations for the president to the rest of the National Security Council.

As the administration prepared for the presidential campaign of 1976, Ford found himself caught in the middle of the intense debates about post-Vietnam foreign policy. On the one side, conservatives dismissed détente as weakness, if not outright appeasement, and as responsible for the loss of American power and prestige in the world. They sought a return to

President Ford, National Security Advisor Brent Scowcroft, Counselor John Marsh, Deputy Assistant for National Security Affairs William G. Hyland, and Chief of Staff Dick Cheney monitor the evacuation of American citizens from Beirut on June 19, 1976. Courtesy of the Gerald R. Ford Presidential Library.

military superiority, confrontation, and a hard line on communism. Liberals, on the other side, questioned America's role in the world and sought a rethinking of the fundamental basis of policy. Guided by the type of internationalist views held by Scowcroft and his desire to maintain continuity in policy, Ford began the bicentennial year defending his policy. In January he declared that "détente is in the best interest of the country. It is in the best interest of world stability, world peace." Yet, by March, he was looking to distance himself from the term, stating during the Illinois primary that "we are going to forget the use of the word détente." Instead, Ford sought to emphasize the achievements brought about by negotiations and the need for moderation in the making of foreign policy. What mattered were results, not terminology.[39]

Ronald Reagan's challenge in the Republican primaries embodied attacks on détente and what he saw as the increasing Soviet threat. Reagan represented an emerging new political force in the nation—neoconservatives. They were mainly former liberal academics or government officials who feared cultural changes at home and what they saw as the decline of American power abroad. Aligned with traditional conservatives who had never changed their views on Soviet behavior through the Committee on the Present Danger, they argued that the Soviet Union had embarked on an effort to gain military superiority over the United States as part of a plan to gain world dominance, and that the Kremlin's apparent reciprocity of restraint through arms control and other agreements was merely a ploy to take advantage of détente and lull Washington into a false sense of security. Reagan and his supporters viewed the Soviet Union through the axioms of the Cold War, seeing communism as an expansive evil. Moreover, Reagan rejected the idea that American power was declining and that therefore détente and the Nixon Doctrine were necessary accommodations to new international realities. For Reagan, the only proper course of action was to return to the policy of containment fully backed by military superiority and a willingness to take the offensive once again to save the free world.

On March 22, 1976, a minicrisis broke out concerning American policy in Europe that illustrated the differences between the administration and its conservative opposition. That day's Evans and Novak column in the *Washington Post* reported that at the December 1975 meeting of American ambassadors to European nations in London, State Department counselor and key Kissinger deputy Helmut Sonnenfeldt had declared that an "organic" relationship between the Soviet Union and Eastern Europe was necessary to avoid World War III. Quickly dubbed the "Sonnenfeldt Doctrine" by critics, it seemed to confirm their fears of a United States sellout of the Eastern European nations behind the Iron Curtain.

The context for Sonnenfeldt's remarks was a discussion of ways to prevent an unwanted conflict in central Europe while keeping communism out of Western Europe. In doing so, the State Department counselor stated that the "Soviets' inability to acquire loyalty in Eastern Europe is an unfortunate historical failure because Eastern Europe is within their scope and area of natural interest." The problem was that the Soviet Union was unable to "establish roots of interest that go beyond sheer power." Because the Kremlin relied on the "presence of sheer Soviet military power" to control Eastern Europe, "the desire to break out of the Soviet strait jacket" has caused tension and instability. Détente was designed to deal with this "present unnatural relationship," which might "sooner or later explode, causing World War III. This inorganic, unnatural relationship is a far greater danger to world peace than the conflict between East and West." It, therefore, "must be our policy to strive for an evolution that makes the relationship between the Eastern Europeans and the Soviet Union an organic one."[40]

Reagan immediately seized upon the leak of Sonnenfeldt's remarks to attack the Ford administration and its policy of détente. He argued that Ford and Kissinger had been too willing to grant concessions to the Soviet Union at Helsinki and that Sonnenfeldt's statement was in line with Washington being unnecessarily accommodating to Moscow's interests and the stabilization of Soviet control over Eastern Europe. It was appeasement all over again. The Sonnenfeldt Doctrine, Reagan declared, "put the seal of approval on the Red Army's World War II conquests." Furthermore, the administration had allowed the United States to fall behind in the arms race, in effect making it the number-two military power in the world as the Soviets continued to take advantage of American policy and arms agreements. Congressional critics charged that détente, as practiced by the administration, was encouraging the "consolidation of Soviet dominion, and all that means, over the peoples and nations of Eastern Europe."[41]

The administration acknowledged that the use of the term "organic" was unfortunate and could convey the wrong message, but the administration also insisted that critics were misinterpreting both what was said and American policy toward Eastern Europe. First, there was no Sonnenfeldt Doctrine. Second, administration officials strove to assure those concerned that the United States continued to support greater freedom in Eastern Europe. In writing to members of Congress who raised concerns, Scowcroft insisted that the administration "strongly supports the aspirations for freedom and national independence of peoples everywhere—including Eastern Europe," and that it opposed any notion of "so-called spheres of influence by any power." This was made clear in the agreements reached at Helsinki and was a policy that the nation "will continue to pursue with patient persistence and from which the United States will not waiver."[42]

It was upon the understanding of how to achieve the goal of greater freedom in Eastern Europe that the disagreement was found, between the patient persistence of détente and the aggressive confrontation of containment. The administration was pursuing an evolution of the East-West relationship from one based on force to one based on other means that would serve to bring about agreements between the superpowers and reduce Soviet domination over Eastern Europe. It saw this as a more productive and prudent course and one that better served American interests by controlling the costs of the arms race, by maintaining cohesion in the Western alliance, by gaining concessions from Moscow, and by hopefully creating greater stability in the Third World by curbing Soviet challenges to Western interests.

Yet Scowcroft privately acknowledged that détente was a double-edged sword that left the administration open to criticism. Unlike containment as practiced since the late 1940s, détente's achievements were not always visible or easily measured beyond the SALT agreement or trade deals. The policy of détente was based on the understanding that the era of American domination of the world and military superiority over the Soviet Union was at an end. The initial surprises of the trips to the Soviet Union and China, the early success in terms of trade and arms agreements, and the rapidity of change led to heightened expectations by the public that more agreements could be easily reached and to their overconfidence in the process. Over time, however, there was a diminishing return, particularly with the failure to secure SALT II in 1975.

In an implicit criticism of Kissinger, Scowcroft noted that there were negatives associated with the policy of détente. Some started to believe that the period of hostility between the superpowers was over. This led the United States, Scowcroft believed, to let down its guard in a manner that Moscow could use to its advantage. Linkage had been oversold as a deterrent to Soviet support for radical nationalist movements and as a means of controlling change in the Third World, to the point that by the end of the 1970s the Soviets were claiming that the balance of power in the world had changed.

Ford was able to turn back Reagan's challenge and secure the nomination, but in part this was achieved by moving to the right, by no longer using the term *détente*, and by accepting some of its critics' positions. The most polarizing issue, the SALT II agreement, was put on the back burner so as not to arouse conservative ire, while across the board it became necessary to deemphasize good relations with the Soviet Union in order to defeat Reagan. Ford downplayed any efforts toward securing better relations with the Soviet Union and emphasized the need for reciprocity from Moscow if future progress were to be made.

Scowcroft found the influence of the political campaign on policy troubling. He believed another SALT agreement was possible in 1976, but the growing criticism of the Soviet Union for domestic political gain undermined the negotiations. Moreover, he wanted the president to run on his foreign policy achievements, including Helsinki, and defend the wisdom of great-power negotiations in creating a safer, more peaceful world. Scowcroft believed the policy was correct, and he was convinced that a clear explanation of its value would persuade the public and build support. Doing otherwise was giving in to a growing sentiment in the wake of the Vietnam War that the United States should no longer accept the duty of being a great power and take on the burdens of world leadership and instead should succumb to the reckless attacks on détente. Most troubling for Scowcroft was the fact that Ford agreed to a plank in the party platform at the Republican Convention, "Morality in Foreign Policy," which was proposed by the Reagan forces. It was a direct criticism of the administration's policies, specifically the Helsinki Accords, going so far as to praise Solzhenitsyn's criticisms of the Soviet Union.

In the general election, the president faced another set of criticisms and challenges to his foreign policy. In combination with the experience in Vietnam, the congressional disclosures of illicit covert actions and American support for brutal dictatorships, and new legislation that required human rights to be a component of American policy, liberals were able to appropriate the nation's bicentennial celebration into their critique of foreign policy. This served to legitimize alternative views about America's role in the world and made possible Jimmy Carter's efforts to redirect American foreign policy away from the logic of the Cold War, to rethink American commitments abroad, and to place a new emphasis on morality.

On one level, Carter's view on foreign policy did not differ greatly from the Ford administration's. Carter believed that the Vietnam War demonstrated that the period of U.S. domination of world affairs had passed and that the nation had to adjust to the new realities of world politics. However, Carter and Ford diverged on the centrality of East-West relations. Carter, like Church and other liberal critics, saw the Cold War as an anachronistic approach to the issues that confronted the nation as the world became more interdependent. The Vietnam War demonstrated both the limits of American power and the need to adjust America's approach to the Third World. While the easing of tensions with the Soviet Union and China was welcomed, and the pursuit of arms control was seen as necessary and correct, the problem with détente for liberals was that it focused almost exclusively on the rivalry with the Soviet Union as a means to managing change. Stability, prosperity, and the protection of

American interests, they argued, demanded that the United States work in collaboration with other nations. Central to this was the need to promote the protection of human rights in order to repair America's image and credibility in the world.

Therefore, a key theme of Carter's 1976 presidential campaign was the pursuit of a new direction in relations with the rest of the world, with human rights as the central organizing tenet of his message. Linking his call for change to the bicentennial celebration of the American Revolution and the Declaration of Independence, he argued that the real strength of the United States rested in its ideals and promised to return to the values of the Founding Fathers. In his formal announcement that he was running for president, Carter asserted that "our government can and must represent the best and the highest values of those who voluntarily submit to its authority," and he envisioned a world where the United States would "set a standard within the community of nations of courage, compassion, integrity, and dedication to basic human rights and freedoms."[43]

The central flaw in past American foreign policy, according to Carter, was that it too narrowly focused on the Soviet Union and did not encompass all of the nation's interests and values. He saw the United States as "strongest and most effective when morality and a commitment to freedom and democracy have been most clearly emphasized in our foreign policy."[44] As Carter stated in his first major speech on foreign policy in 1976, the recent actions of the United States had weakened the moral standing of the nation. "Every successful foreign policy we have had," Carter declared, "was successful because it reflected the best that was in us. And in every foreign policy that has failed—whether it was Vietnam, Cambodia, Chile, Angola, or the excesses of the CIA—our government forged ahead without consulting the American people, and did things that were contrary to our basic character." It was, therefore, "the responsibility of the President to restore the moral authority of this country in its conduct of foreign policy." Carter concluded that "policies that strengthen dictators or create refugees, policies that prolong suffering or postpone racial justice weaken that authority. Policies that encourage economic progress and social justice promote it."[45]

In accepting the Democratic nomination for president, Carter noted that there was a new mood in the nation. "We have been shaken by a tragic war and by scandals and broken promises at home." It was now time "for America to move and to speak not with boasting and belligerence but with a quiet strength, to depend in world affairs not merely on the size of an arsenal but on the nobility of ideas." Carter promised new leadership based on America's historic values, a rejection of compromises with right-wing dictatorships, and a foreign policy based upon American freedom and liberty, cooperation with allies, and less reliance on military power.

Peace and security from attack were the foremost responsibilities of any president. But, Carter opined, "peace is not the mere absence of war. Peace is the unceasing effort to preserve human rights . . . a combined demonstration of strength and good-will." The United States, Carter continued, "was the first nation to dedicate itself clearly to basic moral and philosophical principles: that all people are created equal and endowed with inalienable rights to life, liberty, and the pursuit of happiness." This "created a basis for a unique role of America—that of a pioneer in shaping more decent and just relations among people and among societies. Today, two hundred years later, we must address ourselves to that role."[46]

Building upon the connection with the bicentennial of the United States, these ideas were consistent themes throughout Carter's campaign as he constructed an alternative narrative to the national security state. The United States had to stand up for the values and principles set out in the Declaration of Independence and protect freedoms around the world. Carter was sure, "when people are put in prison without trial and tortured and deprived of basic human rights that the President of the United States ought to have a right to express displeasure and do something about it. . . . I want our country to be the focal point for deep concern about human rights around the world."[47]

Scowcroft agreed that morality had to be part of the calculus in making policy, but he felt that the liberals did not understand the necessity of balancing morality with force or of maintaining a credible threat to use military power. The push for humanitarianism without acknowledging the dangers presented by America's enemies was, for Scowcroft, an abdication of responsibility as a nation and dangerous to its interests. The peace and prosperity of the United States depended upon working with allies, protecting American interests, and countering the power and influence of Moscow. This was a complex relationship that could not be reduced, in Scowcroft's view, to moral maxims or just the respect for human rights. The United States had an obligation to lead the world and to exert moral leadership, but the latter had to be secondary to containing the Soviet Union and its expansion, which threatened the United States and its allies. The proper role for idealism was to ensure that Americans understood the necessity and obligations of world leadership.

These contrasting views were central to the presidential campaign, specifically to the candidates' second debate on foreign policy. Throughout the fall 1976, Carter criticized both the policy of détente in a manner similar to Reagan and the central tenets of containment. He claimed that the Russians gained more than the United States from the various agreements; that America's allies showed "a deep concern . . . that the United States has abandoned a long standing principle: to consult mutually, to share responsibility for problems"; and that he saw no reason why the

United States should have participated in the Helsinki meetings which "ratified the take-over of eastern Europe by the Soviet Union." At the same time, he rejected a return to containment, since that policy led to a rejection of morality in policy making. Rather, it created a militarized posture, interventions in the Third World that might lead to another Vietnam, the support of right-wing dictatorships, and covert operations such as the ones in Chile. "Our government should justify the character and moral principles of the American people," Carter stated, "and our foreign policy should not short-circuit it for temporary advantage." All of the actions in the Third World carried out in the name of containment, he claimed, were counterproductive. While they might provide immediate gains, the long-term impact was negative.[48]

Ford again sought to defend his policies without endorsing the concept of détente. Guided by Scowcroft's extensive preparation, the president countered Carter's charges by noting that the goal of American policy was to prevent Soviet expansion while reducing the danger of confrontation and nuclear war—to move policy beyond confrontation to a more stable and viable relationship that would allow for the peaceful resolution of problems between Washington and Moscow. More had been gained in the past few years from hard bargaining than from almost three decades of dangerous confrontation. At the same time, the administration had worked to strengthen the Western alliance through greater consultation and mutual efforts to reduce the military tensions in central Europe and open contacts between East and West. Without discussing Helsinki, Ford made it clear that détente had not meant an acceptance of spheres of influence in Europe, and that the United States continued to support the aspirations of Eastern Europeans for freedom.

An internationalist policy, in Scowcroft's view, equaled a more moral approach to foreign policy than Carter's vision. How you evaluate morality depended on the goals set and what the United States wanted to achieve. The country had to deal with the world as it was, and change had to come from practical measures and a responsible course. Nothing was more moral, in his estimation, than avoiding the specter of nuclear war, and if the United States wanted to have peace, then negotiations with the Kremlin and arms control agreements were necessary. What was moral about rejecting Helsinki, an agreement that thirty-five other nations, including the Vatican, had signed? The road to freedom for Eastern Europe was found in easing tensions and Soviet fears so that controls would loosen and people would gain a greater ability to travel, express their views, and take action. Confrontation only hardened the existing divisions and gave a weapon to those who wanted to keep Eastern Europe in a vise grip of Soviet control. Finally, to achieve a policy of nonintervention, it was necessary to have strong allies and regional powers. Change would have to come gradually, but greater human rights could only be achieved when Third World nations gained enough political stability for increased trade and economic growth.

During the debate, all of this careful analysis and presentation of American policy was undone when Ford, responding to a question by Max Frankel of the *New York Times* on détente, stated that there was no Soviet empire in Eastern Europe. The question accepted the premise of the critics' view that the Soviet Union had gained the better of the United States from détente, including the assertion that the United States had signed "in Helsinki, an agreement that the Russians have dominance in Eastern Europe" while the United States bailed out Soviet agricultural failures. In his response, Ford began by pointing out the benefits of arms control and grain sales, and then turned to the heart of the question, the Helsinki Accords. He rejected the notion that the United States had granted the Soviet Union domination of Eastern Europe. The president continued by asserting that "there is no Soviet domination of Eastern Europe, and there never will be under a Ford Administration." When Frankel asked for clarification, Ford dug himself in deeper, arguing that the people of Eastern Europe "did not consider themselves dominated by the Soviet Union."[49] It was one of the greatest political gaffes in American history. For many, it confirmed the critics' point that, through the process of détente, its proponents had fallen out of touch with the realities of Soviet power and the threat it presented, and they were pursuing a policy that was fraught with danger.

For Scowcroft, there was no question that what Ford meant to say was that the spirit of the Eastern Europeans was indomitable and could not be controlled or crushed by the Soviets. Ford stubbornly insisted that he had in fact said just that, and it took days to convince him otherwise and to issue a clarification. With that, all of the subtlety, nuance, and value of détente were swept aside amidst the clamor for clarification and the denunciations of Ford's inability to recognize the reality of the Soviets' military and political dominance of the satellite nations of Eastern Europe. Ford's defeat in November signaled the final end to détente.

CONCLUSION

Scowcroft was proud of the foreign policy accomplishments of the Ford administration and attributed them to following the central tenets of his internationalist vision. The United States had taken on its "duty to bear the burden of leadership, to help build a world that is safer, more prosperous, and more just."[50] It successfully navigated the central tension, in Scowcroft's worldview, between the belief that American world leadership was essential to peace and prosperity and the need to recognize the limits of power and avoid the hubristic overreach that had led to the debacle in Vietnam. Because of this, the United States had restored the nation's credibility and had regained the trust of its allies and the respect of its adversaries. It was at peace after almost a decade of war in Vietnam. The tensions of the Cold War were loosened, and relations with European allies and Japan were strengthened, allowing the United States to continue to play the role of leader of the free world. Moreover, American military strength and preparedness were unsurpassed, and progress had been made in the areas of arms control and in reducing the danger of another war in the Middle East. All of this was the result of vision, diplomacy, and a balancing of power with interests and values.

Scowcroft gave the president a great deal of credit for these accomplishments. He thought Ford was "ideally suited" for conducting foreign policy at the end of the Vietnam era. "He was a man for his time because he restored the United States to normality following a time of great internal turmoil," and he provided the necessary consistency and caution in making foreign policy.[51] Ford would be best remembered for restoring dignity to the presidency after Watergate and for helping the nation to heal in the wake of the bitter disputes over the Vietnam War.

These were not, however, the only significant accomplishments, nor the most long lasting, of the Ford administration. Although bitterly attacked at the time, Scowcroft's wisdom in pushing for full American participation in the CSCE summit and endorsement of the Helsinki Accords would be the ultimate positive outcome of détente. It was to the advantage of the United States to pursue containment through negotiations as it allowed room to maneuver and to influence Soviet actions. In the process, the policy of détente created political space for change while opening up contact with Eastern Europe, and it set forth a standard of behavior and expectations that eroded the power of the Soviet client governments and Moscow's domination over the Warsaw Pact nations. Without the outright hostility of the West, it became harder for the Soviet Union to justify strict control over Eastern Europe and harsh measures against dissidents.

Ultimately, détente in general and Helsinki in particular paved the way for the end of the Cold War and the collapse of the Soviet Union. What Ford thought he had said, or what he meant to say, in his debate with Carter was correct. The people of Eastern Europe had not consented to Soviet control, and the United States did not accept the status quo on the other side of the Iron Curtain. An internationalist vision carried forth through patient, cautious negotiations had brought about an enormous achievement that would only be fully appreciated when Brent Scowcroft was again national security advisor in 1989.

NOTES

1. Gerald R. Ford, *A Time to Heal* (New York: Harper & Row, 1979), 326–27.

2. Memo, 29 October 1974, National Security Advisor (hereafter NSA): Memorandum of Conversation, Box 6, Gerald R. Ford Presidential Library, Ann Arbor, Michigan (hereafter GRFL).

3. Memo, 29 October 1974, NSA: Memorandum of Conversation, Box 6, GRFL.

4. Memo, 29 October 1974, NSA: Memorandum of Conversation, Box 6, GRFL.

5. Zbigniew Brzezinski and Brent Scowcroft, *America and the World: Conversations on the Future of American Foreign Policy*, moderated by David Ignatius (New York: Basic Books, 2008), 273.

6. *Department of State Bulletin*, 17 March 1975 (Washington, DC: Government Printing Office, 1975), 328.

7. *Department of State Bulletin*, 7 April 1975, 434, and 28 April 1975, 544 (Washington, DC: Government Printing Office, 1975).

8. *Public Papers of the Presidents: Ford 1975* (Washington, DC: Government Printing Office, 1976), 605.

9. *New York Times*, 7 May 1975.

10. Memo, 25 April 1975, NSA: Memorandum of Conversation, Box 11, GRFL.

11. *New York Times*, 7 May 1975.

12. Ford, *A Time to Heal*, 275.

13. Ford, *A Time to Heal*, 276.

14. Kissinger to Ford, May 1975, "Strategy for Your Discussions with the Shah of Iran," Briefing Memorandum for Kissinger, 9 May 1975, Savage Files, Box 3, GRFL; see also Kissinger to Ford, 5 July 1975, VIP Visits: Indonesia, Kissinger-Scowcroft Files, Box A6, GRFL.

15. Henry Kissinger, *White House Years* (Boston: Little, Brown, 1979), 653–57.

16. Memorandum of Conversation, "NSC Meeting: Chile" (NSSM 97), 6 November 1970, Chile Declassification Project, Fourth Tranche, 13 November 2000, National Archives, College Park, Maryland (hereafter NA).

17. "Current Policy and the Environment That Shaped It," 8 September 1971, NSSM 108, National Security Council, Box 11, Record Group 273, NA.

18. Kissinger to Popper, 27 April 1974, Chile Declassification Project, Department of State, Box 4, NA.

19. Memorandum of Conversation, 18 July 1975, Chile Declassification Project, Department of State, Box 7, NA.

20. Memorandum of Conversation, 8 June 1976, Chile Declassification Project, Ford Library, Box 1, NA.

21. Memo, 29 October 1974, NSA: Memorandum of Conversation, Box 6, GRFL.

22. Executive Session, Senate Foreign Relations Committee, 19 September 1974, Wolthuis Files, Box 2, GRFL.

23. *Face the Nation*, 9 November 1975, Nessen Files, Box 64, GRFL.

24. Memo, 13 October 1975, NSA: Memorandum of Conversation, Box 16, GRFL.

25. Ford, *A Time to Heal*, 218–19.

26. Douglas Brinkley, *Gerald R. Ford* (New York: Times Books, 2007), 110.

27. Memo, 28 August 1974, NSA: Memorandum of Conversation, Box 5, GRFL.

28. Memorandum, "The CSCE and Western Europe: Pluses and Minuses," 18 July 1975, NSA: Conference on Security and Cooperation in Europe (hereafter CSCE), Box 44, GRFL.

29. Central Intelligence Agency, "Weekly Report: Special Review," 30 August 1974, NSA, CSCE, Box 44, GRFL.

30. "Conference on Security and Cooperation in Europe (CSCE)," Trip Briefing Books and Cables for President Ford, Box 10, GRFL.

31. Quoted in Ford, *A Time to Heal*, 300.

32. Ford, *A Time to Heal*, 298.

33. Statement by the President, NSA: CSCE, Box 44, GRFL.

34. Statement by the President, NSA: CSCE, Box 44, GRFL.

35. *Public Papers of the Presidents: Ford*, 1975, 1043–44.

36. Ford, *A Time to Heal*, 306.

37. Brent Scowcroft, interview by author, 17 July 2009.

38. Brzezinski and Scowcroft, *America and the World*, 259–60.

39. Quoted in James Mann, *Rise of the Vulcans: The History of Bush's War Cabinet* (New York: Penguin Books, 2004), 71.

40. Rowland Evans and Robert Novak, "A Soviet–East Europe 'Organic Union,'" White House Central Files (hereafter WHCF): CO 1–4, GRFL.

41. "REPUBLICANS: The Kissinger Issue: Whose Alamo?" *Time*, 19 April 1976; Leo Ribuffo, "Is Poland a Soviet Satellite? Gerald Ford, the Sonnenfeldt Doctrine, and the Election of 1976," *Diplomatic History*, July 1990, 394; Senator James Buckley to Henry Kissinger, 22 March 1976, WHCF: CO 1–4, GRFL.

42. Scowcroft to Buckley, 6 April 1976, WHCF: CO 1–4, GRFL.

43. Jimmy Carter, "Formal Announcement," in U.S. Congress, *The Presidential Campaign 1976* (Washington, DC: Government Printing Office, 1978), 1:4.

44. Jimmy Carter, *Keeping Faith: Memoirs of a President* (New York: Bantam, 1982), 142.

45. Jimmy Carter, "Our Foreign Relations," *The Presidential Campaign 1976*, 1:111.

46. Jimmy Carter, "Our Nation's Past and Future," *The Presidential Campaign 1976*, 1:347–51.

47. Quoted in Zbigniew Brzezinski, *Power and Principle: Memoirs of the National Security Adviser* (New York: Farrar, Straus & Giroux, 1983), 125.

48. Jimmy Carter, "Personal Questions," *The Presidential Campaign 1976*, 1:953–54.

49. Ford, *A Time to Heal*, 422–23.

50. "Ford Goals," Special Files: Second Debate, 6 October 1976, GRFL.

51. Kenneth W. Thompson, ed., *The Ford Presidency* (Lanham, MD: University Press of America, 1988), 311.

3

⊸◎⊷

Internationalism Under Fire

W hen the Ford presidency ended, General Scowcroft thought that his government service had also come to an end. It was not just that the Democrats now controlled the White House. Scowcroft was willing to serve the other party in the right circumstances, and he was young enough to be certain that he would see another Republican administration in Washington. The fact was that senior foreign policy officials did not get a second chance in another administration. Not since Henry L. Stimson was called back to Washington by Franklin D. Roosevelt in 1940 to serve a second term as secretary of war, after also serving as secretary of state under Herbert Hoover and secretary of war in William Howard Taft's administration, had a former secretary of state, secretary of war, secretary of defense, or national security advisor left office and then returned in a similar position under another president.[1]

There was no reason to think Scowcroft would be the exception. He disagreed with Carter's campaign attacks on Ford's conduct of foreign policy, his emphasis on human rights, his criticism of past U.S. policies in the Third World, and his apparent direction in American foreign policy. At the same time, he had been on the receiving end of the leading Republican candidate Ronald Reagan's blistering attacks on détente and the Ford administration's policies, and he feared that Reagan's growing adherence to the emerging neoconservative critique of American foreign policy represented a rejection by a significant part of the Republican Party of the main tenets of internationalism that had guided the United States since World War II and for which Scowcroft had become the leading spokesperson. Being so closely identified with a policy that was under attack from both the left and the right, it appeared that his direct service to the nation that had begun thirty years earlier was over.

Scowcroft turned his attention to writing, private business, and the life of an expert commentator. Upon leaving office, the former national security advisor joined the Atlantic Council, a Washington, D.C., think tank and public policy group dedicated to the support of NATO, good trans-Atlantic relations, and U.S. leadership of that community's central role in world affairs. A nonpartisan organization, it reflected the internationalist views held by Scowcroft and brought together individuals from both sides of the Atlantic to meet for discussions, the study of challenges facing them, and the production of works designed to influence public discussions and policies. His main focus was on his traditional areas of expertise: the Soviet Union, containment, arms control, and a growing interest in the Middle East. Through Atlantic Council publications, he promoted his ideas on and approach to international relations as an alternative to the Carter and Reagan administrations' policies. In 1982, Scowcroft joined Kissinger Associates, an international consulting firm for large corporations, where he would work for the next six years. Both positions allowed him to stay in touch with critical international issues and developments and with like-minded individuals.

Scowcroft was also called upon by Carter and Reagan to assist on the issue of arms control, and again by Reagan to examine what went wrong leading up to the Iran-Contra scandal. Having established a reputation of probity, loyalty, effectiveness, and bipartisanship, it was not surprising that both presidents would call upon him to assist them at different times. Scowcroft's internationalist views, expertise, and integrity were what Carter and Reagan sought, and he held to his core convictions while ably serving them.

All of these traits and beliefs were the same ones possessed by Stimson during World War II and explain his selection by Franklin D. Roosevelt to again serve the nation at a critical juncture. Few men gained so much respect and alienated so few people during their time in office as Stimson and Scowcroft. To the World War II generation, Stimson was seen as the "consummate American statesman" and as the person who "personified the bipartisanship and practical idealism" that came to shape containment and American internationalism.[2] These descriptions could have been penned about Scowcroft as well, and he was a worthy heir to Stimson's legacy. With the nation's faith in the conduct of its foreign policy again shaken in the wake of the Iran-Contra affair, the newly elected President George H. W. Bush sought to restore confidence in the nation's dealings with the world. This led him to bring Scowcroft back to the White House for a second service as national security advisor.

REPRESENTING THE CENTER

Scowcroft had mixed opinions about Carter's foreign policy, although he characteristically kept his most critical views and opposition to specific policies private. On the positive side, he publicly endorsed Carter's signing of the Panama Canal treaties and worked on behalf of their passage in the Senate. The treaties represented for Scowcroft a wise accommodation to legitimate nationalist sentiments and the concerns in Latin America over U.S. dominance. The negotiations that led to a final agreement were a bipartisan effort by many administrations to find a solution that protected American interests in the security of the Panama Canal while bringing to an end direct U.S. control. As Ronald Reagan led the opposition to the treaties, Scowcroft's support was important for gaining Republican votes in the Senate. Scowcroft was disappointed with Republican attacks on the treaty, seeing them as shortsighted and misplaced, but he thought the final passage was a sign that the two parties could still work together on foreign policy issues.

The former national security advisor also served Carter as a member of the General Advisory Committee to the Arms Control and Disarmament Agency after he left office. Scowcroft was pleased that Carter did not abandon the work of the Ford administration in its efforts to secure arms control agreements with the Soviet Union and gave whatever support he could to the ongoing negotiations. Carter reached a SALT II agreement in 1979, and although he failed to obtain its ratification by the Senate, both the United States and the Soviet Union agreed to adhere to the terms it set out. Critics charged that the agreement weakened the United States and emboldened the Soviet Union to further challenge U.S. interests in the Third World. Setbacks in Nicaragua, Iran, and Afghanistan that year seemed to confirm those predictions, and it was in these areas that Scowcroft shared the concerns of Carter's opponents.

Carter's criticism of past American foreign policy and his advocacy of a foreign policy based on human rights greatly worried Scowcroft. Ford, in Scowcroft's estimation, had handled well the unique challenges of his presidency, having come to office in the wake of the Watergate scandal and the defeat in Vietnam. Scowcroft believed that Ford had done a great deal to ameliorate the political crisis in the nation that he inherited. The president reestablished stability and trust in the government after Watergate, he oversaw the final end to the Vietnam War without further domestic division or unrest, and he greatly reduced international tensions and aided the cause of peace through the Helsinki Accords. Scowcroft found these to be significant achievements given the circumstances of Ford's presidency. Still, he thought it was inevitable that the nation would engage in the self-criticism that Carter represented regarding the Vietnam experience.

For Scowcroft, however, that reexamination and reevaluation should have led to a recommitment to Cold War internationalism, albeit without the hubris that had led to Vietnam, rather than to an overly idealistic policy based on criticism of the United States that was impossible to achieve and was dangerous to American interests. Scowcroft was well aware of the shortcomings of American policy in Vietnam, blaming it on an exaggerated sense of American power to influence events and manage the world, but he feared a swing of the pendulum too far in a different direction. Carter's human rights policy represented unwise self-flagellation motivated by guilt and an abdication of responsibility, and it thereby threatened American interests.

In the wake of the Vietnam War, many liberals sought to move beyond détente to an abandonment of the Cold War structure and containment in relations with the Third World. They saw the Soviet threat as exaggerated, they rejected various forms of American intervention, and they believed that the national interest was best advanced through the promotion of human rights, reform, and self-determination, even if the latter led to socialist or communist rule. In particular, critics of prior American policy rejected the idea of a bipolar world where the United States represented freedom in a struggle with an evil, totalitarian enemy. During the 1976 campaign, Carter made himself the leader of this critique, and it came to shape the central parts of his foreign policy.

The president articulated his criticisms of past American actions and his new policy based on human rights during his May 22, 1977, commencement address at Notre Dame University. Indicating his intention to break from past policy, Carter declared that it was time for the United States to have a foreign policy "that is democratic, that is based on fundamental values, and that uses power and influence . . . for humane purposes. We can also have a foreign policy that the American people both support and, for a change, know about and understand." Continued support of right-wing dictators and intervention in the Third World in the name of anticommunism contradicted American ideals and hurt the nation's self-interest. It was vital that the country place its faith in democracy and overcome its "inordinate fear of communism which once led us to embrace any dictator who joined us in that fear." The fundamental problem with containment, the president stated, was that "for too many years we've been willing to adopt the flawed and erroneous principles and tactics of our adversary, sometimes abandoning our own values for theirs. We've fought fire with fire, never thinking that fire is better quenched with water." It was time to acknowledge that "this approach failed, with Vietnam the best example of its intellectual and moral poverty."[3]

The United States had to forge a new policy toward the world, one based on a belief in self-determination and democratic values, not confrontation and reaction to communism. Carter announced that he would implement a new approach based upon a commitment to "human rights as a fundamental tenet of our foreign policy." The old policy was, according to Carter, built on an inaccurate reading of American history, of the development of democracy, and of the challenges in the world. "The great democracies are not free because we are strong and prosperous." Rather, the president argued, "we are strong and influential and prosperous because we are free." Following a foreign policy based on human rights did not dictate a set of "rigid moral maxims" for decision making, but it did require an abandonment of the bipolar Cold War approach, a tolerance for change and diversity among nations, and a policy "rooted in our moral values, which never change."[4]

Scowcroft rejected this response to the Vietnam debacle. He believed that there was no easy way out of the central paradox of being a great power faced with an enemy who had the capacity to destroy your nation and the values and systems you supported, and the need, therefore, to at times support governments that were not democratic. The lesson to be learned from Vietnam was caution and making sure that such a commitment was worth the cost and was achievable, not embarking on campaigns to reform the world and transform other governments. This required that a central component of containment be the support of right-wing dictators, even though this went against the belief in and promotion of democracy. For Scowcroft, only time would solve the dilemma through the political and economic development of the Third World.

It was essential that the United States provide international leadership, and it was Washington's obligation to combat and contain the Soviet Union. At the same time, Scowcroft recognized that there were limits to American power, that the United States did not have all of the answers to every problem, and that it could not transform the world unilaterally. It was just as dangerous to get caught up in its own moral righteousness in criticizing Third World governments as it was to believe it could do whatever it pleased through military intervention. There had to be restraint, good judgment, cooperation with allies, and caution in order to avoid another tragedy like Vietnam by undertaking a campaign to reform other nations. The United States should promote democracy, freedom, and its values where it could, Scowcroft believed, as that served the national interest, but it had to balance that quest with humility about its capacity to promote change and an acknowledgment that it could be wrong and did not have the solutions to all problems in other lands. "Ought we to stand by our principles? Yes," Scowcroft answered. That was one of the central issues at stake in the Cold War, and it was important that the United

States actively engage with other countries to create international institutions and structures that promoted these values. "But we can't remake the whole world at once,"[5] Scowcroft recognized, and efforts to do so would prove costly to the nation.

In the implementation of his human rights policy, Carter took a very moderate approach. In all, aid was only cut to thirteen nations based on human rights considerations, as the administration relied more on persuasion and rewards rather than sanctions in carrying out its policy. Carter's policy of human rights did undo the Nixon Doctrine and linkage of containment to the building up and support of regional powers to provide stability and security in different areas of the world without direct American military involvement. Yet, in two celebrated cases in nations that had been linchpins of the Nixon Doctrine, namely the ouster of the Shah of Iran and the overthrow of Anastasio Somoza in Nicaragua by the communist-led Sandinistas, the policy of human rights was seen by critics as leading to the downfall of staunch American allies due to Carter's unwillingness to intervene to save their regimes.

The shortcomings of the Nixon Doctrine were exposed when the Shah of Iran fell and an Islamic republic replaced his rule. The Iranian Revolution raised again the question of containment in the Third World. Carter refused to intervene directly to save the Peacock throne, fearing a repeat of the Vietnam experience. But how was the United States going to protect its interests in the region, promote stability, and ensure Western access to Middle Eastern oil in the Persian Gulf and Saudi Arabia? The questions became more urgent in the fall of 1979, with a second oil embargo driving up the price of gas at home, the taking of the American embassy in Tehran by radical students in November and the holding of sixty-six American personnel hostage, and the Soviet invasion of Afghanistan the following month.

Carter, under considerable criticism at home over these setbacks and the appearance that America's enemies were gaining ground around the world, changed his policy, returning to containment and a hard line against the Soviet Union. He quickly condemned the Soviet intervention in Afghanistan and took a series of steps designed to punish Moscow and protect crucial American interests in the Middle East. Covertly, the United States began to send aid to the anti-Soviet mujahideen rebels and others in an effort to thwart the Russians' ability to establish control over Afghanistan. Employing the idea of linkage, the president drastically curtailed East-West cooperation. Carter placed an embargo on the sale of new technology and further grain sales to the Soviet Union, he put the passage of SALT II on hold, and he announced that the United States would boycott the Summer Olympics in Moscow.

In his boldest step, the president announced the Carter Doctrine in his January 1980 State of the Union address. Declaring the Persian Gulf an area vital to American security, he stated that the United States would rely on its own resources to protect the Gulf and Western access to Middle East oil. Carter opined that the "implications of the Soviet invasion of Afghanistan could pose the most serious threat to world peace since the Second World War" and that any denial of Persian Gulf oil to the United States and its allies "would threaten our security and provoke an economic crisis greater than the Great Depression." He declared, therefore, that any effort by an "outside force to gain control of the Persian Gulf region will be regarded as an assault on the vital interests of the United States" and would be "repelled by the use of any means necessary, including military force."[6] The president backed up his claim with requests for increased military spending, weapons building, aid to regional allies, and greater American forces in the Indian Ocean. In addition, he froze all Iranian assets in the United States; imposed a trade embargo, including on military supplies already purchased; and broke diplomatic relations with Tehran.

Scowcroft supported Carter's announcement that the Persian Gulf was an area vital to the security of the United States and his pledge to defend its allies and access to the region's oil. The developments in the Gulf and Carter's new policy served, however, to convince Scowcroft of Carter's misplaced attention on human rights and the folly of abandoning containment and the central tenets of internationalism. While the Soviets had not instigated the unrest in Iran, Scowcroft believed that Moscow would be the beneficiary of America's loss of a crucial ally, and of greater instability in the region and the world. He deemed this a crucial turning point. The outside force the United States worried about was the Soviet Union, but disruptions could come from within the region, as the Iranian Revolution demonstrated. The main focus of American foreign policy was starting to shift from central Europe to the Middle East, as was Scowcroft's work.

In 1979, Scowcroft, along with John C. Campbell and Andrew J. Goodpaster, wrote a report for the Atlantic Council's Special Working Group on the Middle East. Responding to the OPEC oil embargo of 1973 and 1974, the current withholding of oil from the United States, and the fall of the Shah, the report highlighted the critical importance of Middle Eastern oil to the West in terms of both the Cold War and economic necessity, and the need for good relations with the oil-producing states of the Persian Gulf. "The Middle East is of the utmost importance to the US for three reasons," the study, entitled *Oil and Turmoil*, stated: "oil, security, and conflict settlement." The U.S. attention to the Middle East had to go beyond its traditional support of Israel. With Great Britain having pulled back as the regional stabilizer and protector of the Gulf, it was now a "primary requirement of American policy . . . to maintain a position in the Middle East, in cooperation and good relations with key Middle Eastern countries, that will ensure the availability of oil over the coming decade, prevent the extension of Soviet control, and bring about sufficient stability in the region" to achieve "these aims." To do so, it required that the American public realize the crucial importance of the Persian Gulf to national security and support the increased military presence and diplomatic efforts necessary to maintain access to Middle Eastern oil.[7]

This was linked, in Scowcroft's view, to the need to strengthen NATO, Western credibility, and deterrence capacity. Again writing for the Atlantic Council, along with Kenneth Rush and Joseph Wolf, Scowcroft was critical of the state of the North Atlantic Treaty Organization and its ability to respond to threats to the West. The authors believed that due to Carter's weakness and the erosion of the American position in the Third World, the United States faced a new era of Soviet expansion and hostility. The problem was exacerbated, they wrote, by the lack of cohesion in NATO, and they warned that the "allies cannot continue to be content with random, uncoordinated ad hoc responses, which themselves can constitute challenges to the unity of the alliance." Washington had to again assume global leadership among the free world nations and take responsibility for an "effort to maintain and strengthen alliance unity."[8]

A renewed cohesion was "a fundamental NATO imperative. Both short and long-term improvements can be sought under an acceptance of a common threat." It would not always be easy to convince people after the period of détente that this was necessary and that the Soviet Union remained a threat in Europe as well as in other parts of the world. It was true that a recommitment to the alliance "may be difficult for political leaders to accept in the 1980s. But real progress must be made . . . if NATO is to endure as an effective deterrent at a time when deterrence is of utmost importance."[9]

Scowcroft was not convinced that a Republican presidential victory would solve this problem, and he played no role in the 1980 presidential campaign. He shared Ronald Reagan's staunch anticommunism position and agreed with his criticisms of Carter's human rights policy, but he was uncomfortable with Reagan's and the neoconservatives' approach to the Soviet Union and the arms race. In his campaign for the presidency in 1980, Ronald Reagan criticized both the policy of détente and Carter's policy of human rights for weakening the United States and leading to perceived Soviet gains in Africa, the Middle East, and Latin America. Reagan saw the world in Manichean terms, with the Soviet Union, what he called in 1983 the "evil empire," responsible for the unrest and anti-American activity in the world. He held to an idealized view of the United States as the "City on the Hill," an exceptional nation whose ideals, values, and institutions were sought by others yearning to emulate the United States. Concomitantly, he rejected any criticism of the U.S. role in the world, particularly of the Vietnam War, as defeatism, and he actively sought to overcome the so-called Vietnam syndrome. Reagan believed the latter stemmed from the self-criticism of that period and led to an unwillingness of the United States to use its power abroad to protect its friends and confront its foes.

Reagan promised to return to the verities of the Cold War, to challenge the Soviet Union, and to restore American power and prestige in the world. In particular, he planned to rebuild the nation's strength through an arms buildup and to reverse ostensible Soviet gains by aiding anticommunist forces around the world. Candidate Reagan claimed that the United States had fallen behind in land-based missiles and was threatened by a window of nuclear vulnerability that had to be closed. In what became known as the Reagan Doctrine, he sought a rollback of Soviet influence and power by aiding, both covertly and overtly, so-called freedom fighters who were battling against communism.

In addition to his bipolar, Cold War worldview, Reagan also adopted some of the neoconservative critique of American foreign policy that had developed during the 1970s in response to the American defeat in Vietnam and the policy of détente. Most importantly, the neoconservatives and Reagan criticized Nixon's and Ford's pursuit of détente as concessions, a one-way street whereby Moscow gained all the advantages against a weakened and chastened Washington. Carter's policies only worsened the situation by attacking American allies in the Third World while doing nothing to replace totalitarian communist regimes. Neoconservatives rejected any limits on American power or the idea that U.S. power was in relative decline, both key premises behind the internationalists' lessons from the Vietnam War and the strategy of détente. Rather, Reagan and his neoconservative allies sought to engage the world, as they saw it, from a position of strength, sure of the correctness of their views, the justice of their goals, and the transformative power of the nation.

Moreover, Reagan shared the neoconservative belief that the United States should act alone in the world if necessary to carry out its foreign policy agenda and achieve its goals. This unilateralism was connected to the idea that the United States was an exceptional nation and a transformative power that could expand freedom in the world and export democracy. Thus, Reagan and the neoconservatives drew very different lessons from the fall of Saigon than did the proponents of détente or the war's critics. To Reagan, the Vietnam War was "a noble cause" and a proper application of the policy of containment.[10] The only problem, from Reagan's perspective, was that the United States lost its will to fight, withdrew, and failed to achieve a victory in defending South Vietnam from communist aggression.

Once in office, Reagan carried through on his campaign promises. He proposed a large increase in defense spending that included a new mobile MX ICBM missile system with ten nuclear warheads on each, the B-1 bomber, and an expansion of the American navy. The military buildup was accompanied by new talk about rejecting deterrence and mutual assured destruction in favor of superiority and being prepared to wage "winnable" nuclear war.[11] The capstone to this approach came in 1983 with Reagan's announcement of his Strategic Defense Initiative (Star Wars) that would be able to destroy nuclear ballistic missiles before they reached the United States. In addition, the president began to implement the Reagan Doctrine by providing support to the anti-Sandinista contras in Nicaragua and the mujahideen in Afghanistan, while at the same time reasserting American support for many of the dictatorships that Carter had criticized, in Chile, El Salvador, the Philippines, and South Africa, and providing them with military and financial aid. The president sought to roll back Soviet influence and reassert American hegemony in the Third World.

Reagan's actions led to widespread public and congressional opposition. Antinuclear protests took place all across the country and in Western Europe. Many people feared that the breakdown of arms talks and the growing tensions between Moscow and Washington might lead to nuclear war. There were massive demonstrations in major cities, such as the protest in New York City's Central Park on June 12, 1982, that drew a half million people, and grassroots political organizing arose to stop the nuclear buildup and freeze the development of new weapons. Democrats in Congress, while passing much of the increased military spending, held up many of the new weapons, including the MX missile, which they saw as unnecessary and destabilizing.

Similarly, Reagan's support for the contras, along with renewed aid to the military dictatorship in El Salvador, spurred broad opposition at home. Polls showed that the American public did not share the administration's interpretation of the events in Central America as representing a Soviet beachhead that threatened the United States, and they feared that Reagan's sending military advisors to El Salvador and aid to the contras might escalate into another Vietnam. Congress moved to restrict American support in both cases, and in 1984 the second Boland Amendment cut off all direct or indirect American support for the contras, a restriction that Reagan sought to get around through covert and illegal means.

THE SCOWCROFT COMMISSION

Scowcroft had never been comfortable with Reagan's approach to the Cold War. While the administration was willing through the Reagan Doctrine to go it alone in pursuing containment and to support forces in the Third World that were battling Soviet-backed governments, Scowcroft believed it was necessary to work with allies and that negotiation with the Soviets was the best means for managing containment and increasing American influence in the world. In 1983 and 1984, he produced two reports, one at the behest of the administration and the other for the Atlantic Council, which challenged the fundamental tenets of Reagan's policies and reasserted the necessity of returning to internationalist approaches to the difficult questions of the arms race, containment, and the American response to revolutionary nationalism.

The contrast in the two approaches was greatest in terms of the question of an arms buildup. Reagan sought confrontation with Moscow, a reassertion of American military power through an arms buildup, and the use of force to transform the Soviet system. Scowcroft, on the other hand, believed that security was best achieved through arms control, stability, and international agreements that lessened the risk of war and provided opportunities for American institutions and values to spread and have influence.

For Scowcroft, the Reagan administration's arms buildup had lost sight of the central problem that faced the nation and the world, namely the possibility of a nuclear war that could destroy humanity. Scowcroft believed, in direct contrast to much of the administration's rhetoric about the feasibility of winning and surviving a nuclear exchange with the Soviet Union, that one could not talk or act so cavalierly about the possible use of nuclear weapons. As a policy maker, "there was the ever-present thought that if either side made a serious mistake, it could be a catastrophe for humanity."[12] This meant that arms control and stabilizing the Cold War were vital to national security. A "nuclear war, involving few or many nuclear weapons, would be a tragedy of unparalleled scope for humanity. It is wrong to pretend or suggest otherwise," Scowcroft stated in 1983. It was vital, therefore, to maintain a policy based on deterrence because the "devastating nature of nuclear warfare" would lead to "mass destruction."[13]

These realities, Scowcroft was convinced, made ongoing negotiations and arms control talks a necessity, not a choice. It was essential to know what the Soviets were thinking and doing, and what they were capable of achieving, in order to bring stability to the question of nuclear weapons, reduce the risk of accidental war, and maintain sufficient American deterrence credibility to contain Soviet expansion without getting the United States or the Soviet Union into a situation that could escalate out of control. To act otherwise was to abdicate the responsibilities of leadership and the defense of national security.

After two years of bitter partisan fighting, growing frustration among advocates for the modernization of American missiles with delays in gaining congressional approval, and a large and still growing nuclear freeze movement aimed at stopping the new buildup of arms, Reagan decided in late 1982 to take a different approach to weapons by forming a bipartisan commission to study missile basing options and make recommendations in early 1983. On January 3, 1983, the president announced that Scowcroft would chair his Commission on Strategic Forces (the Scowcroft Commission) to review the strategic modernization program for the next generation of intercontinental ballistic missiles and the basing alternatives for that system.[14]

Due to his expertise, stature, and respect on both sides of the political aisle, Scowcroft was a logical choice to achieve the goals of finding a moderate approach and building a political consensus over what new missile systems to build and how to base the ICBM system. This fit with Scowcroft's belief that weapons systems and force modernization should be treated as technical issues rather than as ways to achieve political goals. Yet Scowcroft fully understood the political implications of different approaches to these questions and the decisions made concerning weapons systems. In particular, he feared that Reagan's approach was a return to the thinking of strategic superiority and represented a dangerous effort to win the arms race, and he saw the commission's work as an opportunity for the nation to turn away from that path. Scowcroft believed that modernization was necessary, but as part of a broader effort to achieve stability in the arms race and deterrence based on sufficiency and credibility. The former national security advisor's own preference was to return to the approach of the Ford years. He therefore went beyond the charge to the commission by linking the building of new weapons to arms control agreements.

For three months, the Scowcroft Commission held twenty-nine full commission meetings with members of Congress, the military, and over two hundred other experts on arms, as well as numerous smaller conferences in its review of U.S. strategic policy and forces. Working toward the goal of creating a "broad national consensus" on the future of the nation's ICBM forces and their basing requirements, the commission listened to all sides of the debate and developed a comprehensive proposal that was integrated in such a way that it could work only if taken as a whole, not by selecting particular parts that matched preconceived ideas or prior positions.[15]

While the commission's final report was unanimous and was endorsed by seven additional notable former officials who served as senior consultants to the commission,[16] it clearly bore Scowcroft's stamp in making recommendations that sought to create stability in the area of nuclear weapons, link deterrence with arms control, and act with a "calm persistence" to uphold the credibility that made stability possible and deterrence viable. In the first paragraph of the report, the importance of maintaining a credible deterrent against the threat of an aggressive, totalitarian adversary was set out as a basic assumption that shaped the urgency and necessity of the commission's undertaking. At the same time, it was stated that "the Commission believes that effective arms control is an essential element," along with deterrence, in preventing nuclear war.[17]

The purpose of a nuclear arsenal was meant primarily to be defensive in nature, the commission argued, in order "to deter attack on the United States or its allies." There could never be any doubt that the United States was "able, and prepared, if necessary, to use" nuclear weapons if forced to by the Soviet Union. But a mere reliance on force was not enough to ensure the safety and long-term interests of the nation. Arms control agreements were essential to reducing the risk of war, limiting the buildup of weapons, managing the risk of misunderstandings, controlling costs, and channeling necessary modernization efforts onto paths of maintaining agreements and stability rather than causing alarm and fear. "Stability," the report concluded, "should be the primary objective both of the modernization of our strategic forces and of our arms control proposals" so that both sides moved "in directions that reduce or eliminate the advantage of aggression and also reduce the risk of war by accident or miscalculation." Thus ICBM modernization was important as a deterrent and "to encourage the Soviets to reach stabilizing arms control agreements and to redress perceived U.S. disadvantages in strategic capabilities."[18]

To these ends, the Scowcroft Commission recommended that the best means for modernizing the ICBM force had three components: "initiating engineering of a single-warhead small ICBM, to reduce target value and permit flexibility in basing for better long-term survivability; seeking arms control agreements designed to enhance strategic stability; and deploying MX missiles in existing silos now to satisfy the immediate needs of our ICBM force and to aid that transition" by eliminating the Soviet advantage in land-based missiles and ensure the American deterrent. The report stressed that all three aspects of the recommendation were integrally related and needed to be accepted as a package, as "they point toward the same objective—permitting the U.S. and encouraging the Soviets to move toward stable ICBM deployments over time in a way that is consistent with arms control agreements having the objective of reducing the risk of war." No single part of the proposal could accomplish these objectives or work alone.[19] Specifically, the report recommended that a new single-warhead ICBM should be ready by the early 1990s, and it should be able to operate out of hardened silos or hardened mobile missile launchers; that one hundred MX missiles should be deployed in existing Minuteman silos as replacements for existing missiles as a modernization of the force; and that new arms control talks should be started to guide this modernization process into an agreement for long-term stability in missiles between the United States and the Soviet Union.

The final section of the Scowcroft Commission's report focused on arms control. Stability would be gained by having future ICBM deployments of smaller, single-warhead missiles to make it easier to reach equal levels of warheads rather than counting launchers, missiles, and tonnage. Past arms control efforts, the SALT agreements and the current START proposals, focused on limiting only launchers and missiles. This provided incentives for putting multiple independently targeted reentry vehicles (MIRVs) on missiles and building the launchers and missiles as large as possible, thus leading to the construction of larger missiles that could carry more warheads. The new goal, the commission argued, should be an evolution toward ICBM forces that encouraged each side to look at the "survivability of its own forces in a way that does not threaten the other."[20]

The report concluded with a Scowcroft-inspired plea for consensus on strategic deployments and arms control. The nation had failed to ratify an arms control agreement for over a decade due to disagreements between the executive branch and Congress and wrangling between the two parties. The outcome was that there was no treaty covering offensive missile systems and no sustainable strategic modernization program for American ICBM forces. "Such a performance, as a nation, had produced neither agreement among ourselves, restraint by the Soviets, nor lasting mutual limitations on strategic offensive weapons." The commissioners recognized that there would still be conflicting perspectives on different elements of the difficult issues at hand, but they firmly believed that compromise and consensus were the only means for moving forward toward greater stability and reduced risk. "If we can begin to see ourselves, in dealing with these issues, not as political partisans or as crusaders for one specific solution to a part of this complex set of problems, but rather as citizens of a great nation with the humbling obligation to persevere in the long-run task of preserving both peace and liberty for the world, a common ground may finally be found."[21]

The establishment of the Scowcroft Commission indicated the beginning of a change in direction in Reagan's policies. The president started to mix growing indications of moderation and willingness to negotiate with Moscow with his bellicose rhetoric. On March 8, 1983, he labeled the Soviet Union the "evil empire" in a speech to the National Association of Evangelicals, and later that month he announced his plans for the Star Wars defense system. Yet, the next month, he endorsed the Scowcroft Commission's report, calling upon Congress to take action quickly in support of the proposals because they "will preserve stable deterrence and thus protect the peace, and they will add solid incentives and credibility to our efforts to negotiate arms reductions that can pave the way to a more secure and peaceful future." He went on to say in his message to Congress that, "obviously, the best way to nuclear stability and a lasting peace is through negotiations." The task in front of the nation was to maintain its deterrence capability, show its resolve, and move forward in the manner outlined by the commission.[22]

The acceptance of the Scowcroft Commission's recommendations represented a significant compromise by the president. Reagan was yielding to his critics on the idea of superiority and was returning to a policy of mutually assured destruction and deterrence, scaling down the number of warheads and types of missiles he sought, and agreeing to resume arms negotiations as part of a comprehensive approach to containment rather than winning the Cold War. Central to this new direction was Reagan's agreement with the Scowcroft Commission that "the attainment of stability at the lowest possible level of forces" was the goal.[23] This meant the reduction of overall force levels, while still permitting the modernization of weapons to provide for a credible deterrent, at the center of strategic planning.

Congressional Democrats Al Gore (D-TN) and Norm Dicks (D-WA), writing for a group of ten members of the House of Representatives, welcomed the president's new position and hoped it would lead to a new "American policy on nuclear weapons and arms control . . . based on a durable bipartisan consensus" that focused on integrating new weapons systems with arms control in "the pursuit of stability." Still, many had concerns about the MX missile and sought assurances from the administration that the "trend toward more highly MIRVed ICBMs" be reversed and that "a less threatening force based on single-warhead missiles, ideally in a program orchestrated through arms control," move forward as the Scowcroft Commission recommended. They called for an explicit plan that would demonstrate how the MX missile would fit into arms control talks and a stable U.S.-Soviet relationship, and for the president to establish a bipartisan follow-up group to the Scowcroft Commission to provide advice on how to accomplish its goals and monitor the progress being made on the proposals.[24]

Due to the Scowcroft Commission's recommendations, and arguments that the MX missile was an indispensible part of a comprehensive approach along with a new single-warhead missile and arms control, Congress approved the controversial new weapon. In turn, Reagan asked the members of the Scowcroft Commission to continue to serve until January 1984 to assist with the discussions, to ensure that progress was made in implementing the recommendations made in April, and to maintain the bipartisan approach to weapons modernization and strategic arms reduction talks. As senators Sam Nunn (D-GA), William Cohen (R-ME), and

Chuck Percy (R-IL) wrote Scowcroft, "Much of the progress towards consensus" on the modernization of America's ICBMs and arms control "is due to the spirit of consultation, coordination and compromise between Congress and the Administration fostered by the Scowcroft Commission Report and recommendations."[25]

It was still hard to see in 1983 if these recommendations would lead anywhere. Reagan's continued use of harsh rhetoric and the Star Wars proposal were met by anger in the Soviet Union and alarm in the Kremlin that the United States was seeking superiority and a first-strike capability. Arms control talks had come to a halt, and the fear of a superpower conflict was at a point not seen since the Cuban Missile Crisis in October 1962. When a Soviet fighter shot down a Korean airplane in September, the Reagan administration's response was loud and strident, and relations between Moscow and Washington reached their nadir. In November, the confrontation reached the brink when the Soviet military concluded that a NATO military exercise was a cover for a planned first-strike nuclear attack by the United States. The Kremlin put its nuclear forces on high alert and prepared for the worst. Caution prevailed in the end, and the crisis passed, but many on both sides were shaken by the event. Senate leaders turned to Scowcroft to make sure that the administration did not abandon the course his commission had set out, reminding him that a bipartisan consensus had formed and that unity would be necessary to ease tensions and prevent the tragedy from derailing efforts for arms control that were underway.[26] Progress, however, was being made, and Scowcroft's prestige, demeanor, and reputation were critical in achieving the compromises reached in 1983, which set the groundwork for Reagan's more moderate tone and approach that began in 1985 and culminated in his later negotiations with the new Soviet premier Mikhail Gorbachev.

CRITIQUING THE REAGAN DOCTRINE

While Reagan began moderating his policy toward the Soviet Union and on arms control, he continued to wage the Cold War in the Third World, particularly in Central America, and to pursue the goals of the Reagan Doctrine. Reagan saw the events in Nicaragua and El Salvador as critical to his efforts toward reasserting American power and prestige in the world, regaining U.S. credibility with friendly governments, and rolling back communism. He was convinced that the Sandinista victory in Nicaragua resulted from Soviet actions and that the ongoing revolution in El Salvador represented Moscow's efforts to further expand communism in the Western Hemisphere. As the State Department's February 1981 white paper on El Salvador, entitled *Communist Interference in El Salvador*, concluded, the ongoing insurgency represented "a textbook case of indirect armed aggression by Communist powers through Cuba."[27] In response, the administration sent military aid and advisors to San Salvador and at the same time began funding the anti-Sandinista contras to help overthrow the government in Managua.

Both efforts met considerable opposition in the United States. Polls showed that over 60 percent of the American public disapproved of the president's policies, and Congress moved to tie aid to El Salvador to improvements by its government on human rights and free elections. As the civil war in El Salvador dragged on, Reagan turned more of his attention to Nicaragua and aiding the contras. The official justification for aid was so that the contras could stop the alleged flow of weapons from Nicaragua to the El Salvadoran rebels, but the real goal was to remove the Sandinistas from power. The more aid the administration sent, the more domestic opposition grew, as fear of another Vietnam made the public wary of Reagan's policy.

As concerns mounted that the president's actions were the first steps toward an escalation of American involvement in the region, Congress, on December 21, 1982, passed restrictions on aid to the contras that barred the CIA and Defense Department from using any funds to help overthrow Nicaragua's government. This first Boland Amendment lasted only six months, and Congress restored limited aid the next year. With new revelations on the extent of CIA involvement with the contras and the scope of American involvement in the effort to drive the Sandinistas from power, on October 3, 1984, Congress passed the second Boland Amendment, cutting off all funding for the contras from State, Defense, or the CIA and prohibiting "any other agency or entity 'involved in intelligence activities' from directly or indirectly supporting military operations in Nicaragua."[28]

Unwilling to give up on his policy of supporting the contras, Reagan instructed his staff to find other ways to fund them. The National Security Council staff, led by Lieutenant Colonel Oliver North, began a secret project of raising funds from friendly allies such as Taiwan and Saudi Arabia, and private individuals. Money was funneled through secret Swiss bank accounts, dummy corporations, and an organization called Project Democracy. The latter owned various assets in Central America that were used to move money, supplies, weapons, communications equipment, and other necessities to the contras—all in clear defiance of the congressional ban on U.S. involvement.[29]

With debate over the growing American involvement in Central America leading to deep divisions in the nation, Scowcroft entered the fray in hopes of putting forth a policy position that would create a consensus on how to deal with the problems to America's south. Concerned that the

Reagan Doctrine was driven more by ideology and wishful thinking than by a considered and thorough analysis, Scowcroft addressed the question of American interests and policies in the Caribbean Basin and how best to respond to the unrest and upheaval in the region. Written with James R. Greene, the report's title, *Western Interests and U.S. Policy in the Caribbean Basin*, indicates its departure from Reagan's viewpoint. Whereas the administration was acting alone and against the wishes of its allies in its interventions in El Salvador and Nicaragua and rejected all opposition and alternatives, Scowcroft sought to place American policy in the larger context of a global approach to the problems the West faced. Writing before many of the revelations concerning the extent of American covert support for the El Salvadoran military and the contras, much less the Iran-Contra affair, Scowcroft's sustained and methodical critique of the assumptions and implementation of the Reagan Doctrine in Central America predicted the failure of the policy and the need for change.[30]

Scowcroft agreed with the administration that there was a new Soviet assertiveness in the region in the wake of the Sandinista victory, that any expansion of communism in the Caribbean Basin was a threat to U.S. interests, and that Moscow's influence had to be contained. The question was the reason for the Soviet gains and how best to respond. Scowcroft differed fundamentally with the administration in interpreting the lessons of the Vietnam War. For the United States to succeed, Scowcroft believed, it had to follow a policy based on its interests and ability to influence events, not one predicated on an idealistic and ideological position that ignored local conditions, the role of nationalism, and legitimate grievances among the nations of Central America. American policy had to be "realistic in its objectives." It was essential that Washington "accept . . . [a] new assertiveness and nationalism in the Basin . . . to help reduce the dangers of Soviet inroads." Scowcroft warned that "a policy that fails to take into account different local realities or constraints that are either inevitable or too costly to remove will falsely raise expectations. This result will be a cycle of disillusionment and retreat" that will alienate supporters and friends and strengthen the forces the United States seeks to contain. By contrast, "a policy that sets modest, incremental goals can be both effective and sustain interest and support over the long run."[31]

The United States needed to discern the difference between nationalism and communism, understand the roots of upheaval and demands for change, and develop policies that worked with local countries to meet their needs while protecting American security, economic, and political interests in the region. The Sandinistas' success in overthrowing the Somoza dictatorship and the insurgency in El Salvador had indigenous roots and causes. That Cuba and the Soviet Union would provide aid and try to take advantage of these situations was no surprise, but it was critical to understand the proper cause and effect that had brought revolution and unrest to Central America. Basing policy, Scowcroft wrote, on a "lack of sound knowledge, empathy, and deep understanding of cultures other than its own was a crucial problem—perhaps the single most critical one—for the United States in Indochina."[32] Thus Washington had to learn and understand the history and culture of Central America, and the differences among the nations in the region, rather than trying to impose a policy built on a bipolar worldview of monolithic communism.

Finally, the report on the Caribbean Basin took up the question of American unilateral action. Scowcroft argued that to achieve success, the United States could not act alone. It was critical to work with local governments and other allies to construct a policy that could address the problems of the region in a manner that yielded real solutions and undercut the appeal of radical ideas and proposals. In so doing, the unrest and frustration that the Soviet Union exploited to gain influence would be curtailed. The administration's policy had none of these elements and was thus exacerbating the exact problem it sought to eliminate and was creating more opposition to the United States abroad and dissent at home. Again, drawing upon the Vietnam experience, Scowcroft noted that "a policy that does not retain broad popular support at home and congressional approval will not obtain the material resources needed to sustain that policy over time. If it combines enlightenment, realism, and consistency, U.S. policy may elicit that support."[33]

Unfortunately, from Scowcroft's vantage point, his prescriptions had no impact on the administration's behavior, as Reagan remained adamant in maintaining support for the contras as the centerpiece of his Central American policy and the Reagan Doctrine. The crisis for American foreign policy only deepened when this covert and illegal activity was married to Reagan's Iran initiative. Together, they would produce a policy failure that damaged American credibility and prestige and eroded faith in American institutions and world leadership.

THE TOWER COMMISSION

An additional source of funding for the administration's covert war against Nicaragua was money received through the secret and illegal sale of weapons to Iran that was then diverted to the contras. The starting point on the road to arms sales to Tehran began with Reagan's Middle East policy and actions in Lebanon. At the same time that the president was enacting the Reagan Doctrine in Central America, he was seeking to contain and roll back perceived Soviet expansion in the Middle East. These efforts led Reagan, after his initial opposition to Israel's invasion of

Lebanon in June 1982, to try to use the situation to strike a blow at Syria's influence and power in the region, and in the process undercut Soviet prestige and policies. Damascus was the capital in which the Russians had the most influence, and Reagan reasoned that he could use the crisis in Lebanon to discredit the Soviet Union and keep it from gaining more friends. To that end, Reagan dispatched over eight hundred marines to Beirut as part of an international peacekeeping force designed to defend the Israeli-backed, pro-West Christian government of Lebanon.

The American forces found themselves with no clear mission in the middle of a civil war among multiple factions. In April 1983, a terrorist attack on the U.S. embassy killed seventeen Americans. Reagan ordered retaliatory air attacks and bombardment from navy ships in the Mediterranean against terrorist strongholds and increased the marines' presence to over 1,400. On October 23, 1983, an enormous truck bomb blew up the marine headquarters, killing 241 Americans and wounding many more in the worst terrorist attack to that time against the United States. In February 1984, the troops were withdrawn from Beirut, ending the direct American intervention. The hostility to the United States remained, and after the marines left, seven Americans were taken hostage in Beirut between March 1984 and June 1985, mostly held by Hezbollah, a pro-Iranian Shiite terrorist group.[34]

Reagan grew frustrated by his administration's inability to secure the release of the hostages. The president had adopted a hard-line position against terrorism, including opposition to any negotiations or concessions to terrorists in exchange for the release of hostages during the 1980 campaign, and he had reiterated the position many times after coming to office. Yet no threats worked or appeared credible since sending U.S. troops back into Lebanon was politically out of the question. Still, Reagan was determined to secure the release of the hostages. Lacking a stick with which to free the hostages, the president was open to ideas that a carrot might work, even though this was in direct contradiction to his public pronouncements and policy.

Iran, in the middle of a bloody conflict with Iraq, desperately needed spare parts and replacements for much of its American-made weaponry left over from the Shah's military. In 1985, representatives of the Iranian government approached the United States with an offer to trade arms for hostages, setting off a chain of ill-conceived and illegal activities by the Reagan administration known as the Iran-Contra affair. Similar to the efforts to aid the contras, the Iranian initiative was run out of the National Security Council, cutting out Congress and many within the executive branch.

Starting in August 1985 and lasting until word leaked in November 1986, the United States sent over two thousand antitank and antiaircraft missiles to Iran, either through Israel or directly, in return for guarantees that these weapons deliveries would lead to the release of hostages in Lebanon. Complete with clandestine meetings, middlemen, false identities, and hidden gifts smuggled into Iran inside books, these covert activities violated the still existing ban on the sale of weapons to Iran, the policy of not dealing with terrorists, the nation's declared neutrality in the Iran-Iraq War, and the requirements for informing Congress of covert operations. The diversion of funds from the arms sales to the contras in violation of the Boland Amendment added to the illegal activities of Reagan's national security staff. To make matters worse, the policy was doomed from the start, as only three hostages were released and three more were taken during this time.

Once the story broke, it severely damaged Reagan's credibility and America's standing in the world. In an effort to restore confidence in the nation's foreign policy and the National Security Council, Reagan announced on December 1, 1986, the establishment of the President's Special Review Board (the Tower Commission), to be chaired by former senator John Tower along with Brent Scowcroft and former senator and secretary of state Edmund Muskie. Because the primary focus of the board's inquiry was "a comprehensive study of the future role and procedures of the National Security Council (NSC) staff in the development, coordination, oversight, and conduct of foreign and national security policy,"[35] as well as the provision of recommendations for improvement, Scowcroft was the key member of the group, and his views shaped its findings.

The *Tower Commission Report* was somber and critical, placing the blame on the president for failing both to demand a proper review of the Iranian initiative and to maintain control over the implementation of the policy to free the hostages through Iran. His staff was criticized for not following proper procedures, for a willingness to circumvent Congress and legal restraints, and for overstepping their proper roles. In the process, the NSC staff had poorly served the president and had given him bad and incomplete advice that led to serious political risks and illegal actions. The Tower Commission concluded that the "arms transfers to Iran and the activities of the NSC staff in support of the Contras are case studies in the perils of policy pursued outside the constraints of orderly process." In doing so, the "Iran initiative ran directly counter to the Administration's own policies on terrorism, the Iran/Iraq war, and military support to Iran. The inconsistency was never resolved, nor were the consequences of this inconsistency fully considered and provided for. The result taken as a whole was a U.S. policy that worked against itself."[36]

The problems, the report found, stemmed from the actions of the individuals, not from the NSC structure or system. Long-established procedures for decision making and the implementation of policy were

ignored or deliberately avoided, NSC principals were not given the opportunity to review and evaluate the policy, "applicable legal constraints
were not adequately addressed," and, once begun, the initiatives were
not subjected to regular reviews and analysis. In addition, the NSC staff
"assumed direct operational control" instead of allowing the proper
agencies, State, Defense, and the CIA, to implement the policy. Of course,
having circumvented the normal process of discussion and decision
making, and having ignored the objections of Secretary of State George
Schultz and Secretary of Defense Caspar Weinberger, the NSC had to
work around these departments and run the operation itself if it was
to be carried out. In a dramatically understated summation, the Tower
Commission concluded that "the result was an unprofessional and, in
substantial part, unsatisfactory operation."[37]

Reagan defended the Iranian effort by claiming that the purpose was
to establish high-level contacts, encourage more pro-West groups within
Iran, and improve the position within Iran of particular factions seeking
better ties with the Iranian military. Furthermore, he claimed that the
United States was never dealing directly with terrorists but with people
believed to have influence with the kidnappers. In this sense, it did not
contradict his stated position of no negotiations with terrorists. While
the Iran initiative was originally described as part of building a larger
strategic relationship with Iran, the other elements never developed, and
it quickly became, the report stated, only "a series of arms-for-hostages
deals." It was true that, "strictly speaking, arms were not exchanged for
hostages" but for cash, but "time and again U.S. willingness to sell was
directly conditioned upon the release of hostages."[38]

The Tower Commission deemed the sought-after strategic opening
with Tehran defensible, but not the dealing in arms. In its most damning
assessment, the report stated that "as arms-for-hostages trades, they could
not help but create an incentive for further hostage-taking. . . . The arms-
for-hostages trades rewarded a regime that clearly supported terrorism
and hostage-taking." Even if the Iranians could have freed the hostages,
the policy was a mistake, and it of course "was not genuine." The price
demanded for the hostages was constantly raised with little to show for
the weapons sent. In the process, it "raised questions as to whether U.S.
policy statements could be relied upon," it damaged American credibility
with its allies, and it gave ammunition to critics of the United States in the
Middle East. "This sad history is powerful evidence of why the United
States should never have become involved in the arms transfers."[39]

Scowcroft's vision of how the National Security Council should func-
tion in relation to the proper policies of the nation shaped the Tower
Commission's recommendations. The primary fault in the Iran-Contra
affair, the commission found, rested with the president and how he used

the National Security Council. It was Reagan's desire to free the hostages and maintain aid to the contras that produced the Iran initiative and led the NSC to illegal actions that circumvented other executive agencies and Congress. Yet "the president appears to have proceeded with a concept of the initiative that was not accurately reflected in the reality of the operation," and he was unaware of the way "the operation was implemented and the full consequences of U.S. participation." In such a "high-risk operation and so much at stake, the President should have ensured that the NSC system did not fail him. He did not force his policy to undergo the most critical review of which the NSC participants and the process were capable. At no time did he insist upon accountability and performance review."[40] Given this, what the NSC system does best—comprehensive policy analysis, assessment, discussion, and providing context, alternatives, and follow-up—was not utilized.

The Tower Commission endorsed maintaining the National Security Council as presently constructed. The problem was not a structural one, but one of how the system was used and a disdain for opposing views. The report, therefore, offered a model for National Security Council operations based on Scowcroft's direction during the Ford administration. The key was that the national security advisor "should present his own views, but he must at the same time represent the views of others fully and faithfully to the President." This would only work if the national security advisor had the trust of the president and the other NSC principals. "He, therefore, must not use his proximity to the President to manipulate the process so as to produce his own position" or "interpose himself between the President and the NSC principals" or "exclude the NSC principals from the decision process,"[41] as the Tower Commission found that Reagan's national security advisors Robert McFarlane and Vice Admiral John Poindexter had done throughout the Iran-Contra fiasco.

Moreover, the national security advisor must have direct access to the president without having to go through another official, or the NSC system would not work. Moreover, the special assistant to the president for national security should not be a public figure or try to "compete with the Secretary of State or the Secretary of Defense as the articulator of public policy," but rather must operate offstage and "promote cooperation rather than competition among himself and the other NSC principals." Finally, it was necessary to "focus on advice and management, not implementation and execution" of policy that properly belongs with State, Defense, and the CIA. To act otherwise was to put objectivity and the NSA's role as impartial coordinator and advisor to the president at risk.[42]

For Scowcroft, the findings of the Tower Commission demonstrated the faults of the neoconservative approach to foreign policy, the volatility of the Reagan Doctrine, and the dangers of straying away from the principles of internationalism. Scowcroft believed that President Reagan was "an incurious President; he is not fundamentally interested in foreign policy; he is not at all interested in details." Rather, Reagan thought in broad terms with grand themes and beliefs, he trusted in the unilateral ability of the United States to bring positive change to a waiting world, and he was convinced of the moral correctness of America's actions at all times. Because of this, he did not oversee policy implementation; he was too trusting of his advisors, who cast policies in scenarios that played to Reagan's desires; and he was too hands-offs in his management, which provided the opportunity for subordinates to take his general directives into areas that violated the law and public trust and hurt American policy and prestige abroad.[43]

The combination of poor policy and a willingness to deceive Congress and others to reach idealistic ends made abuses of power almost inevitable. The diversions of funds, the misuse of the NSC, the violations of congressional restrictions, and the illegal sale of arms were all significant problems. Scowcroft, however, thought the worst aspect of the scandal was that Reagan had violated his own policies and ideals. He had pledged to restore American power and prestige in the world, to regain the credibility of the United States, and to make it again a great power that was respected for its might and its values. Moreover, he had promised to never negotiate with terrorists and those who took hostages, positions that were, to Scowcroft, right and popular. "Then he turned on that policy in secret and did the very opposite. That was the most damaging aspect of the Iranian issue."[44]

The Iran-Contra scandal also exposed a fundamental tension in Reagan's thinking and the neoconservative approach to foreign policy. Was the goal the containment of communism and Soviet power, or was it to increase American influence and spread democracy, including rolling back perceived Soviet gains? The former goal could be realistically pursued and achieved within acceptable costs and limits, while the latter was an idealistic hope that could not easily be aligned with the realities of other nations, the power of the United States, and the tolerance of the American people. Thus, it had to be pursued covertly and, in the end, illegally, with great damage to the United States, in terms of greater anti-American sentiment, loss of confidence in American leadership and credibility, and increased distrust of Washington and its leaders.

THE ROAD BACK TO WASHINGTON

The Iran-Contra scandal played out amid renewed discussions of the relative decline of American power. The impetus was the publication of Paul

Kennedy's *The Rise and Fall of the Great Powers* at the end of 1987. Starting around 1500, Kennedy analyzed the factors that had led to the rise and then decline of great Western powers, from Spain and the Netherlands to France and Great Britain. He argued that what originally made them powerful was their control of economic resources and their capacity for the production of goods. Each power, in turn, had fallen victim to what he termed "imperial overstretch." In an effort to protect the wealth and power they had gained, the nations expanded their control over more territory, built up their military, and took on more commitments than they could afford in a self-defeating strategy designed to preserve a position of dominance. This set off an economic decline that made their empires unsustainable and required retrenchment at the same time that another power was emerging in a dominant position. The theory seemed to explain many of the problems the United States faced, with its military bases spanning the globe from commitments made decades earlier, its economy suffering from budget and trade deficits by the end of the 1980s, its policies seemingly stymied by defiant small nations, and its dominating post–World War II influence waning. While still a great power, Kennedy argued that a relative decline had set in, and the nation would have to adjust its policies and expectations accordingly.[45]

No matter how much the administration claimed that Kennedy was wrong, that the United States was an exceptional nation, not an empire, and was therefore not subject to the same forces that had undermined previous great powers, the American public was unhappy with Reagan's foreign policy and the direction in which he had taken the United States abroad. Chastened, Reagan began to retreat from many of his policies. It was the president's good fortune that his second term in office coincided with the emergence of Mikhail Gorbachev as the head of the Soviet Union. The new Soviet leader's openness to different approaches to East-West relations, in conjunction with Reagan's desire to negotiate on arms, began a series of summit meetings and negotiations that culminated in a December 1987 intermediate-range nuclear forces (INF) treaty that for the first time reduced the number of nuclear weapons on both sides. The INF treaty was in line with the aims of the Scowcroft Commission's recommendations to pursue modernization and strategic stability through arms negotiations rather than a nuclear buildup and a quest for strategic superiority. This led to an easing of tensions on other issues in Europe that would soon transform the world and take attention away from the failures in policy marked by the Iran-Contra affair.

In Central America, the administration was forced to accede to a peace process headed by Costa Rica's president, Oscar Arias, who managed to gain agreement among all heads of state for a cease-fire in the region and the promise of elections in Nicaragua to resolve the political disputes there. With the public more opposed to his policy than ever, and Congress unwilling to provide new support to the contras, Reagan had to admit defeat and the failure of the Reagan Doctrine to accomplish its goals. The policy ideas outlined by Scowcroft in 1984 turned out to be the way to peace in Central America, even if the United States could take little credit for the outcome.

Out from under the cloud of Iran-Contra, and with tensions in Europe noticeably eased, talk began to emerge in 1988 that the Cold War was ending. Ironically, as Reagan was backing away from his hard-line position to one that was akin to the strategy of détente, a myth began to emerge among his boosters that it was Reagan's military buildup and confrontational stance that had prompted Gorbachev's compromises and reduced tensions between Washington and Moscow. Relations had improved, and Gorbachev, seeking to enact desperately needed domestic reforms to try to save a Soviet system that was failing, sought a reduction in the costs and dangers of the Cold War. On both sides, sufficiency in terms of defense rather than victory through arms became the approach. In the most celebrated moment, Gorbachev spoke at the United Nations on December 7, 1988, Pearl Harbor Day, and announced that he would reduce the size of the Soviet army and be guided by the idea of freedom of choice in government in Eastern Europe, signaling an end to Soviet interventions in the satellite nations.

It fell to George H. W. Bush to respond to this latest Soviet initiative and the events it would unleash. As Reagan's vice president, Bush was concerned about the loose administrative style that had led to the Iran-Contra scandal, the often bitter divisions within the foreign policy team that had led to principals being cut out of the decision making, what he considered the too-easy embrace of Gorbachev, and the damage done to American prestige and credibility outside of Europe. As a conservative, Bush sought to reestablish trust in the structure of the government and faith in the individuals who made foreign policy. To ensure that the problems of the Reagan White House were not repeated, Bush turned to Scowcroft to be his national security advisor. Committed to restoring the main tenets of post–World War II American foreign policy, the two men would be the last of the containment generation to guide American foreign policy, and they oversaw the final success of internationalism and the end of the Cold War. Like Stimson, Scowcroft's second chance would lead to his greatest achievements.

NOTES

1. Stimson and Scowcroft were the only two officials to serve two different administrations in a senior foreign policy position in the twentieth century. The last

person prior to Stimson to do so was his law partner Elihu Root, who was William McKinley's secretary of war and Theodore Roosevelt's secretary of state. General George Marshall served as secretary of state and secretary of defense, but he held both positions in the Truman administration. Since Scowcroft left office in 1993, Colin Powell and Donald Rumsfeld have served two different presidents, Powell as national security advisor to Reagan and secretary of state for George W. Bush, and Rumsfeld as secretary of defense for presidents Ford and George W. Bush. Henry Kissinger held the positions of national security advisor and secretary of state at the same time from 1973 to 1975. Stimson remains the only person to serve in these positions in a Republican and a Democratic administration.

2. David F. Schmitz, *The First Wise Man* (Wilmington, DE: Scholarly Resources, 2001), xii–xvii.

3. *Public Papers of the Presidents: Jimmy E. Carter, 1977* (Washington, DC: Government Printing Office, 1978), 954–62.

4. *Public Papers of the Presidents: Carter, 1977*, 954–62.

5. Zbigniew Brzezinski and Brent Scowcroft, *America and the World: Conversations on the Future of American Foreign Policy*, moderated by David Ignatius (New York: Basic Books, 2008), 93.

6. *Public Papers of the Presidents: Carter, 1980* (Washington DC: Government Printing Office, 1981), 162–79.

7. John C. Campbell, Andrew J. Goodpaster, and Brent Scowcroft, *Oil and Turmoil: Western Choices in the Middle East* (Boulder, CO: Westview Press, 1979), 12, 9.

8. Kenneth Rush, Brent Scowcroft, and Joseph J. Wolf, *Strengthening Deterrence: NATO and the Credibility of Western Defense in the 1980s* (Boston: Ballinger Publishing, 1982), 253–54.

9. Rush, Scowcroft, and Wolf, *Strengthening Deterrence*, 259.

10. Marilyn Young, *The Vietnam Wars* (New York: HarperCollins, 1991), 315.

11. See Robert Scheer, *With Enough Shovels* (New York: Random House, 1982).

12. Brzezinski and Scowcroft, *America and the World*, 4.

13. *Report of the President's Commission on Strategic Forces (the Scowcroft Report)*, (Washington, DC: Government Printing Office, 1983), 1.

14. The other members of the Scowcroft Commission were Nicholas Brady, former senator from New Jersey; William Clements, former governor of Texas and deputy secretary of defense; Dr. John M. Deutch, dean of science at MIT and former director of research at the Department of Energy; Alexander M. Haig, Jr., former secretary of state and supreme Allied commander in Europe; Richard Helms, former director of the Central Intelligence Agency; John H. Lyons, vice president of the AFL-CIO and chairman of the defense subcommittee of its executive council; William J. Perry, former undersecretary of defense for research and engineering; Thomas C. Reed, special assistant to the president and former secretary of the Air Force; Vice Admiral Levering Smith, former director of special projects for the Navy; and R. James Woolsey, former undersecretary of the Navy.

15. Scowcroft to Reagan, 6 April 1983, *Report of the President's Commission on Strategic Forces* (Washington, DC: The Commission).

16. The seven senior counselors were Harold Brown, former secretary of defense and secretary of the Air Force; Lloyd N. Cutler, former counsel to President Carter; Henry A. Kissinger, former secretary of state and national security

advisor; Melvin R. Laird, former secretary of defense; John McCone, former director of the Central Intelligence Agency; Donald H. Rumsfeld, former secretary of
defense; and James R. Schlesinger, former secretary of defense.

17. *Report of the President's Commission on Strategic Forces*, 1–2.

18. *Report of the President's Commission on Strategic Forces*, 1–3, 12.

19. *Report of the President's Commission on Strategic Forces*, 14–15.

20. *Report of the President's Commission on Strategic Forces*, 24.

21. *Report of the President's Commission on Strategic Forces*, 25–26.

22. *Public Papers of the Presidents: Ronald W. Reagan, 1983* (Washington, DC:
Government Printing Office, 1984), 563–65.

23. Reagan to Foley, 11 May 1983, White House Office of Records Management
(hereafter WHORM): National Security-Defense, 125120, Box 8, Ronald Reagan
Presidential Library, Simi Valley, California (hereafter RRPL).

24. Gore et al. to Reagan, 2 May 1983, WHORM, National Security-Defense,
Box 8, 125120, RRPL.

25. Nunn, Cohen, and Percy to Scowcroft, 9 September 1983, WHORM, National Security-Defense, 171320, RRPL.

26. Nunn, Cohen, and Percy to Scowcroft.

27. Department of State, *Communist Interference in El Salvador*, Special Report
No. 80, 23 February (Washington, DC: Government Printing Office, 1981).

28. President's Special Review Board, *The Tower Commission Report* (New York:
Times Books, 1987), 56.

29. *The Tower Commission Report*, 58.

30. James R. Greene and Brent Scowcroft, *Western Interests and U.S. Policy in the
Caribbean Basin: Report of the Atlantic Council's Working Group on the Caribbean Basin*
(Boston: Oelgeschlager, Gunn & Hain, 1984).

31. Greene and Scowcroft, *Western Interests and U.S. Policy*, 26, 21.

32. Greene and Scowcroft, *Western Interests and U.S. Policy*, 55.

33. Greene and Scowcroft, *Western Interests and U.S. Policy*, 22.

34. *The Tower Commission Report*, 18.

35. *The Tower Commission Report*, 100.

36. *The Tower Commission Report*, 62.

37. *The Tower Commission Report*, 62–63.

38. *The Tower Commission Report*, 64–65.

39. *The Tower Commission Report*, 65–66.

40. *The Tower Commission Report*, 79.

41. *The Tower Commission Report*, 91.

42. *The Tower Commission Report*, 91–92.

43. Kenneth W. Thompson, ed., *The Ford Presidency* (Lanham, MD: University
Press of America, 1988), 314–16.

44. Thompson, *The Ford Presidency*, 314–16.

45. Paul Kennedy, *The Rise and Fall of the Great Powers* (New York: Random
House, 1987).

4

✧

Internationalism Triumphant: The Fall of the Berlin Wall and the End of the Cold War

Brent Scowcroft had developed a close friendship as well as a good working relationship with George H. W. Bush when Bush was director of the CIA under President Ford. The two men, both flyers, shared similar worldviews shaped by World War II, the successes of the early Cold War, and the challenges of the Vietnam era. Conservative internationalists, they believed that the United States had to act as a world leader, contain the Soviet Union, extend American power and influence globally, support Europe and key allies, and work through international organizations designed to implement American ideas around the world. The proper use of American power would bring about stability and a more peaceful international system that would allow for the growth of American influence, ideas, and trade. The Vietnam War taught the need for restraint in using American force and the necessity of a clear mission with definable and obtainable goals that had the support of the American people. Changes in the international system had to be managed and controlled so as not to lead to the rise of forces hostile to the United States. Scowcroft and Bush became so close that the national security advisor purchased a condominium in Kennebunkport, Maine, near the Bush family compound.

Scowcroft believed that Bush, having served as ambassador to the United Nations, chief of the Liaison Office in China, director of the Central Intelligence Agency, and vice president, came to the office of the presidency with a wealth of experience and understanding of foreign policy, and that he understood the world better than any other president. The two men thought so much alike and worked so closely together that

President Bush and General Brent Scowcroft fish from the Fidelity off the coast of Kennebunkport, Maine, on August 28, 1989. Courtesy of the George H. W. Bush Presidential Library.

they cowrote a foreign policy memoir of the Bush administration. *A World Transformed* has a unique structure that alternates back and forth within the chapters between sections written by Bush or by Scowcroft, and it also includes context and background parts that they wrote together.

Their friendship, mutual understanding, and close working relationship placed Scowcroft at the head of Bush's foreign policy team, even with James Baker, Bush's longtime friend from Texas, as secretary of state. This allowed Scowcroft to manage the national security process and shape the policies of the Bush administration. Scowcroft had the president's complete confidence, and it was taken as a given that when Scowcroft gave an order, it had Bush's endorsement. As Scowcroft has noted, he believed that at the top level "it's all personality," and he had "a very close relationship with President Bush." This allowed him to disagree with the president when he thought it was necessary, because it was "important that the national security advisor tell the president what you think he or she needs to know, not what he wants to hear. And that can be tough."[1] Scowcroft's own assessment was that the process he fostered allowed strong people to express "their views forcefully, under a President who joined the debate but sought to draw out the various arguments, not stifle them. Underlying it all was a sense of camaraderie that kept the discussion within bounds. When the President made the decision, debate ended immediately and attention turned to executing it."[2]

The national security advisor's reputation and work habits were also a key asset in creating a cooperative foreign policy process and setting the tone of the administration's foreign policy. Scowcroft earned the trust of all who worked for him with his work ethic (usually spending fifteen to sixteen hours a day in the office), discipline, open leadership style, loyalty to those who worked for him, well-mannered behavior, and well-known modesty. As Robert Gates, who served Scowcroft as deputy national security advisor, recalled, Scowcroft was especially effective because he made sure the system functioned at its best during the crises, challenges, and dramatic moments of change that faced the Bush administration. "The strong individuals who ran State, Defense, CIA, and the other key institutions of national security trusted Scowcroft as no other National Security Adviser has been trusted—to represent them and their views fairly, to report to him on meetings accurately, to facilitate rather than block their access to the President." Scowcroft's "lack of egotism and his gentle manner," Gates wrote, "made possible the closest working relationships with other senior members of the national security team."[3]

Future national security advisor Condoleezza Rice, whom Scowcroft recruited from Stanford to work for him on the National Security Council from 1989 to 1991 as a Soviet expert, agreed with Gates's assessment. Scowcroft's National Security Council, she recalled, was a flat organization where special assistants had direct contact with him and the president. It was not a hierarchical organization, but one where his staff was encouraged to present their views. Access was never limited, and Rice saw him almost every day. This provided a great sense of cooperation, coordination, and purpose and assured everyone that their opinions would be heard and respected.[4]

As the momentous political changes unfolded in Eastern Europe that would confront the Bush administration in its first year in office, Scowcroft employed a framework for policy that reflected his internationalist viewpoint and concerns along with his inherent caution and deliberate approach. Rice recalls that Scowcroft was careful about the use of power, and in that sense he was something of a realist, but he did not hold to realism as a coherent view of how international relations worked or as a singular approach that guided him in making policy. Rather, he was convinced that caution, moderation, and conciliation were the right approaches to the changes taking place in the communist world.[5]

Scowcroft was critical of Reagan's response to the Soviet Union. He thought the previous administration had lacked a clear policy and had simply been reacting to events, placing all of its efforts into arms reduction in its final years and claiming an end to the Cold War. But the Cold War was far from over. Soviet troops remained in Eastern Europe, Germany was divided, and the Warsaw Pact remained intact. Scowcroft sought to shift the focus in relations from arms control talks with the Soviet Union to the developments behind the Iron Curtain. He wanted the United States to have a policy that engaged the changes taking place in Eastern Europe, that shaped the course of events, and that helped move the needle toward undoing the post–World War II division of Europe. Gorbachev had created an opening and a great opportunity, but much work still needed to be done if a fundamental reshaping of the political map were to occur. It was Bush and Scowcroft who crafted the policies that guided these remarkable changes to a peaceful end.

Scowcroft did not foresee the rapid pace of change that would take hold in 1989 and lead to the fall of the Berlin Wall in November 1989. His goal in dealing with the remarkable political upheavals taking place was to set a course of "encouraging, guiding, and managing change without provoking backlash and crackdown," and thereby ensure that change continued in a manner that brought forth stability, served U.S. interests, and fostered long-term peace.[6] Above all, he sought to consolidate Western gains while avoiding a Versailles Treaty outcome with a bitter, defeated Soviet Union that would remain hostile to the West and continue to be a destabilizing force in the world. The tenets of internationalism under the prudent leadership of Bush and Scowcroft guided American foreign policy making at this critical moment and helped to bring about a peaceful cessation of Soviet domination of Eastern Europe, the reunification of Germany, and an end to the Cold War—all without violence or war.

EASTERN EUROPE

When Scowcroft returned to Washington in January 1989, the world remained the "familiar bipolar one of superpower rivalry." Scowcroft believed that the Reagan administration, having first gone too far to one extreme with its bellicose attacks on the Soviet Union and its attempts to win the Cold War through an arms race during its first term, had swung too far in the other direction at the end of its second term to a position "marked by what I considered an unwarranted assumption that the changes in Soviet attitudes and rhetoric, or perhaps the accession of Gorbachev to power, signaled the end of the forty-year confrontation between East and West." Specifically, he found Reagan's proposals for eliminating all ballistic missiles "insane," and the president's desire for disarmament "a mighty dubious objective for grown-ups in this business," since these efforts did not provide a structure for greater stability. It troubled Scowcroft that the administration was fueling talk that the Cold War was over without thinking through what that actually meant in terms of the two alliances (NATO and the Warsaw Pact), nuclear weapons and conventional forces, and political differences. It was undeniable, however, that there was unrest in Eastern Europe and demands for change. Planning, not "wishful thinking," had to be carried forward on a deliberate basis, and Scowcroft was "determined that we should err on the side of prudence."[7]

There was reason for optimism, and Scowcroft believed the United States was operating from a strong position. "Post–World War II policies toward the Soviet Union" had been "extraordinarily successful," and containment was "vindicated" as people rejected communism for freedom. The direction of U.S.-Soviet relations was favorable, and it "would be unwise thoughtlessly to abandon policies that have brought us this far." Given the changes taking place in the Soviet Union and Eastern Europe, Scowcroft thought it was vital to consider what the United States could do to further the positive trends. The United States could "be standing at the door of a new era in our relationship with the USSR, with potential for significantly reducing military forces and resolving long-standing international disputes." Nonetheless, it was important to remember that the Soviet Union remained "an adversary with awesome military power whose interests conflict in important ways with our own" and that the outcome of the dramatic changes underway remained unknown.[8]

In sum, Scowcroft was cautious. There were numerous good reasons for this, Scowcroft believed. The Cold War was not over, despite Gorbachev's different rhetoric and approach to the United States. Historically, every time there were signs of political liberalization behind the Iron Curtain, the Soviet Union crushed the movement and reasserted its control. It happened in East Germany in 1953, in Hungary in 1956, and in Czechoslovakia in 1968. A pattern had emerged of ferment for change followed by Soviet repression, and Scowcroft deemed it too early to tell if the pattern would change. The period of détente had also led to high hopes that the political environment was changing, only to see the old guard again take control. Scowcroft was wary of the "danger of excessive expectations," and he worried that the United States would be swayed by rhetoric and the surface appearance of change. This led him to be "very hard-nosed about Gorbachev." The Cold War was about Eastern Europe, "and the Soviet army was still there."[9] Scowcroft wanted to be sure that American actions encouraged liberalization at a rate that did not bring about a Soviet reaction and military crackdown as had occurred in the past.

Events moved quickly, and there was often little time for reflection on their meaning or the proper response. Yet Rice recalls that she and Scowcroft talked about the historical precedents, most notably John Foster Dulles and Hungary in 1956. They worried that the United States might raise hopes and expectations behind the Iron Curtain that could not be satisfied. The biggest concern was not to encourage something in Eastern Europe that the United States was unprepared to back up. If events went too far too fast, Rice believed, the Soviet Union could crack down, and there was nothing the United States could do to prevent that. As Eastern Europe was unraveling in a positive manner, Scowcroft was determined that the United States not do anything to tempt Moscow to take action. Given the bad historical analogies and previous failures to sustain change, the Bush administration had to be careful what it said.[10]

There were also military concerns. Critics later would say that the Bush administration was too timid and that the Soviet Union had no option but to allow the changes to play out. Yet the Soviet Union had over 1.5 million troops in Europe, and over thirty thousand nuclear weapons. Moscow's choices might not have been good, but they existed, and a conflict could still destroy the world. Washington, therefore, did not want to back Moscow into a corner and provoke a nuclear response. There was no guarantee that hard-liners in the Kremlin would not ultimately prevail, as their counterparts in China did that summer during the Chinese crackdown on dissent in Tiananmen Square. Scowcroft understood the stakes for the Soviet Union. The Cold War had started in Eastern Europe, Scowcroft realized, and Soviet forces were still there. This was a key strategic and political interest of Moscow's, and the American response had to be handled carefully.

Nobody knew what direction Gorbachev was ultimately going to take, but it was clear to Scowcroft that the Soviet leader's objective was to save communism, not end the Cold War. Glasnost and perestroika were seen by Gorbachev "not as leading toward democracy but as a way to increase the efficiency and effectiveness of the Soviet Union."[11] Gorbachev was trying to rejuvenate the system and increase productivity, Scowcroft believed, not to make it democratic but to maintain power. As Rice noted, she and Scowcroft thought that, since Gorbachev was unwilling to assert Soviet power to stop the political changes that were taking place, the most important thing was to not back him into a corner. It was crucial not to make a mistake when events were going the way Washington wanted.[12]

For all of these reasons, Scowcroft believed that the United States needed to find a delicate balance. It should focus on what was transpiring in Eastern Europe and encourage the political groups seeking liberalization, but only at a rate that did not bring about a Soviet backlash. Scowcroft therefore ordered a series of strategic policy reviews in order to get ahead of the ferment that was building inside the Warsaw Pact countries. As Scowcroft explained, he had two goals for the policy reviews. First, he sought to change the focus of American policy toward the Soviet Union from arms control to the events in Eastern Europe, and in the process alter the political situation that Washington confronted. The United States, he argued, should seek a reduction of conventional forces in central Europe so as to reduce or eliminate the presence of the Red Army. "That would create a better environment for political evolution there."[13]

Rice noted that policy reviews are generally launched to prevent something from happening, to provide time to change out the bureaucracy and get new people in place, and in this case to slow things down and not rush into any decisions. Yet, the Eastern European review that she headed up turned out to be an important policy change. Previously, American policy had been premised on the idea that you favored Eastern European states that had developed a distance from the Soviet Union, notably Romania and Yugoslavia. With the political changes developing in Poland, the yardstick for support became how much internal liberalization had occurred. The review made this break and led to a fundamental shift in policy that foreshadowed Washington's support for the political revolution that was taking place in Eastern Europe.[14]

Second, this policy shift fit with Scowcroft's desire to revise the American approach to the individual states of Eastern Europe. The new approach was to "encourage the movement from within [Eastern European nations] to broaden the system to make it more open."[15] Scowcroft agreed that the United States should reverse its policy and encourage the people who were trying to liberalize their nation's political structures. This meant that Romania went from receiving the most support to the least, and Poland and Hungary moved to the top of the list of Eastern European countries the United States supported. Scowcroft knew that Gorbachev was pushing for reform in Eastern Europe, in part "as a prod to recalcitrants inside the Soviet Union who were standing in the way of his own reforms."[16] Yet the Soviet leader failed to realize that the communist governments had no political legitimacy, and that the more liberal they became, the greater their chances were of being overthrown.

While these developments could present problems, they also provided an opportunity to the United States, and Scowcroft did not want to miss any chance for positive change. He thought Poland would see the most rapid transformation and liberalization because the communist regime had never fully reestablished its control after the unrest in 1981 and the imposition of martial law. It should therefore be the primary focus of the new American policy. The Catholic Church, headed by the Polish Pope John Paul II, was providing moral leadership in the quest for political freedom, while the labor union Solidarity was consistently challenging the power and legitimacy of the government. By 1989, the Communist Party agreed to share some power with the union, a development that Scowcroft hoped the United States could encourage. The administration "saw real possibilities in the way Solidarity was behaving."[17] It would be the test of whether 1989 signaled a new era and was different from the earlier years of hope in Eastern Europe.

With Scowcroft taking the lead, the administration's discussions and policy in 1989 focused on his two policy objectives. In the first major meeting of senior policy makers, the national security advisor explained his understanding of the situation the United States faced and what it could do to influence a favorable outcome in Europe. The internationalist policies adopted after World War II had worked for four decades, containing Soviet power and allowing the West to prosper. It now appeared that the endgame of the Cold War might be in sight. The upheavals in Eastern Europe were not solely anticommunist in nature, Scowcroft opined. The Russian Revolution, and then the results of World War II, "had frozen the process of the restructuring of Eastern Europe following the collapse of the Austro-Hungarian Empire after World War I. It appeared that we were witnessing the incipient collapse there of Soviet domination—the successor in many ways to Austria-Hungary." What did this revival of nationalism mean, how quickly would it progress, and how would the Soviet Union respond? Scowcroft then turned to another crucial outcome of World War II, a divided Germany. In a prescient observation, Scowcroft was the first to ask what the implications were of "its potential reunification as Moscow's control ebbed?"[18]

Scowcroft did not expect concrete answers to all of these questions, as it was impossible to know where Gorbachev was heading and what would develop in the Eastern European nations. The most important goal was to keep in mind the larger picture of what the United States sought and what was at stake, and to create an environment that would help foster positive change. Seeking stability in the arms race at the lowest possible number of weapons was central, as was building a relationship with Moscow that would lessen the chance of conflict by reducing forces in Eastern Europe. Both objectives appeared possible given the changing political landscape in the Eastern European nations. It was vital, however, to make sure that the United States took the initiative and that it put forward positions that Gorbachev could accept, or at a minimum would not reject outright.

Scowcroft noted that the interpretative analysis he had set out and the conclusions drawn from it—to reorient Soviet policy with a focus on Eastern Europe, to encourage and prepare for political change, to envision an end to the Cold War, and to create an atmosphere of trust with Moscow by not challenging its power when it was vulnerable—"was cautious and prudent, an appropriate policy in a period of turbulence and rapid change, but it proved surprisingly durable and established a valuable framework for the conduct of policy."[19] It helped to achieve the goal of moving "liberalization forward, but at a pace that would be under the Soviets' reaction point."[20] Still, Scowcroft did not think change would happen as fast as it did. But he did understand early on that, if there was no Soviet backlash or crackdown by the communist regimes, then Gorbachev was undermining the foundation of the Soviet empire.

The Bush administration's policy was articulated in a series of speeches in April and May. The first was delivered on April 17 and focused on the new approach to Eastern Europe. Given that the topic of the address was freedom in Poland, the president traveled to Hamtramck, Michigan, a city surrounded by Detroit, which had a high percentage of workers of Eastern European and Polish descent. On April 5, the Polish government signed a historic agreement that ended its sole control of power. It legalized Solidarity, created an office of president and a one-hundred-seat senate, and allowed the political opposition to the communists to compete for these seats as well as for over one-third of the positions in parliament. Bush declared that the dramatic changes taking place in Poland were a result of its yearning for freedom and that the United States stood with the people of that nation in their quest for democracy. "Let no one doubt the sincerity of the American people and their government in our desire to see reform succeed" in Eastern Europe. It was there that the Cold War had begun, "and if it is to end, it will end in this crucible of world conflict." The United States welcomed the agreements that were reached in Poland to recognize the Solidarity labor union and to allow for a free opposition press, the rights of independent political organizations, and the holding of elections.[21]

The United States sought, the president emphasized, "to promote the evolution of freedom—the opportunities sparked by the Helsinki accords and the deepening East-West contact." For real change to come, Bush insisted, political openness must be matched by economic reform. The United States was prepared to provide assistance in terms of greater trade, tariff relief, loans, and other financial measures, and further help would be provided commensurate with political and economic liberalization. What was at stake was not just a new and prosperous Poland, but a free and stable Europe. "If Poland's experiment succeeds, other countries may follow," the president opined. Guided by a dedication to freedom, if the United States was wise "and ready to seize the moment, we will be remembered as the generation that made all Europe free."[22]

This was, Scowcroft believed, a significant first step, because it addressed "the central questions of the Cold War" and directed American policy to "try to capitalize on the signs of thaw in the communist states of Europe and to steer events in productive directions, but at a speed Moscow could accept."[23] The next month, Bush spoke at the Texas A&M University commencement ceremonies, where he outlined the Soviet side of his new policy, "Beyond Containment," his desire to find a resolution to the East-West conflict, and the need to imagine a post–Cold War world.

Rice recalled that George Kennan was on her and Scowcroft's minds at the time. She reread the Mr. X article, "Sources of Soviet Conduct," and discussed it with Scowcroft as he was preparing the "Beyond Containment" speech. Kennan, Rice noted, wanted to deny the Soviet Union an easy course of external expansion, which would eventually make it turn inward and have to deal with its own internal contradictions. In the late spring of 1989, she and Scowcroft believed that was what they were witnessing. Mounting pressures had forced Moscow to confront the internal problems of the nation. But was the Soviet Union really going to stay on the sidelines and allow Soviet power to be eliminated in Eastern Europe?[24]

In a speech crafted mainly by Scowcroft, the president began by recalling the establishment of the policy of containment and the belief that "the Soviet Union, denied the easy course of expansion, would turn inward and address the contradictions of its inefficient, repressive, and inhumane system." The policy worked, the president declared, and the "Soviet Union is now publicly facing this hard reality." Moscow now "says it seeks to make peace with the world and criticizes its own postwar policies." Bush welcomed these words and stated that it was his desire to "move beyond containment to a new policy for the 1990s—one that recognizes the full scope of change taking place around the world and in the Soviet Union itself." He sought a new era of relations with Moscow through the "integration of the Soviet Union into the community of nations. And as the Soviet Union itself moves toward greater openness and democratization . . . we will match their steps with steps of our own."[25]

To achieve this break with the past would require concrete measures. Bush called on the Kremlin to take such positive steps as a reduction of its conventional forces in Europe, abandonment of the Brezhnev doctrine and support for self-determination in Eastern Europe, cooperation with the West in resolving ongoing conflicts around the world, respect for the Helsinki agreements, and support for democratic and human rights. He also extended an invitation to move toward arms reduction to reduce the risk of nuclear war. The United States recognized that "a new breeze is blowing across the steppes and the cities of the Soviet Union," and Washington was ready to be a partner in bringing the Cold War to an end. He reminded his audience that, in 1945, it had been a Texas A&M graduate who was the first American to shake hands with a Soviet soldier at the Elbe River. "Once again, we are ready to extend our hand. Once again, we are ready for a hand in return."[26]

The final speech, delivered at the graduation ceremony at the Coast Guard Academy on May 24, focused on U.S. security strategy in the context of a changing world. Communism was entering into the last days of that failed system, Bush asserted, while democracy was in the ascendancy. "Never before has the idea of freedom so captured the imagination of men and women the world over, and never before has the hope of freedom beckoned so many," from the trade unionist in Poland to the students in China's Tiananmen Square who held the world transfixed by their actions. Where did the United States want to see the world go, and what would be the security issues in a new international system?[27]

Bush envisioned "a growing community of democracies anchoring international peace and stability and a dynamic free-market system generating prosperity and progress on a global scale." These were the values of the United States, and they gave the country its strength. Promoting and advancing this change, and moving beyond containment to build a stable relationship with Moscow, would do more to advance the security of the United States than any weapons. The president declared that he was ready to explore every opportunity to advance this vision and transform the world.[28]

There were, however, new security challenges emerging that would have to be confronted. Too many nations in the Middle East and Asia were acquiring highly destructive weapons that made them a threat to their neighbors and to international stability. In addition, "It is an unfortunate fact that the world faces an increasing threat from armed insurgencies, terrorists, and . . . narcotics traffickers—and in some regions, an unholy alliance of all three." The starting point for dealing with these dangers was the reduction of arms, peace in Europe, and an effective American deterrent "that promotes stability at the lowest feasible level of armaments." Positive steps by the Soviet Union to reduce its weapons and troops in central Europe and abandon its offensive strategy for one of cooperation with the West would allow the United States to focus on these emerging problems and regions, and, "provided we seize the opportunities open to us, we can help others attain the freedom that we cherish."[29]

These were exhilarating times, and Scowcroft was optimistic about the changes on the horizon and the end of the Cold War in Europe. Policy changes had been implemented. Aid was starting to flow to Poland and other countries, Gorbachev was promising unilateral reductions in troops, arms talks with the Soviets were proceeding, and political change in Eastern Europe was progressing much faster than anyone could have imagined. The focus of American policy was now on constructing a framework "designed to reduce the threat of war and bring real peace" by encouraging the liberalization underway in the Warsaw Pact nations.[30] While in Europe for NATO meetings, Bush summarized the American position in a speech in Mainz, West Germany. Due to forty years of Cold War, the president declared, democracy was dormant in half of Europe. "But the passion for freedom cannot be denied forever. . . . The time is right. Let Europe be whole and free." He pledged American support for "self-determination for all of Germany and all of Eastern Europe." The president sought a strengthening of the "Helsinki process to promote free elections and political pluralism in Eastern Europe," a reference to the parts of the 1975 Helsinki Accords that President Ford had signed which stipulated respect for human rights, freer travel, and expanded trade, and a reduction of military forces on the continent to form what he called a "commonwealth of free nations" in Europe. Bush praised the political reforms in Poland and the removal of barriers on the Hungarian-Austrian border, and he called for the barbed wire to be removed everywhere. "Let Berlin be next—let Berlin be next!" he declared. The Berlin Wall "stands as a monument to the failure of communism. It must come down."[31] A new vision of Europe was driving American policy.

Still, Scowcroft saw a need for caution. Although the achievement of America's Cold War goal of liberating Eastern Europe and putting an end to the Soviet threat in Europe was coming into view, he did not know how hard the United States could push or what might upset the Kremlin and cause a change in course. A perfect example of the problems the administration faced was posed by the annual marking of Captive Nations Day in July. Begun in the 1950s to highlight the Soviet occupation of Eastern Europe and to express the moral support of the United States for freedom in those lands, by the 1980s it was a ritual event that garnered little attention. As Rice recalled, there was always a strident declaration issued by Washington. To do so in the midst of the dramatic changes in Eastern Europe would sound like a call to arms and an attack on the Soviet Union. The routine was suddenly a potential misstep.[32] It was still unclear exactly what would transpire, and as the events in Tiananmen Square would demonstrate, the emergence of a post–Cold War world would not be without its trials and setbacks.

TIANANMEN SQUARE

Immediately after the 1988 election, Scowcroft had hoped that Bush could visit China in the opening weeks of his presidency, particularly after it was announced that Gorbachev would be going to Beijing in mid-May. The national security advisor believed it was important to enhance U.S.-Chinese relations and to impede a potential Sino-Soviet rapprochement. Xiaoping Deng's economic reforms during the 1980s had begun to open up China's markets and introduce capitalist practices, but they were misunderstood by many in the United States as a move toward political liberalization as well. Scowcroft, realizing that "at no time was [Deng] offering fundamental political change," wanted the Chinese leaders to know that the Bush administration looked forward to a cooperative relationship based on mutual interests. Scowcroft was also aware that demands for political change were growing in China, particularly among students, and that a split had developed within the Chinese Communist Party "between those who backed market reforms and greater openness and those who demanded orthodoxy and retention of absolute political control by the Party."[33] He wanted to assure the Chinese that these political issues were not the concern of the United States and that the Bush administration had no intention of disrupting good relations over China's internal policies and practices.

Scowcroft had played a role in U.S.-Chinese relations from the early 1970s. He traveled to Beijing in 1971 as part of the American team that prepared the way for Nixon's historic trip to China, and in 1972 he was part of the president's entourage on the visit that ended over two decades of diplomatic isolation by the United States of the People's Republic of China. The primary accomplishment of Nixon's diplomacy, in Scowcroft's estimation, was the United States' "understanding with China" to "join together to oppose Soviet hegemony." Allowing the "communist Chinese to assume the China seat in the UN" was a first step toward bringing Beijing into the American-created post–World War II international system. This came at a crucial time in the Cold War when the United States was withdrawing from Vietnam and seeking to maintain its influence in East Asia.[34]

Scowcroft first met Deng in 1975 when he and President Ford visited China, and he met him again in 1981 when they returned to China as private citizens. His work for Kissinger Associates kept Scowcroft involved in American-Chinese economic relations as a consultant throughout the 1980s, and he remained in contact with all the key leaders of the Chinese government. Through all of his work and contacts, Scowcroft considered himself an expert on China and on how best to nurture this important and tricky relationship.

Scowcroft's understanding of China's past and the importance of that history to the decision making of current Chinese leaders guided his thinking: "If you look back at Chinese history," Scowcroft observed, "you find periods of going from a highly centralized, very tightly knit country to chaos." Beijing, he believed, worried about a return of this pattern, and that fear was a driving force in its decision making. Scowcroft was aware "that the Chinese leadership" was "deeply fearful of instability." This kept party leaders from opening up the political system at the same time that they were pursuing economic reform. Scowcroft was sympathetic to this fear and believed it had to be accounted for in any policies toward China.[35] The Chinese government could not tolerate political challenges or reforms at the same time that it was engaged in economic development, and it feared that the process could move beyond its control.

Instability could come from internal forces or from an external attack, making China also deeply wary of the outside world and sensitive to any criticism. There was no doubt in Scowcroft's mind that the Chinese leadership continued to "bear a grudge against the West" stemming from "the humiliation of the nineteenth century. That's deeply burned into their historical consciousness."[36] Therefore, it was exceedingly important to Scowcroft that caution be used in any dealings with China. It was fine to make it known "that we believe democracy is the way to go, and we're prepared to help anybody who wants to go in that direction." The choice, however, was up to Beijing, not Washington, and policy could not be made with that overt intent. The United States should encourage democracy "and help others who seek to emulate the best parts of our democracy," but "we should not seek to impose it."[37]

Bush, too, had extensive experience with China. He had served a year in Beijing as the chief of the U.S. Liaison Office—the head American diplomat to China prior to official diplomatic recognition—as well as head of the CIA, and he had visited China again while vice president under Reagan. During that time, he had developed a close relationship with Deng, who called him *"lao pengyou*, an old friend" during one of his visits, in recognition of Bush's understanding of China and the importance of U.S.-Chinese relations.[38] Scowcroft and Bush firmly believed that trade between the United States and China "had helped lead to the quest for more freedom. If people have commercial incentives, whether it's in China or in other totalitarian systems, the move to democracy becomes inexorable."[39] These attitudes made developing a response to the Tiananmen Square massacre very difficult for the administration.

Scowcroft believed that relations between the United States and China were critical and had to be handled with great care. The issues of political change in Eastern Europe and China, he believed, demanded different approaches. The different histories of the areas, the role of nationalism, and the issue of government legitimacy had to be taken into consideration. The Chinese government had greater political legitimacy than the communist regimes in Eastern Europe, and the issues involved in the Chinese protests did not have international implications. For these reasons, the Bush administration had a very different view of China than of the nations in Eastern Europe. The reforms in China under Deng Xiaoping were an effort to solidify the legitimacy of the party's rule through its economic program. The leaders in Beijing had concluded that the best way to preserve stability and retain the allegiance of the people was to improve the standard of living of the Chinese. Gorbachev, Scowcroft thought, was trying to do something similar, but his reforms extended beyond the Soviet Union to Eastern Europe, as he also had to contend with the Cold War with the United States. The Chinese were focused on their internal problems, while Gorbachev had both his internal problems and the external issues in Eastern Europe.

Initially, it appeared that an early trip to China was not feasible. The president's schedule precluded any state visit in the first half of 1989, and planning turned in a different direction before Japanese Emperor Hirohito died on January 7, 1989. While there was some opposition due to the emperor's role in World War II, Bush decided to attend the February 24 funeral. This allowed him to travel to China the next day for two days of discussions with China's leaders. As Scowcroft noted, this trip made Bush the first "president to travel to Asia before Europe—a sign of priorities for the new era."[40]

Scowcroft and Bush met with both Chinese premier Li Peng and Deng Xiaoping, among other senior officials. Li thanked Bush for U.S. support of Chinese reforms and expressed his hope for continued growth in the friendship between the two countries, especially in terms of American investments and trade relations. Yet he noted that the party believed that economic reforms demanded centralized control by the government, and he warned the president that China would not tolerate interference in its policies. Criticism "smacks of interference in China's internal affairs," he said, "and we are not happy about it." Li acknowledged that this was not the case with the new administration, and he wanted to speak in a frank manner to ensure the continuation of good relations.[41]

Deng focused on Chinese history and the accumulated problems with the outside world over the past 150 years, while emphasizing that "the Chinese people pay great attention to history." Since the Opium Wars, he stated, China had been "subjected to humiliation and invasion by foreign powers interfering in its internal affairs." The two nations that had hurt China the most were Russia, with the territory it had seized, and Japan, due to the millions of lives it had taken and the physical damage it had wrought during World War II. Deng focused particularly on the Yalta agreements, which "severed Outer Mongolia from China" and placed parts of Manchuria under Soviet control. He told Bush he was not trying to offend the United States by bringing up the agreements Roosevelt had reached with Stalin. Bush assured him that he was not troubled by this since he did not "like Yalta either."[42]

The point of Deng's comment was to highlight the difficult security situation China faced, a problem that grew with the Soviet military support of India and its base agreements in Vietnam, and to assure the United States of its friendship as a balance against the Russians. The strategic situation, in Deng's words, "is very unfavorable for China," and it faced an "encirclement" that had grown worse over time. It was for these reasons that Chairman Mao and Zhou Enlai had reached out to the United States and sought greater contact and support. Deng's words did much to assuage the administration's fears about Gorbachev's upcoming visit, and Bush left China "optimistic that we had laid some important groundwork for a productive period in our diplomatic relations." The president wanted the Chinese leadership to know that he was not interested in "lecturing and rhetoric." The United States could not ignore human rights issues, but it could continue to encourage the progress China had made while making clear its views on other issues without "unleashing an endless barrage of public criticism."[43]

This promising start to relations with China would soon be severely tested by student protests in China. Sporadic demonstrations by Chinese students began in 1987 with calls for political reforms to match the economic changes. Hard-liners in the party ousted Hu Yaobang, Deng's apparent successor, because he appeared to support further liberalization of Chinese society. Hu's death on April 15, 1989, led to demands for more change and set off large antigovernment demonstrations. As the protests grew, thousands of students came to Tiananmen Square, the center of China's capital. While acknowledging the party's authority, the students delivered a list of demands that called for greater freedoms, more democracy, a crackdown on corruption, and other political reforms. The government sent in the police to break up the demonstrations, and Deng went so far as to accuse the students of deliberately creating turmoil in society. On April 26, the party attacked the students for "counterrevolutionary" activity, a move that only fueled student anger and increased the size of the demonstrations.

On the sixtieth anniversary of the May 4 movement, the largest demonstrations took place, with tens of thousands of students and others occupying the square. In the midst of this turmoil, Mikhail Gorbachev arrived in China on May 15. In anticipation of the foreign coverage of the visit, hundreds of students began a hunger strike. Government officials met with the students and tried to persuade them to leave so as not to disrupt the ceremonies planned for Gorbachev and embarrass the party. Despite the threats and negotiations, the protest continued to build, with nearly a million people involved by the time Gorbachev left on May 18. After the Soviet leader's departure, Premier Li Peng warned the students that they were creating chaos and that the government would not tolerate the situation much longer. At the same time, the leading proponent of moderation and negotiation with the students, party general secretary Zhao Ziyang, lost his power. Li announced the imposition of martial law on May 19, and soldiers were called into the capital in preparation for a showdown.

As the government's position hardened, divisions appeared among the protestors. Many left due to a lack of progress or fear of reprisals, and others called for an end to the occupation of Tiananmen even while they still sought greater democracy and reform. The most determined of the students stayed on, showing their defiance on May 30 by building a thirty-three-foot statue, the "Goddess of Democracy," in the image of the Statue of Liberty, directly across the street from the gate to the Forbidden City and its portrait of Mao. The crisis reached its climax on June 4 when the People's Liberation Army, using deadly force, drove the protesters out of Tiananmen Square in a brutal and bloody move that killed over two thousand people and injured thousands more, and put an end to the demonstrations and further calls for reform.

Scowcroft was horrified by the images he saw of the crackdown in Tiananmen Square, and he knew that an immediate public statement and expression of U.S. abhorrence was necessary. But he believed the response had to be tempered with the knowledge of how sensitive China was to criticism and the need to maintain relations with China for both commercial and security reasons. Bush concurred. He sought a "measured response" that demonstrated that the military actions by the Chinese government were unacceptable to the United States but that did not sever relations with Beijing or impact economic relations in a way that would hurt the Chinese people. The president was conscious of China's displeasure over foreign criticism and was adamant that the United States had to remain "engaged with the Chinese government, if we were to have any influence or leverage to work for restraint and cooperation, let alone human rights and democracy. While angry rhetoric might be temporarily satisfying to some, I believed it would deeply hurt our efforts in the long term."[44] Scowcroft and Bush knew that the people of the United States were appalled by the massacre and would seek condemnation and punishment. The question they faced was how to express that anger while maintaining relations with China.

The fact that party hard-liners were blaming foreigners, particularly Americans, for China's troubles compounded the difficulty of formulating a response. The outpouring of support in the United States for the demonstrators made the United States, as the American embassy in Beijing noted on June 4, "an intrusive actor in this Chinese situation." The embassy further reported that "the Chinese have at all levels signaled us to watch our step or else."[45] Thus any action by the United States had the potential to bring further reprisals against the demonstrators and to strengthen the position of those Chinese leaders who opposed reform.

The administration did take strong measures. On June 5, President Bush denounced the brutal suppression of the Chinese demonstrators in Tiananmen Square, who were "advocating basic human rights, including the freedom of expression, freedom of the press, freedom of association." He noted that he had urged the Chinese government to show restraint and that the United States could not "condone the violent attacks and cannot ignore the consequences for our relationship with China." In response, he announced the suspension of military visits by U.S. and Chinese officers and all weapons sales to China, both by the government and by private contractors; he promised to look sympathetically on all requests by Chinese students in the United States to extend their stays; and he offered humanitarian assistance through the Red Cross to those injured by the Chinese Army. Further, the administration moved to deny China credits from the World Bank and pressured other nations and international institutions to cut off loans to Beijing. When asked why he did not go further and impose economic sanctions on trade, Bush replied that he believed commercial contacts were what had led to the push for freedom in China, a momentum he did not want to undermine: "I don't want to see a total break in this relationship and I will not encourage a total break in the relationship." While the United States asserted its commitment to democracy, it was important that it encourage peaceful change and "recognize the fact that China does have great pride in its own history."[46]

In spite of his genuine anger over the military crackdown, the president, Scowcroft recalled, wanted to communicate directly with the Chinese leaders to avoid severing contact and "to try to explain to them the enormity, in the eyes of the world, of what they had done." Scowcroft, as national security advisor, concurred, arguing that the United States "had too much invested in the China situation to throw it away with one stroke." As Bush wrote in his diary on June 10, "I want to preserve the relationship, but I must also make clear that the US cannot condone this kind of human rights brutality."[47]

Therefore, President Bush quickly reached out to the Chinese. In Scowcroft's words, the administration's tone was, "Look, we don't like what you did. We don't agree with what you did. But our relationship is so important for both of us that we must see our way through this." It would take some time, and the administration incurred severe criticism for its approach, but "we salvaged the relationship," which to Scowcroft was absolutely necessary for American economic interests and stability in East Asia.[48] He saw no chance that China was going the way of Eastern Europe or the Soviet Union. The Communist Party in China remained firmly in control and had the support of the army and much of the peasantry. Scowcroft perceived the political situations as vastly different. The changes underway in Eastern Europe were part of a political evolution in states where the governments lacked legitimacy, not a revolutionary confrontation with power. The situations were just not the same, and they called for different policies.

The Chinese leadership was angered by the American sanctions and public criticism, accusing the United States of interfering in China's internal affairs, and refused to talk directly to Bush. To break this impasse, Bush decided to send a letter to Deng setting out his concerns and views in an effort to remain engaged with China. He began by noting his great respect for Deng and the leadership he had provided to China, as well as for his knowledge of Chinese history, culture, and tradition, and Bush acknowledged Deng's fears of outside interference and encirclement. But the president asked Deng to understand the American reverence for freedom and democracy, the principles the United States was founded on, and how they shaped its understanding of world events. "It is not a reaction of arrogance or of a desire to force others to our beliefs but of simple faith in the enduring value of those principles and their universal applicability."[49]

That was the "fundamental problem." On the one hand, the student demonstrations in China had "captured the imagination of the entire world," only to see their hopes dashed in bloodshed. Given the values of the United States, it had to respond, and there were demands for even more forceful actions. "I have resisted this clamor, making clear that I did not want to see destroyed this relationship that you and I have worked hard to build." In an indication that he was ready to move past Tiananmen, Bush wrote that "I will leave what followed to the history books" and asked if he could send a special emissary to express his views and help repair relations. The president concluded with a personal appeal to Deng: "We must not let the aftermath of the tragic recent events undermine a vital relationship patiently built up over the past seventeen years."[50]

Scowcroft delivered the letter to China's ambassador to the United States, Han Xu. They had first met on Scowcroft's visit to China in 1971 when they had worked together in preparation for Nixon's visit. Han was stationed in Washington throughout most of the 1970s and 1980s, and the two men became friends during this period. Scowcroft was confident that Han would not leak the content of the president's letter and that he would help facilitate repairing relations. In less than twenty-four hours, Deng indicated his willingness to accept an emissary from Bush. The president selected Scowcroft because of his knowledge of China and his past dealings with Deng. On July 1, Scowcroft and Deputy Secretary of State Lawrence Eagleburger arrived in Beijing for highly secret talks with Deng, Li, and Foreign Minister Qian Qichen, which took place in the Great Hall of the People the next day.

Deng began by blaming the United States for the tensions in relations. Washington apparently did not understand how serious a threat the demonstrators presented to the government. He argued that the real "aim of the counterrevolutionary rebellion was to overthrow the People's Republic of China and our socialist system." In response, the United States had taken action that "cornered China" and added to its sense of encirclement.

China had not done anything to harm American interests or to threaten the United States, yet Washington had punished China by interfering in its internal affairs and had "injured Chinese dignity." China would not be deterred from "putting down the counterrevolutionary leaders" and "punishing those instigators of the rebellion . . . in accordance with Chinese laws," and the Chinese "would never allow outsiders to interfere in their internal affairs, no matter what the consequences."[51]

The Chinese leader did, however, leave the door open for a return to good relations. President Bush's decision to send Scowcroft was a "wise and cool-headed action" that showed there was "still hope to maintain our originally good relations." Deng used a Chinese proverb to explain how he thought the two nations could resolve their difference. "It is up to the person who tied the knot to untie it. Our hope is that in its future course of action the United States will seek to untie the knot." The elder Chinese statesman continually referred to the president as his friend and to his belief that they both shared the hope of a restoration of cooperation between the two nations.[52]

Scowcroft cast his response in the recent history of U.S.-Chinese relations, noting that despite the different cultures and systems, the two countries had made great strides since President Nixon's 1972 visit. While there had been problems along the way in the relationship, the trend "has been a steadily deepening one." This stemmed from a combination of good relations meeting the best interests of both sides and "because we respect the diversity between our two societies." The mutual benefits derived from the relationship—in strategic terms regarding the Soviet Union and regional stability, and in economic terms, with trade increasing from nonexistent in the mid-1970s to over ten billion dollars annually—remained. Moreover, increased contact had led to a growing admiration in the United States "for the Chinese people and the efforts of the Chinese government to encourage economic reform."[53]

It was in this context of "deepening cooperation and growing sympathy that the events of Tiananmen Square had imposed themselves." Scowcroft fully expressed the abhorrence of the administration to the bloody crackdown and sought Chinese understanding of the U.S. response and the political climate in which the administration was operating. The perception by the American people of the demonstrations in Tiananmen Square, "rightly or wrongly," was that they were an "expression of values which represent their most cherished beliefs, stemming from the American Revolution. . . . We, like you, hold deeply to the tenets of our own struggle for independence." The history of the United States, Scowcroft declared, was an effort to expand freedom, and "Americans, naturally and inevitably, respond emotionally when they see these values promoted elsewhere." China's crackdown produced a reaction in the

United States "which is real and with which the President must cope. That is the crux of the problem President Bush faces."[54]

Bush imposed sanctions that he believed were appropriate given the recent events in China, Scowcroft said, but it was a measured response because the president did not desire a permanent rupture of the growing ties between the United States and China. "President Bush shares the feeling of the American people," Scowcroft told the Chinese, "but he also believes deeply in preserving the relationship between our two countries. He wants to manage events in a way which will assure a healthy relationship over time." This was not easy for the president, and depending on future developments, it might not be possible to sustain. "You have protested these actions of his, while the Congress and much of the US press have attacked him for not acting strongly enough." In fact, Congress had passed more stringent sanctions on the eve of Scowcroft's departure for China.[55]

Scowcroft concluded by assuring Deng and the others that Bush was "very sensitive to Chinese concerns regarding the actions he must take to preserve control over the course of events in the United States," but he also noted that the president was "not omnipotent in his ability to control such events." His position would be "strengthened were the Chinese leaders likewise to try to be sensitive . . . to the reality that what you do and the way you do it will have a major impact on opinion in the United States and throughout the Western world."[56] The message was clear. The administration planned to take a long-term approach to the crisis and looked forward to a restoration of normal relations. That was why economic sanctions were not imposed and why trade continued across the Pacific.

Deng replied from his own historical perspective. The Chinese Revolution was fought for independence, he stated, and the party would not tolerate any foreign interference in China's affairs. Before he left the meeting, he repeated that it was up to the United States to take actions to repair relations. Li Peng was more conciliatory, noting that he understood the historical differences in culture and values of the two nations, and that the "concern of the Americans could not be denied." Washington was wrong, however, if it thought it could direct China to follow its views and practices, and it should remember the old saying "that emotion is no substitute for policy." The demonstrations threatened to bring anarchy to China, and the government was seeking to maintain stability in a manner similar to other governments, including the United States during the 1960s.[57]

The talks were tense throughout, and it was apparent that the differences in culture had led to a gulf in perceptions. As Scowcroft observed, the Chinese resentment of "foreign 'interference' was omnipresent" throughout the meeting, and their concern was "security and stability." The American interest in questions of freedom and human rights had no impact. Still, Scowcroft believed it was "a most useful trip." The purpose was not to resolve the differences between the two nations but to "keep open the lines of communication with a people inclined to isolate themselves and whose long experience with foreigners had engendered xenophobia." Each side had expressed its views, and the concerns of the United States were presented forthrightly. Just as importantly, Scowcroft recalled, he had emphasized to the Chinese, "beneath all the turmoil and torment, how important the President thought the relationship was to the national interests of the United States." He believed the personal meetings "cultivated a degree of trust by each side in the motives of the other," which kept the door open for a restoration of good relations.[58]

Demands for additional sanctions against China continued throughout the year, and Congress passed greater restrictions on arms sales, satellite technology, and exports in the fall. President Bush worked hard to prevent Congress from passing overly stringent economic sanctions and obtained a clause in the legislation allowing him to lift the sanctions if it was in the national interest to do so. Congress also overwhelmingly approved the Pelosi Bill, named after California congresswoman Nancy Pelosi, to allow Chinese students studying in the United States to renew their visas indefinitely until it was deemed safe for them to return home. Bush had already announced his support for the idea, but he and Scowcroft opposed the legislation because they saw it as Congress micromanaging foreign policy and feared that action through congressional legislation rather than executive prerogative would be seen as confrontational in Beijing and might lead China to end the exchange program, an outcome that nobody wanted. Bush, therefore, vetoed the bill.

As the months passed in 1989, the president grew frustrated with the lack of progress in easing tensions and decided to send Scowcroft to Beijing again to try to move relations forward. Scowcroft sought to develop a "road map" that would lead the two nations "back from the brink" on which they had been poised since June.[59] Scowcroft and Eagleburger returned to China in December to continue the process of restoring relations. This trip was not secret, but Scowcroft, realizing that it would be controversial, decided not to announce it until the two men were already in Beijing. While the main explanation given for the meetings was to brief China on the recent summit in Malta between Bush and Gorbachev and on developments in Europe, the most important goal was actually to "stop the erosion of Sino-American relations and to initiate a mutual process of actions" that would address the concerns on both sides. Disagreements remained, but Scowcroft believed that it was not in America's interests to continue to isolate China, since that only played into the hands of the faction in the Communist Party that sought to end reforms and return China to a position of international isolation.[60]

The trip got off to a bad start for Scowcroft when the Chinese, who wanted to publicize the meeting extensively, allowed CNN to cover the toasts at the end of the welcome dinner. Scowcroft, not wanting to insult his hosts and jeopardize the whole trip, went ahead with his toast, even though he knew it would appear that he was "toasting those the press was labeling 'the butchers of Tiananmen Square.'" Scowcroft's reference to "negative forces" that "seek to frustrate our cooperation" overshadowed his critical comments about the events in June, and he was broadly criticized for his decision to raise his glass to the Chinese leaders. Nonetheless, Scowcroft found the visit "productive" in getting Sino-American relations back on track and "healing the wounds of June."[61]

Scowcroft's message was that President Bush was "strongly committed to close relations with China," but that he "suffered loud, widespread, misguided criticism in the U.S. because of that commitment." The president had vetoed the Pelosi bill, had fought against congressional sanctions, was working toward restoring military sales, and had authorized this visit as a sign of his determination to move beyond the Tiananmen crisis. Scowcroft stressed that it was imperative for China to take some steps toward improving relations, as Bush might not be able to hold off further congressional action without some signs of progress. Tangible action, such as ending the harassment of the U.S. embassy, resuming the Fulbright and Peace Corps programs, and providing assurances against weapons sales to the Middle East, would allow additional U.S. steps.[62]

He found that the Chinese were ready to improve relations and that they understood Bush's political problems. Party General Secretary Jiang Zemin said he was aware of the steps Bush was taking and that it was time for the two nations to focus on areas of mutual interest and "not let ideology come between us." He invoked Zhou Enlai's view that it was important "to find common ground while reserving our minor differences." Deng Xiaoping added that China did not see the United States as a rival and believed that good Sino-American relations were vital to international stability and peace.[63]

Upon Scowcroft's return to Washington, the road map toward good relations became a plan. China made a series of gestures to assuage negative opinion in the United States, including a resumption of the Peace Corps and Fulbright programs, a muting of anti-American propaganda, assurances that it would not sell weapons to the Middle East, a lifting of martial law in Beijing, and the first release of people arrested after Tiananmen. Bush was able to sustain his veto of the Pelosi bill in the Senate, and he moved forward with the relaxation of sanctions. In 1990, the administration lifted the suspension of weapons and technology sales to

China and agreed to a resumption of World Bank and other multilateral lending, especially those loans aimed at promoting China's efforts at reform and integration into the world economy. The next year, Bush sought congressional approval of most-favored nation status for China, putting relations on the track they have followed since. Tiananmen, in the end, represented only a brief detour on the road to greater normalization of relations between Washington and Beijing rather than the turning back that Scowcroft had so greatly feared.

THE FALL OF THE BERLIN WALL

Shortly after his return from his first trip to Beijing, Scowcroft and Bush were scheduled to travel to Europe for a Group of Seven (G-7) meeting. Due to the unfolding political events in Eastern Europe, and to show U.S. support for the political changes in the region, visits to Poland and Hungary were added to the beginning of the trip, and the meetings in Warsaw and Budapest overshadowed the summit. In sharp contrast to the events in China, on the day after the massacre in Tiananmen Square, June 4, Solidarity was victorious in Poland's elections for the National Assembly. President Bush's visits to Poland and Hungary, Scowcroft asserted, were part of the continuing effort to craft "an appropriate response to the remarkable transformation taking place" in those nations. While it was seen as vital that the United States demonstrate its support for the reform movements, there were problems that had to be considered. On the one hand, there were limits to what the United States could offer to assist the process of change or reward liberalization. Scowcroft was well aware that "the days were over when the United States could pick up the check for everything: a new Marshall Plan was not possible."[64] On the other hand, the danger of a crackdown still remained, as the events in China illustrated all too clearly. The Soviet Union had a large military presence in Eastern Europe and had not criticized China for its actions. The administration did not want to embarrass Moscow by outwardly celebrating the collapse of communism in Eastern Europe. It therefore continued the policy of providing encouragement, aid, and support for change, but the administration recognized that it was the people of Poland and elsewhere who were the key actors in bringing about the reforms that were taking place.

In Poland, the discussions focused "on the best next steps for Poland's evolution into a non-Communist state with a market economy," and on persuading Solidarity and the communist leaders to continue to cooperate in the political transformation taking place. Bush met for over two hours with Polish leader General Wojciech Jaruzelski and encouraged him to continue on the road to reform. Their meeting was followed by a luncheon hosted by the president at the American ambassador's residence, which brought together for the first time Communist, Catholic, and Solidarity leaders, a group that included many people Jaruzelski had jailed earlier in the decade. The remarkable nature of this meeting was dramatized when Solidarity spokesperson Janusz Onyszkiewicz "clinked champagne glasses with Jaruzelski [and] observed that if one took into account that a year before he had been in prison, this was indeed quite a change." As Scowcroft saw it at the time, the meetings were a "graphic demonstration of the role the United States was playing as midwife at a critical moment in the strained but peaceful evolution of Eastern Europe from autocracy to pluralism."[65]

The symbolism could not have been greater. Poland was the country where in many ways the Cold War had begun, and now the president of the United States was in Warsaw working toward its end. Bush spoke to Poland's National Assembly and reiterated the promises he had made in Hamtramck while praising the role of the people in bringing about peaceful change. Scowcroft came away from the visit optimistic about the "prospects for making this difficult transition work successfully." The United States had demonstrated its support for political reform through peaceful change without provoking the Soviet Union and had helped bring the two sides in Poland together in a process for change. After the visit to Hungary, Scowcroft concluded that the changes taking place could not be reversed. There was a fundamental shift of attitudes occurring, "something I was becoming convinced would not be denied. Reform now seemed to be determined, deliberate, and without the bitterness or thirst for revenge which might trigger renewed repression."[66]

As one who had studied history, Scowcroft knew that "dying empires rarely go out peacefully." Thus, he and the president recognized that a meeting with Gorbachev was necessary. Events were moving rapidly, and it was imperative to try to prevent any misunderstandings concerning American policy. Rather than a summit, the president wanted the talks to take place in a more informal setting to exchange ideas and views. After weeks of secret negotiations, it was agreed that the meeting would be held at sea off the coast of Malta in early December, an echo of the Atlantic Charter meeting of Franklin D. Roosevelt and Winston Churchill in August 1941. The purpose, according to Scowcroft, was "a trust-building meeting" between Bush and Gorbachev.[67]

The pace of change in Europe quickened in the fall of 1989. Gorbachev, facing resistance from hard-liners at home, gave even more room for Eastern European leaders to move ahead so that he could present his own pace of change as moderate. This step encouraged the Bush administration, which elected to avoid any rhetoric or appearance of interference that would upset the Soviets at a time when the political evolution be-hind the Iron Curtain was moving in a favorable direction. More could be gained by saying less. The end of Soviet control over Eastern Europe was within sight.

A potential stumbling block appeared in Washington in September in the person of Boris Yeltsin, Gorbachev's biggest political adversary. A Russian reformer, and celebrated drinker, he was highly critical of Gorbachev for his moderation and called for more reform at a quicker pace. Yeltsin was on a speaking tour in the United States and asked to see President Bush. This request left Scowcroft in an uncomfortable posi-tion similar to the one he had experienced during the Ford administra-tion when the question of allowing Alexander Solzhenitsyn to visit the president had caused a political uproar. How could the administration allow Yeltsin to visit without embarrassing Gorbachev? How would Gor-bachev, and his conservative critics of reform, react to Yeltsin coming to the White House? What would be the impact on the reform movement if the president refused to see him? Would it create criticism at home that the United States did not support the changes taking place in Russia?

It was decided to allow Yeltsin to come, without any public ceremony, by entering the White House through the West Wing basement and hav-ing a meeting with Scowcroft. President Bush would stop by to say hello and would be able to control how long he stayed. Little went as planned. Yeltsin arrived half an hour late and protested as soon as he got out of his car that he was not at the entrance used for seeing the president. Condo-leezza Rice, who was there to meet him, told him that the appointment was with "General Scowcroft." Yeltsin refused to move if he could not meet with the president, saying he did not even know who Scowcroft was and wondering if he was important enough to meet with. After arguing with him, Rice finally told him he could leave, that General Scowcroft was a busy man. Yeltsin relented and went upstairs to the meeting, where he promptly launched into a one-hour monologue during which Scowcroft dozed off.* As he was leaving the White House, Yeltsin spotted some re-porters and got out of his car to hold a press conference. There were no negative ramifications, but it lowered the administration's estimation of Yeltsin.[68]

At the same time, the main themes of Bush's "Beyond Containment" Soviet policy were laid out by Scowcroft in National Security Directive

---

* Scowcroft was well known for working long hours, but also for falling asleep briefly in meetings. President Bush was so impressed by his ability to "awaken as though he hadn't missed a beat of the discussion" that he created the Scowcroft Award for Somnolent Excel-lence, which was presented at the annual cabinet dinner to the person who demonstrated the best "sleep-and-recovery" method (Bush and Scowcroft, *A World Transformed*, 33).

23. The changes taking place inside the Soviet Union opened up the possibility that a new era was emerging. "We may be able to move beyond containment to a U.S. policy that actively promotes the integration of the Soviet Union into the existing international system." This could only happen, however, through "the demilitarization of Soviet foreign policy." The immediate future was uncertain and would require a steady approach by Washington that did not respond to every Soviet move or declaration, but rather to concrete action and changes. The United States "will be vigilant, recognizing that the Soviet Union is still governed by authoritarian methods and that its powerful armed forces remain a threat to our security and that of our allies. But the United States will challenge the Soviet Union . . . to behave in accordance with the higher standards that the Soviet leadership itself has enunciated." In the end, the "goal of restructuring the relationship of the Soviet Union to the international system is an ambitious task. The responsibility for creating the conditions to move beyond containment to integrate the Soviet Union . . . lies first and foremost with Moscow. But the United States will do its part . . . to work to place Soviet relations with the West on a firmer, more cooperative course than has heretofore been possible."[69]

The political systems in Eastern Europe continued to unravel at an unforeseen pace. The climax came when East Germans began arriving at West German embassies in Czechoslovakia, Hungary, and Poland seeking asylum. On September 10, in response to the growing number of East Germans in the country, Hungary opened its border with Austria, allowing more than ten thousand people to exit and make their way to West Germany. When East Germany's leader Erich Honecker protested, the Hungarians responded that as a signatory of the Helsinki Accords, they were obligated to act as they did.

After much hesitation, and after initially allowing those in foreign embassies to go to West Germany, the Honecker regime closed the borders on October 3, just four days before the fortieth-anniversary celebration of the founding of the German Democratic Republic (East Germany). Gorbachev avoided any criticism of Honecker or any endorsement of his regime during the ceremonies in East Berlin, limiting his remarks to the need for change in the socialist bloc. The central paradox of Gorbachev's whole effort at reform was being exposed. He was working to remove leaders such as Honecker inside the Soviet Union and in Eastern Europe, but, as Scowcroft observed, what Gorbachev did not realize was that, when he pushed for change, he was destroying the actual structures that made the Soviet system work. He failed to recognize the total lack of legitimacy of the communist governments in Eastern Europe, and that "it was not possible to remove the hard-liners and replace them with liberal Communists" and expect the regimes to survive. Scowcroft was convinced that "the situation had passed the point of no return."[70]

The demands for change in East Germany continued to spiral out of the government's control. Demonstrations grew in size, as did the number of people trying to leave East Germany. On October 18, Honecker was forced to resign. Egon Krenz, who replaced Honecker, granted some changes and removed Honecker loyalists from the Politburo, but these moves did not quell the growing dissent. On October 23, West German chancellor Helmut Kohl told Bush that the pace of change was so fast that "none of us can give a prognosis." Gorbachev was encouraging reform, but it was unclear if the new leaders had the determination or wisdom to move forward. Whatever direction it went, Kohl assured Bush that the speculation that a reunified Germany would move away from the West and NATO was "absolute nonsense!" It was only due to the alliance that the developments in the Warsaw Pact nations were taking place. Bush agreed that "the strength of NATO has made possible these changes in Eastern Europe," and he asserted that he did not believe any of the predictions of German neutrality.[71]

The changes being made in East Germany were all too little, too late. On November 9, the government announced that it was relaxing restrictions on its borders with West Germany. An enormous crowd gathered along the Berlin Wall seeking passage through the checkpoints, and that night the wall fell as a barrier. Guards allowed people to cross to West Berlin, climb on top of the wall, walk inside the security perimeter around the wall, and chip off pieces of the concrete divide. It was a sudden and dramatic moment. The most iconic symbol of the Cold War had been breached by ordinary people. As Scowcroft observed, after the fall of the wall, "suddenly anything was possible." What "none of us thought we would see in our lifetimes" was within sight: "A Europe whole and free."[72]

It was Scowcroft who informed Bush that the wall had fallen. The question in the Oval Office was how to respond to this amazing event. Up to this point, the administration's policy had struck the right tone and pace, in tune with the changes taking place and what was possible, knowing when to push and when, as in the past few months, to remain on the sidelines and let events take their course. Bush would have to address the nation, and how he handled this historic moment would be critical to future developments in Europe. Scowcroft advised Bush that he needed to be cautious in his portrayal of the event, that it "was not the time to gloat" about an American victory or a Soviet defeat.[73]

The president decided to hold an informal meeting with reporters in the Oval Office, where he expressed his happiness with the "very good development" in Berlin and the promise of change, noting that it was what the United States had "long encouraged by our strong support for the Helsinki Final Act." But he couched his answers in such a way as not to antagonize the Soviets or produce a backlash in Germany. Reacting to his understated approach, Lesley Stahl of CBS News stated that "this is a sort of great victory for our side in the big East-West battle, but you don't seem elated. I'm wondering if you're thinking of the problems?" She had framed this issue in the exact way that concerned the president. He responded, "I am not an emotional kind of guy." She retorted, "Well, how elated are you?" "I'm very pleased," he said.[74]

This exchange led to a great deal of criticism of President Bush. He was accused of being unaware of the full significance of the event, of being out of touch with the emotional impact of the time and without empathy for the people of East Germany. Most senior officials in the administration, along with leaders in Congress and opinion makers around the country, thought he should go to Berlin in triumph. Bush disagreed. The president's response was that he did not "want to gloat" or dance on the wall.[75] Scowcroft never wavered from his original advice to the president, and he was adamant that it was not the time for claiming victory. Too much could still go wrong.

Certainly Bush had made a mistake in taking the questions sitting down at his desk with his staff behind him rather than at a podium in command of the room, but he had good reasons for his low-key answers and his unwillingness to claim victory. He and Scowcroft knew that the events unfolding in Berlin and elsewhere in Eastern Europe were a strategic defeat for the Soviet Union. East Germany represented reparations for its sacrifice in World War II, a buffer against the West, and a guarantee that there would be no repeat of the invasion of 1941. It was important to take these views into account. In addition, there was more to be done to bring freedom to all of Eastern Europe and an end to the Cold War. While in the West the response to the fall of the Berlin Wall was jubilation, in Moscow it was one of fear and alarm. Gorbachev urged Bush not to "overreact" and told Kohl "to stop talking of reunification." The Soviet leader was worried about where events were leading, that the momentum of change was getting out of his control, and that the whole region could become unstable.[76] For these reasons, Scowcroft believed that not celebrating at the Berlin Wall was mandatory if the United States wanted to continue to facilitate the process of change and not back Gorbachev into a corner or provoke a negative response from the Soviet Union. An unforeseen development "could turn into a crisis very easily. Gorbachev was very frightened by the fall of the Berlin Wall."[77]

Kohl contacted Bush the day after the wall fell to describe the events in Berlin—"It is like witnessing an enormous fair," he told the president— and to thank the United States. It was "an historic hour" that would not have been possible without U.S. efforts. "Tell your people that," Kohl told Bush. The president said he wanted "to see our people continue to avoid especially hot rhetoric that might by mistake cause a problem," and characteristically, Bush and Scowcroft decided not to follow Kohl's suggestion.[78] The president kept to his understated approach. The two men believed that it was best to let events unfold and settle before taking any major steps. Kohl would later tell the president, as Bush recalled, "how outrageously stupid" a triumphant visit by the American president would have been right after the Berlin Wall fell.[79] When the two leaders spoke again the following week, Bush reiterated his concern that the "euphoric excitement in the U.S. runs the risk of forcing unforeseen action in the USSR or the GDR that would be very bad. We will not be making exhortations about unification or setting any timetables. We will not exacerbate the problem by having the President of the United States posturing on the Berlin Wall."[80]

Finally, there was Scowcroft's concern that the opening of the Berlin Wall and the other Soviet setbacks in Eastern Europe might lead to another Versailles. Scowcroft's analysis was that the end of the Cold War represented the end of the era begun during World War I, because it marked the final defeat of the antidemocratic forces that had emerged in Europe in the wake of the Great War and had brought about both World War II and the Cold War. It was imperative to avoid in 1989 a similar outcome to 1919. The Bush administration, Scowcroft said, "didn't want a World War I syndrome again."[81] Instead of triumphalism and talking about a victory for the West or the United States, the message was to be that everybody won because the danger of a war in central Europe or a nuclear exchange between the superpowers was over. According to Rice, by the middle of November 1989, she and Scowcroft thought they were witnessing the endgame of the Cold War, and there was an enormous responsibility to make sure it came out right for all the past forty years of investment in Europe by the United States. It was crucial to avoid a Versailles outcome, to not take an already defeated power and humiliate it.[82]

Events continued to outpace planning. After the fall of the Berlin Wall, the communist rulers in Eastern Europe fell rapidly as the old Stalinist leaders in Bulgaria and Czechoslovakia were forced from power in a similar manner to their brethren in Poland, Hungary, and East Germany. By the time Bush was to meet Gorbachev in Malta at the beginning of December, only Nicolae Ceausescu in Romania remained in power, and he would be removed from office and killed before the end of the year. Moreover, the dominant issue of concern was changing from reform and freedom in Eastern Europe to German reunification.

Bush opened the meeting by setting out a broad range of bilateral issues in an opening statement that lasted over an hour. The president sought to seize the initiative in the talks while also demonstrating to Gorbachev that he could trust that the United States would not take advantage of the changes in Eastern Europe to threaten the Soviet Union. Bush expressed commitment to the following issues: holding a summit meeting in the United States the following June; finding ways to improve economic relations, including granting most-favored nation status to the Soviet Union, at the summit meeting; a desire to resolve the issue of emigration from the Soviet Union; hopes for future arms control arrangements; disappointment with Soviet policy in Central America; joint support for holding the 2004 Summer Olympic Games in Berlin; the need for a conference to discuss a framework for a treaty on climate change; and a willingness to increase student exchanges.[83]

Gorbachev shifted the focus to the question of the Cold War and relations in Europe. He stated that they had reached "a historic watershed" that required them to address completely new problems. The question was whether old Cold War approaches would be followed or new policies developed. The Kremlin was aware that there were many in the United States who saw this as a time of victory, "but what you have said today shows President Bush has his own understanding, which is consistent with the challenges of our times." The two nations needed to "abandon the images of an enemy" and cooperate to solve the new challenges that were emerging. He wanted to "build bridges across rivers rather than parallel them." Bush replied that they were both aware of the quickening pace of the changes taking place, and that the United States had not "responded with flamboyance or arrogance that would complicate Soviet relations. . . . I have conducted myself in ways not to complicate your life. That's why I have not jumped up and down on the Berlin Wall." Gorbachev acknowledged the president's restraint and said he appreciated his cautious approach.[84]

The big issue was Germany. Gorbachev was concerned that Kohl's November 28 ten-point plan for a closer association of the two German states and his call for support for Germany's self-determination of its political future was the first step in an effort at reunification on Western terms. There were many questions to be addressed on this issue, and Gorbachev wanted a joint U.S.-Soviet understanding that "there are two states, mandated by history," and that the four powers from World War II would have the final say concerning developments in Germany. Bush assured Gorbachev that the United States did not seek to accelerate the pace of reunification and that it would act with restraint, but it could not disavow German reunification.[85]

Bush met with Kohl in Brussels right after leaving Malta to inform him of his talks with Gorbachev and of the latter's concern that Kohl was moving too fast toward reunification. The president noted that "Gorbachev's chief problem is uncertainty. . . . We need a formulation which doesn't scare him, but moves forward." Reflecting the approach that he and Scowcroft had agreed to, Bush noted that the United States agreed that the process for German reunification should be self-determination, but the Germans had to "avoid things which would make the situation impossible for Gorbachev."[86] He promised Kohl America's full support and assured him that he was working on getting Soviet forces out of Eastern Europe.

Scowcroft considered Malta a great success. The meeting "worked far better than I had hoped." While no firm agreements were reached, the key was the exchange of ideas on a wide range of topics, as well as the personal relationship and trust that Bush developed with Gorbachev. "I think the relationship between the two leaders changed," Scowcroft said, and they became "comfortable with each other." This would be "very beneficial" in the negotiations to come over Germany.[87] Scowcroft believed they now had "a much more reliable indicator of the perils and opportunities we faced."[88] In addition, the president's meeting with Kohl was a crucial moment in developing trust as they moved forward. The two leaders were in clear agreement about reunification, and Kohl left assured of American support. The meeting "was pivotal," according to Scowcroft, "because Kohl was sort of out on his own. . . . The other allies didn't want German unification, so Kohl was kind of feeling his way." During the meeting, the president said, "I'm not worried. I like your ideas. You go ahead; I'll back you. I'll keep everyone else off your back." In essence, he gave Kohl the green light to move ahead.[89]

GERMAN REUNIFICATION

In all, 1989 had been a historic year of change, and Scowcroft was cautiously optimistic as a new year began. German reunification would shift the strategic balance, and it was important to overcome the resistance of the other powers and keep the process moving forward. All of the established assumptions about Europe and American security had to be reconsidered. "We had to rethink the larger strategic picture of European security," Scowcroft believed, "of our role in it, and of superpower relations." It was uncertain how long Gorbachev could last in power, and the administration hoped to strengthen his political position at home through improved relations while reducing Soviet power in Europe. The changes resembled those "usually only imposed by victors at the end of a major war. It was essential that we avoid another Versailles-type settlement." The agreements reached had to result in a unified Europe that the Soviet Union would accept.[90]

For Scowcroft, this meant a continuation of the main tenets of inter-nationalism that had guided the United States since 1945. "Our first re-quirement was to prevent yet another repetition of the turmoil which had beset Europe in the twentieth century. American isolationism had played its part in those tragedies," and the lesson learned "was that the United States had to continue to play a significant role in European security" through a NATO that included a reunified Germany. This would allow American forces to stay in Europe to provide "security and stability." Maintaining the U.S. "link to European security" became the primary goal.[91] The American vision was a unified Germany consisting of the borders of West Germany and East Germany, incorporated into NATO, and with allied rights to Berlin ended. Washington would allow Kohl, with the assurance of American support, to conduct his own negotiations with East Germany regarding internal questions of reunification, with the expectation that the chancellor would keep Germany in NATO.

Soon after the wall fell, Scowcroft began holding meetings in his office with his senior staff to examine recent developments and where they might lead. There was no expectation of policy recommendations or out-comes, just discussion and reflection so as to fully understand the events that were transpiring. These meetings led to the conclusion that the key to ending the Cold War was German reunification and how that process was handled. It was important to approach the question in such a way that never forced Gorbachev to say no. For that to happen, the Soviet leader would have to trust the United States. Both sides realized it was the end of Soviet power in central and Eastern Europe, but it was crucial that this final outcome not develop in a manner that would humiliate them or fail to take into account Soviet concerns.

Gorbachev wanted all discussions about Germany's political future to be conducted by the four victors of World War II: the Soviet Union, the United States, Great Britain, and France. While seemingly aware that re-unification would happen, he sought to keep a united Germany neutral and out of NATO. The issue was indeed a complicated one, involving two nations, the four World War II powers, and two alliances with foreign troops on German soil. As Scowcroft analyzed the situation, there were two central concerns that had to be acknowledged. First, "there was the problem of unification itself . . . that East Germany was the crown jewel of the Soviet bloc . . . [and] the major achievement . . . out of World War II. And so it was difficult to say, 'Yes, we [the Soviet Union] failed there.'" Moreover, the GDR "was the heart of the Warsaw Pact. It's pretty hard to have a viable Warsaw Pact if East Germany is not in it." The second issue was NATO. From the Soviet point of view, "suppose you let Germany unify—What do you do about membership in NATO?"[92] That was the tough issue for the Kremlin since the loss of East Germany would spell the end of Soviet power in Eastern Europe and the security buffer it had erected after World War II.

Great Britain also feared that a reunified Germany could be a destabilizing force in Europe due to its economic power, its possible demands for border changes, and the fear of its renewed military power. France had similar worries but sought to use German unification as a way to create a stronger Europe as a counter to American influence and power. The United States rejected all of these positions. Scowcroft advised Bush that, while they needed to remain cognizant of Soviet concerns, Germany had to remain in NATO after reunification, and the United States had to continue to view itself as a European power. Scowcroft delivered this message to the allies in a conference in Munich in early February 1990. The United States, he declared, had every intention of maintaining "a substantial military and political presence" in Europe and NATO, as it had "an abiding and permanent interest in European security."[93] Overall, Washington's goal was to maintain stability by demanding respect for the inviolability of the Helsinki agreement on borders while allowing Germany to move forward to one government aligned with the West, and by explaining to its allies that the best assurance for peace was a Germany anchored in NATO.

February was the crucial month. The American position was the "Two-plus-Four" plan developed by the State Department. The two Germanys would work out the political process, while the four powers would only be concerned with the international ramifications of reunification. Scowcroft had reservations concerning this formula because it gave the Soviet Union too much influence in the process and the ability to shape the outcome of reunification in a way that could keep Germany out of NATO. He preferred that the two Germanys reach an agreement and then present it to the allied powers for their endorsement, a process Scowcroft was sure would lead to German membership in NATO. Still, he was concerned about isolating Gorbachev, and Secretary of State Baker assured him that he could get everyone to agree at the outset that reunification was the goal. If that occurred, then Scowcroft believed the Soviet Union would eventually yield on the issue of Germany and NATO.

Baker took the lead in presenting the American plan to the allies and the Soviet Union. He traveled to Moscow in early February to discuss the American position and gain Soviet support for the process. Baker met with Gorbachev on February 9, where the Soviet leader acknowledged that "there is nothing terrifying in the prospect of a unified Germany," and he concurred that the process should be left to the Germans to decide. The question of German membership in NATO was another matter. What was better for the Soviet Union, Baker asked, a Germany tied to NATO with assurances "that there would be no extension of NATO's current jurisdiction eastward," or a neutral Germany that could remilitarize and possibly obtain nuclear weapons? Gorbachev understood the advantages of keeping American troops in Germany, and he did not "want a replay of Versailles either, with Germany rearming." But he was not ready to commit on the issue.[94]

Kohl arrived in Moscow the next day for his own talks with Gorbachev. Baker provided Kohl a summary of his talks with the Soviet leader, emphasizing the need to reassure the Russians on security matters. At Scowcroft's suggestion, Bush wrote to Kohl to reiterate that he had the full support of the United States for German self-determination on reunification and the need for Germany to be in the Western alliance. In a modification of Baker's statement on East Germany's territory and NATO, Bush wrote that it would have a "special military status" with the specifics to be decided later. Bush was, therefore, "deeply gratified by your rejection of proposals for neutrality and your firm statement that a unified Germany would stay in the North Atlantic Alliance." Neutralization was unacceptable, and this had to be made clear to Gorbachev. By providing his unwavering support, Bush sought to prevent Kohl from trading NATO membership for Soviet support for reunification.[95]

Kohl held to his agreements with the United States, and Gorbachev formally agreed that it was up to the German people to decide their political future. Speaking to Bush on the phone three days later, Kohl told him he believed that "the letter you sent to me before I left for Moscow will one day be considered one of the great documents in German-American history. Your support is invaluable." He was pleased with the resolution of the process for reunification, and he would proceed forward with the negotiations. Bush remarked to Kohl that when he had learned that Gorbachev had dropped his objection to reunification, he knew it "must have been an emotional moment for you. The German people certainly want to be together." Regarding the question of Germany remaining in NATO, Kohl said they would "find a solution, but it will be hard work. I told Gorbachev again that the neutralization of Germany is out of the question for me." Bush asked, "Did he acquiesce or just listen?" Gorbachev did not agree, Kohl said. It was "a subject about which they want to negotiate, but we can win that point in negotiations." Bush and Kohl agreed to discuss the matter further at Camp David later that month.[96]

The two leaders met on February 24 to coordinate their efforts concerning reunification, NATO, the Polish border issue, and dealing with Gorbachev. Kohl asked that the United States mediate the issue of borders to assure Poland that there would be no change. This was settled the next month to all nations' satisfaction on the basis of the Helsinki Final Act and the inviolability of the current borders in Europe. Bush insisted that Germany had to be a full member of NATO; he would accept no alternative, and the Soviet Union would have to come to adapt to this reality. In an uncharacteristic statement, the president declared that "the Soviets are not in a position to dictate Germany's relationship with NATO. What worries me is talk that Germany must not stay in NATO. To hell with that! We prevailed, they didn't. We can't let the Soviets clutch victory from the jaws of defeat." Kohl believed it was just a matter of finding out what Gorbachev wanted in exchange for his agreement, a point that could be settled when the president and the Soviet leader met in their upcoming summit, not in a four-power meeting, as it was clear that Gorbachev wanted it to be part of other agreements with the United States. Bush agreed, noting that "Gorbachev has to be provided with face, with standing."[97]

The East German elections held on March 18, 1990, were a triumph for Kohl's Christian Democratic Union. Having pledged that a unified Germany would respect the Oder-Neisse border with Poland and be part of the European Community and NATO, Kohl made it clear that a victory for his party would mean a Germany firmly tied to the West. The new premier of the GDR, Lothar de Maizière, pledged his government to a quick reunification under Article 23 of the West German constitution, a process that would lead to the dissolution of East Germany and its absorption into West Germany. "You're a hell of a campaigner," Bush told Kohl when he called on March 20 to offer his congratulations. The German chancellor responded with thanks for the assistance of the United States, especially for Bush's February letter and Baker's work in Moscow that helped eliminate Soviet objections to a unified Germany.[98] The internal issues of reunification were now settled. The next step, the issue of NATO, would be resolved at the summit meeting in Washington beginning on May 31.

Scowcroft believed that the key to gaining Soviet agreement was to reexamine NATO's mission in a post–Cold War world and its relationship to European security. A post–Cold War NATO had to develop a more political role that would help foster cooperation and partnerships in the new Europe, would help strengthen the ties between former adversaries, and would focus on developing democratic institutions. As for security issues, Scowcroft envisioned NATO helping to reduce the number of offensive forces and the reliance on nuclear weapons in Europe, and developing a truly multinational force. All of this would serve U.S. security needs while reassuring the other nations of Europe that a reunified Germany would pose no threat to them and would allow Moscow to "save face" in reaching an agreement.[99]

With reunification now a fait accompli, the Western allies quickly joined Washington in seeking to include Germany in NATO. Attention turned to the upcoming summit in Washington and to securing Soviet agreement.

The strategy was to use the meeting to hold high-profile events praising Gorbachev for his reforms and for his role in the changes taking place in Eastern Europe, and to provide him with trade agreements and progress on arms talks that conveyed tangible benefits in return for bargaining on Germany's alliance status.

The first day of discussions focused on the future of Europe and Germany. Gorbachev stated that it was necessary for both sides to move beyond suspicion to an era of cooperation. Bush replied that many Americans did not understand the extent of Soviet losses in World War II and the contribution it made to victory, and that he did not seek to diminish the position the Soviet Union had earned. As they moved forward, he did not "want winners and losers." Bush asked Gorbachev to trust him that the United States was not trying to surround the Soviet Union with its military by having Germany in NATO, and that he did not want Moscow to feel "threatened by any power." The president asserted that Germany had learned its lesson and would not return to its old, aggressive ways.[100]

The afternoon session provided the sought-after breakthrough on Germany. Gorbachev began by insisting that Germany could not be part of NATO, as that would lead to an imbalance of power in Europe. Bush acknowledged again that the Soviet Union was more suspicious of Germany of than the United States, and he argued that having Germany in NATO, and therefore tied to a stabilizing U.S. position, was the best means of ensuring future security. Moreover, NATO was to assume a more political role as the Soviet Union and the United States moved beyond the Cold War. Gorbachev remained unconvinced and held to his position that Germany must be neutral or perhaps tied to anchors in both alliances.

Bush tried a different approach by bringing up the Helsinki Final Act, stating that all nations had the right to align with any other country. This meant that Germany should be free to join NATO if it so chose. Bush asked if Gorbachev agreed, and to the surprise of everyone, he said yes. The president sought clarity from Gorbachev to make sure they were agreeing to the same thing. "We support a united Germany in NATO," Bush stated. "If they don't want in, we will respect that," to which Gorbachev replied, "I agree." Scowcroft "could scarcely believe" what happened or figure out why, but he was thrilled with Gorbachev's concession and, the exchange marked the end of the discussions on Germany.[101] The rest of the summit was a success. Gorbachev received the trade agreement he wanted, and progress was made on reducing forces in Europe that would allow for the proposed changes to NATO, although the administration was criticized for going forward with the force reductions at a time when the Soviet Union was clamping down on the Baltic states and their desire for independence. While there were still details to be worked

out, Bush was able to announce that the two powers were in full agreement "that the matter of alliance membership is—in accordance with the
Helsinki Final Act—a matter for the Germans to decide."[102]

For Scowcroft, the Soviet acceptance of a reunified Germany in NATO
signaled the end of the Cold War. The national security advisor believed
that, in the end, Gorbachev accepted a unified Germany in NATO "because he didn't have a better alternative. He toyed around with the idea
of a neutral Germany, but I think he decided that that would be more
dangerous—to have a neutral Germany loose in Europe—than one tied
down by the United States."[103] This outcome was hardly inevitable. The
Soviet Union still had forces in Germany and could have created divisions in the West and an alternative settlement. That it did not was a
result of the Bush administration's adroit diplomacy. This diplomacy was
based on learning from past mistakes and applying the lessons of history
as distilled in the internationalist approach to foreign policy. Bush and
Scowcroft structured the process toward German reunification in a way
that ultimately gave the Soviet Union no veto over anything except the
four-power rights and tied improved relations to German membership
in NATO. Bush's personal diplomacy and Scowcroft's commitment to
consensus, coalition building, and cooperation with allies that brought
forth a free Europe were crucial. There was no repeat of Versailles. "All
had found their stake in the outcome," Scowcroft opined. "It was a shep-
herded victory for peace." Vital to this was the decision to shift the focus
of the NATO alliance "away from the Soviet Union and toward post–Cold
War objectives. This gave Gorbachev the opportunity to argue to his Politburo that NATO had been transformed and was no longer a threat."[104] It
was an extremely well thought-out and implemented policy that brought
an end to the Cold War without bloodshed or violence.

CODA

Scowcroft knew that nationalism and the question of legitimacy were the
Soviets' Achilles' heels, and that once the process of change had begun
it would be difficult for Moscow to control it, as the events in Eastern
Europe demonstrated. The same issues pertained to the internal politics
of the Soviet Union. Gorbachev was trying to revive and save a system
that was failing, but in the process, Scowcroft believed, he destroyed the
sinews that held the Soviet Union together. The Soviet leader was trying
to pursue economic reform, but he could not do it and simultaneously
manage relations with the West. All of this led to growing dissatisfaction
and polarization within the USSR. In 1990, the problem of nationalism
within the Soviet Union erupted, adding to the security concerns already

heightened by the disintegration of the Warsaw Pact. From the Baltic states, especially Lithuania, which sought independence, to the conflicts breaking out in the Caucasus, the non-Russian parts of the Soviet state were threatening the integrity of the nation.

The Baltic republics—Estonia, Latvia, and Lithuania—were of particular concern to the United States. The United States had never recognized their absorption by the Soviet Union in 1940 and had allowed them to operate legations in Washington that purported to represent the pre–World War II governments. The Bush administration cautioned Gorbachev not to use force against those seeking independence, as that would make it very difficult to continue to work with Moscow and improve relations. As Scowcroft noted, the issue of nationalism made Gorbachev vulnerable to the hard-liners in the Communist Party, and it was these people who most strongly opposed him on reform that Washington did not want to see replace him. Too strong a stance in favor of self-determination could produce a military backlash and reverse the course of change.

The question of Lithuania almost derailed the Washington summit. In March 1990, nationalists in Vilnius declared independence, creating a crisis for Moscow. The Soviet Union responded with economic sanctions, cutting off energy supplies, and military maneuvers near the border—all designed to force the breakaway republic to back down. Gorbachev saw the issue as different from the political changes in Eastern Europe, as it represented the potential separation from Moscow of parts of the country and threatened the very existence of the Soviet Union. Bush wrote to Gorbachev urging restraint and negotiations. He acknowledged that the United States had never recognized the incorporation of Lithuania into the Soviet Union and reiterated Washington's support for self-determination, but, he explained, he did not seek to take advantage of the crisis or make the situation more difficult for Gorbachev by issuing public statements. Yet a crackdown on Lithuania would be inconsistent with perestroika and the democratization that was occurring in the rest of Eastern Europe.

The administration's restraint brought strong criticism from members of Congress, the press, and the Baltic-American community, who wanted the United States to publicly support independence. The continuation of the crisis made things difficult for the administration, and Scowcroft told the National Security Council in April to continue working to improve relations with the Soviet Union. It is "hard to explain to Congress why we were negotiating economic arrangements with Moscow that would help their economy at a time when they are using economic leverage to squeeze the Lithuanians."[105] In May, Congress voted to withhold any trade benefits from the Soviet Union until the economic embargo against Lithuania was lifted.

The situation remained unresolved when Gorbachev came to Washington, and the Soviet leader made it clear that achieving an economic agreement was essential to him. A deal was finally struck that had both public and private dimensions. An agreement was signed on a grain and trade package, but it would not be sent to Congress until the Soviets met the conditions regarding emigration necessary to obtain most-favored nation status. Privately, it was agreed that the proposal would be withheld from Congress until Moscow began negotiations with Lithuania and ended the economic sanctions. Gorbachev got what he needed without appearing to negotiate about an internal political matter, while the administration continued to put private pressure on Moscow for a peaceful resolution. Bush paid a steep price in terms of public criticism, but in the end his approach achieved German membership in NATO and maintained good relations with Gorbachev.

Still, the forces of nationalism continued to destabilize the Soviet Union, and by the summer of 1991, the administration feared Gorbachev would be overthrown or that the Soviet Union would collapse, leading to political instability throughout the former empire. The United States warned Gorbachev in July of a possible coup attempt, and Bush traveled to Russia in August to sign a new arms control agreement and bolster Gorbachev's prestige. In Kiev, Bush noted the dangers of too radical a move toward decentralization, "a suicidal nationalism based on ethnic hatred," and, in Scowcroft's words, provided a caution against "the perils of disintegration."[106] It was dubbed the "chicken Kiev speech" by critics who accused Bush of siding with the Soviet Union over Ukraine's desire for independence. Efforts to explain that Bush's comment was aimed at places where violence was breaking out, such as Yugoslavia, and that it would have been inappropriate to give the speech in Moscow in order to avoid precisely the misinterpretation that emerged, satisfied no one.

The unraveling of the Soviet Union could not be prevented as the setbacks for Moscow continued to mount. The Warsaw Pact had dissolved, Germany was reunified and had joined NATO, and more and more republics demanded autonomy or independence, leading to an agreement on a new Union Treaty in July 1991 that shifted a great deal of power from Moscow to the republics. The long-feared coup attempt by the Soviet hard-liners came on August 18, two days before the new political arrangement was to go into effect. The initial information that arrived in Washington late that evening was sketchy, with bogus broadcasts from Moscow that Gorbachev had resigned for health reasons, and it was unclear if the plotters had succeeded or not. Early the next morning, Bush called other allied leaders to gather any information and to let them know he would not endorse the coup, but that he could not condemn it since he might have to work with the new leaders. Speaking on the morning of August 19 from his vacation home in Kennebunkport, Bush called the event "extra-constitutional" and "disturbing," while praising what Gorbachev had done and noting that coups could fail and that the available information was limited.[107]

Once the administration learned that the coup had not yet succeeded and that Yeltsin had taken a defiant stance against it, calling for the affirmation of Gorbachev's position as leader of the Soviet Union, Bush issued a statement condemning the attempted coup. The next day, Bush reached Yeltsin by phone and pledged his "full support for the return of Gorbachev and the legitimate government." On August 21, Bush finally reached Gorbachev, informed him of his actions, and assured him of his support.[108] Even with the failure of the coup, Gorbachev's power had been damaged and Yeltsin's had been enhanced. It was the Russian president who refused to yield to the coup leaders, who stood in front of the tanks, and who was the face of the new, decentralized Soviet system. The republics had gained the upper hand and would not yield again to the Kremlin. The final breakup of the Soviet Union now appeared to be only a matter of time, and the administration actively worked toward ensuring that the end came peacefully, with the Russian Federation in control of the Soviet Union's nuclear weapons.

The denouement came on Christmas Day with Gorbachev's resignation. Gorbachev called Bush that morning to thank him for his friendship, to ask for his support of the republics, and to tell him that the transfer of authority over the nuclear stockpile was under strict control. Therefore Bush could "have a very quiet Christmas evening." The president assured Gorbachev that what he had done "will live in history and be fully appreciated by historians." That night, Bush announced to the nation Gorbachev's resignation, marking the final end of the Cold War. He praised Gorbachev for bringing about "the revolutionary transformation of a totalitarian dictatorship and the liberation of his people from its smothering embrace," and for his contribution "to the remaking of Europe whole and free."[109]

When Scowcroft first assumed his duties as national security advisor in 1975, he never thought he would see the end of the Cold War and the collapse of the Soviet Union in a peaceful manner. Fourteen years later, when he took up the post again in 1989, the situation appeared to be the same. "The world we had encountered in January 1989," Scowcroft recalled, "had been defined by superpower rivalry." Yet, in what seemed like the "blink of an eye, these were gone. We were suddenly in a unique position, without experience, without precedent, and standing alone at the height of power."[110] The key to the peaceful end of the Cold War, Scowcroft believed, was the way President Bush dealt with a world in the process of dramatic changes and took advantage of the forces growing in a careful, thoughtful way. When he was first in office almost twenty years earlier, nobody would have predicted an end to the Cold War and the collapse of the Soviet Union within their lifetime, without a shot being fired. Empires did not end that way. There were many factors, Scowcroft knew, including luck, but Bush's leadership and approach to the developments in Eastern Europe played a significant role.

Scowcroft's response to the lowering of the hammer and sickle from the Kremlin was "one of pride in our role in reaching this outcome. We had worked very hard to push the Soviet Union in this direction, at a pace which would not provoke an explosion in Moscow, much less a global conflagration."[111] Scowcroft's unwavering commitment to the tenets of internationalism was crucial to that outcome. The collapse of the Soviet Union was the culmination of events since World War I—nearly a century of revolution, upheaval, totalitarianism, and war, as well as the internationalist policies developed to confront these threats. The international system was being transformed again, and the United States, in Scowcroft's view, found itself in "an unparalleled situation in history" that presented Washington "with the rarest opportunity to shape the world and the deepest responsibility to do so wisely for the benefit of not just the United States but all nations."[112] How to structure a post–Cold War world was the challenge in front of the Bush administration as the focus of its policies shifted from Europe to the Middle East.

NOTES

1. Zbigniew Brzezinski and Brent Scowcroft, *America and the World: Conversations on the Future of American Foreign Policy*, moderated by David Ignatius (New York: Basic Books, 2008), 262.

2. George Bush and Brent Scowcroft, *A World Transformed* (New York: Vintage, 1998), 211.

3. Robert M. Gates, *From the Shadows: The Ultimate Insider's Story of Five Presidents and How They Won the Cold War* (New York: Simon & Schuster, 1996), 457–58, 574.

4. Condoleezza Rice, interview by author, 3 November 2009.

5. Rice, interview by author, 3 November 2009.

6. Bush and Scowcroft, *A World Transformed*, xii–xiv.

7. Christopher Maynard, *Out of the Shadow: George H. W. Bush and the End of the Cold War* (College Station: Texas A&M Press, 2008), 7, 3; Bush and Scowcroft, *A World Transformed*, xii, 12.

8. National Security Review-3, "Comprehensive Review of US-Soviet Relations," 15 February 1989, Bush Presidential Records, National Security Council: H Files, George H. W. Bush Presidential Library, College Station, Texas (hereafter GBPL).

9. Brzezinski and Scowcroft, *America and the World*, 158–60.

10. Rice, interview by author, 3 November 2009.

11. Brzezinski and Scowcroft, *America and the World*, 159.

12. Rice, interview by author, 3 November 2009.

13. Bush and Scowcroft, *A World Transformed*, 38.

14. Rice, interview by author, 3 November 2009.

15. Brzezinski and Scowcroft, *America and the World*, 158.

16. Bush and Scowcroft, *A World Transformed*, 39.

17. Brzezinski and Scowcroft, *America and the World*, 158.

18. Bush and Scowcroft, *A World Transformed*, 42–43.

19. Bush and Scowcroft, *A World Transformed*, 55–56.

20. Brzezinski and Scowcroft, *America and the World*, 158.

21. *Public Papers of the Presidents: George H. W. Bush, 1989* (Washington, DC: Government Printing Office, 1990), 1:430–33.

22. *Public Papers of the Presidents: Bush, 1989*, 1:430–33.

23. Bush and Scowcroft, *A World Transformed*, 52.

24. Rice, interview by author, 3 November 2009.

25. *Public Papers of the Presidents: Bush, 1989*, 1:540–45; See NSC: NSC PA Files, GBPL, for Scowcroft's writing of critical sections of the speech.

26. *Public Papers of the Presidents: Bush, 1989*, 1:540–43.

27. *Public Papers of the Presidents: Bush, 1989*, 1:600–604.

28. *Public Papers of the Presidents: Bush, 1989*, 1:600–604.

29. *Public Papers of the Presidents: Bush, 1989*, 1:600–604.

30. Bush and Scowcroft, *A World Transformed*, 56.

31. *Public Papers of the Presidents: Bush, 1989*, 650–54.

32. Rice, interview by author, 3 November 2009.

33. Bush and Scowcroft, *A World Transformed*, 86.

34. Brzezinski and Scowcroft, *America and the World*, 114–15.

35. Brzezinski and Scowcroft, *America and the World*, 118.

36. Brzezinski and Scowcroft, *America and the World*, 119.

37. Brzezinski and Scowcroft, *America and the World*, 140.

38. Bush and Scowcroft, *A World Transformed*, 94.

39. Bush and Scowcroft, *A World Transformed*, 89.

40. Bush and Scowcroft, *A World Transformed*, 91.

41. Bush and Scowcroft, *A World Transformed*, 92.

42. Bush and Scowcroft, *A World Transformed*, 95.

43. Bush and Scowcroft, *A World Transformed*, 96–97.

44. Bush and Scowcroft, *A World Transformed*, 89.

45. American Embassy Beijing to Secretary of State, "Chaos within China," June 4, 1989, Bush Presidential Records: National Security Council, GBPL.

46. Press Conference by the President, June 5 1989, Bush Presidential Records: National Security Council, Douglas Paal File (hereafter Paal File): China Scowcroft Trip 1989, GBPL.

47. Bush and Scowcroft, *A World Transformed*, 99.

48. Brzezinski and Scowcroft, *America and the World*, 141.

49. Bush and Scowcroft, *A World Transformed*, 101.

50. Bush and Scowcroft, *A World Transformed*, 101–2.

51. Bush and Scowcroft, *A World Transformed*, 106–7.

52. Bush and Scowcroft, *A World Transformed*, 106–7.

53. Bush and Scowcroft, *A World Transformed*, 107.

54. Bush and Scowcroft, *A World Transformed*, 107–8.

55. Bush and Scowcroft, *A World Transformed*, 108.

56. Bush and Scowcroft, *A World Transformed*, 109.

57. Bush and Scowcroft, *A World Transformed*, 109–10.

58. Bush and Scowcroft, *A World Transformed*, 110–11.

59. Bush and Scowcroft, *A World Transformed*, 158.

60. Secretary of State to all East Asian and Pacific diplomatic posts, "Scowcroft-Eagleburger Mission to China," 14 December 1989, Paal File, China Scowcroft Trip 1989, GBPL.

61. Bush and Scowcroft, *A World Transformed*, 178; "Healing the Wounds of June," Paal File, China Scowcroft Trip 1989, GBPL; Sean Wilentz, *The Age of Reagan* (New York: HarperCollins, 2008), 291.

62. "Talking Points: Introductory Remarks," Paal File, GBPL; Anderson to Eagleburger, 7 December 1989, "China Policy: Strategy for Your Trip," Paal File, China Scowcroft Trip 1989, GBPL.

63. Bush and Scowcroft, *A World Transformed*, 178.

64. Bush and Scowcroft, *A World Transformed*, 113.

65. Bush and Scowcroft, *A World Transformed*, 116, 119.

66. Bush and Scowcroft, *A World Transformed*, 120, 126.

67. Maynard, *Out of the Shadow*, 39.

68. Rice, interview by author, 3 November 2009.

69. National Security Directive 23, "United States Relations with the Soviet Union," 22 September 1989, Bush Presidential Records, GBPL.

70. Bush and Scowcroft, *A World Transformed*, 147.

71. Chancellor Helmut Kohl to President Bush, telephone call, 23 October 1989, NSC: Robert Hutchings File: Country File, FRG (hereafter NSC: RHF: CF, FRG), GBPL.

72. Bush and Scowcroft, *A World Transformed*, 151.

73. Bush and Scowcroft, *A World Transformed*, 149.

74. *Public Papers of the Presidents: Bush, 1989*, 2:1488–90.

75. Brzezinski and Scowcroft, *America and the World*, 7.

76. Bush and Scowcroft, *A World Transformed*, 149–50.

77. Maynard, *Out of the Shadow*, 46.

78. Chancellor Helmut Kohl to President Bush, telephone call, 10 November 1989, NSC: RHF: CF, FRG, GBPL.

79. Bush and Scowcroft, *A World Transformed*, 149–51.

80. Chancellor Helmut Kohl to President Bush, telephone call, 17 November 1989, NSC: RHF: CF, FRG, GBPL.

81. Brzezinski and Scowcroft, *America and the World*, 163.

82. Rice, interview by author, 3 November 2009.

83. "The President's Initiatives during the Malta Meeting, December 2–3, 1989," NSC: NSC Meeting Files, GBPL.

84. Bush and Scowcroft, *A World Transformed*, 164–65.

85. Bush and Scowcroft, *A World Transformed*, 167.

86. Memorandum of conversation, Bush and Kohl, 3 December 1989, NSC: Memcons, Presidential, GBPL.

87. Maynard, *Out of the Shadow*, 51.

88. Bush and Scowcroft, *A World Transformed*, 173.

89. Maynard, *Out of the Shadow*, 73.

90. Bush and Scowcroft, *A World Transformed*, 230.

91. Bush and Scowcroft, *A World Transformed*, 230–31.

92. Maynard, *Out of the Shadow*, 74.

93. Maynard, *Out of the Shadow*, 57.

94. Bush and Scowcroft, *A World Transformed*, 239–40.

95. Bush and Scowcroft, *A World Transformed*, 240–41.

96. Chancellor Helmut Kohl to President Bush, telephone call, 13 February 1990, NSC: RHF: CF, FRG, GBPL.

97. Bush and Scowcroft, *A World Transformed*, 253–54.

98. Chancellor Helmut Kohl to President Bush, telephone call, 20 March 1990, NSC: RHF: CF, FRG, GBPL.

99. Bush and Scowcroft, *A World Transformed*, 293.

100. Bush and Scowcroft, *A World Transformed*, 279–80.

101. Bush and Scowcroft, *A World Transformed*, 282–83.

102. "Issues for Camp David," 1 June 1990, NSC: PA Files, GBPL.

103. Maynard, *Out of the Shadow*, 74.

104. Bush and Scowcroft, *A World Transformed*, 300.

105. Bush and Scowcroft, *A World Transformed*, 224.

106. Brzezinski and Scowcroft, *America and the World*, 114–15; and Bush and Scowcroft, *A World Transformed*, 515.

107. Bush and Scowcroft, *A World Transformed*, 521.

108. President Bush and President Boris Yeltsin, telephone conversation, 20 August 1991; and President Bush and President Mikhail Gorbachev, telephone conversation, 21 August 1991, NSC, Telcons, Presidential, GBPL.

109. Memorandum of telephone conversation between George Bush and Mikhail Gorbachev, 25 December 1991, and "Statement by the President," 25 December 1991, NSC: Nicolas Burns File, GBPL.

110. Bush and Scowcroft, *A World Transformed*, 564.

111. Bush and Scowcroft, *A World Transformed*, 563.

112. Bush and Scowcroft, *A World Transformed*, 564.

5

⚍

The Gulf War and
the New World Order

As the threat of conflict receded in central Europe, a crisis emerged in the summer of 1990 in the Persian Gulf that demonstrated the type of threats that still confronted American interests and challenged the notion that the post–Cold War period would be peaceful or mark the "end of history" following the triumph of liberalism over communism. From Brent Scowcroft's vantage point, it provided an opportunity to consolidate the gains achieved in Europe and to apply the tenets of internationalism to the emerging post–Cold War world. In response to Iraq's invasion of Kuwait, the Bush administration sought to construct what Scowcroft dubbed a "new world order" based on the internationalist principles of American global leadership, great-power cooperation, collective security, the strategic use of international organizations to promote American values and institutions, and the deployment of American power to protect U.S. interests and preserve international stability. Scowcroft acknowledged that the term "new world order" was a gimmicky and unoriginal phrase. Nonetheless, it captured the possibility of the moment to implement the original vision of Franklin D. Roosevelt from World War II for the United Nations and postwar internationalism.

It was Scowcroft who outlined for President Bush what was at stake in the Persian Gulf. He portrayed Iraq's invasion of Kuwait as a threat with implications far beyond the regional challenges posed by Saddam Hussein or the economic consequences for the West's access to oil. How Washington responded to Baghdad's challenge to stability and order could establish expectations, precedents, and patterns of behavior for the post–Cold War international system. Failing to reverse Iraq's conquest and allowing Saddam to absorb a neighboring state would have ramifications far beyond the Persian Gulf. Echoing the Cold War concept of credibility, Scowcroft predicted that other dictators would conclude that aggression could work, and potential victims would see accommodation and appeasement as necessary for survival. Instead, the envisioned new world order would establish the basis for conduct among states and would promote stability and peace, demonstrate the unacceptability of using force to settle disputes, and prove that collective security worked.

The goal remained the same as it had been in making policy in response to the political changes in Eastern Europe: prevent another Versailles-type settlement that led to postwar instability, political upheaval, revolution, and war. The hope was that there would be "no losers, only winners"[1] in the post–Cold War system. For that to occur, the Soviet Union and the United States needed to cooperate in responding to aggression. In addition, the proper lessons from the Vietnam War about the use of American force had to be established. Scowcroft was an adherent to what became known as the Powell Doctrine, named after General Colin Powell, chairman of the Joint Chiefs of Staff during the Gulf War. When the United States needed to commit its military, it should have clearly defined objectives, public support, and an exit strategy, and it should use overwhelming force to accomplish its goals. All of these would be applied during the Gulf War. It was in this manner that Scowcroft and Bush spoke about overcoming the Vietnam syndrome of reluctance to intervene militarily around the world and setting out to establish a U.S.-defined new world order.

THE NEW WORLD ORDER

Since the British disengagement from the area in the 1960s and 1970s, the Persian Gulf had been considered an area of vital interest to the United States. Following the fall of the Shah of Iran, the Carter Doctrine had spelled out the willingness of Washington to take military action to protect American access to oil in the region and defend allied states. During the eight years of fighting between Iraq and Iran that ended in 1988, the United States had tilted toward Baghdad because it saw a victory by the fundamentalist Iranian government as being the greater threat to regional stability and American interests. The Bush administration sought to build on the improved relations with Saddam Hussein that had developed during the 1980s and in so doing to moderate Saddam's behavior, promote regional stability, and develop more cooperative relations with the oil-producing Arab states.

In October 1989, Bush approved National Security Directive 26 (NSD-26) on American policy toward the Persian Gulf. It reasserted the importance of the Gulf as an area "vital to U.S. national security" and proclaimed America's commitment to defend its interests "if necessary and appropriate through the use of U.S. military force." Regarding Iraq, it declared the hope of establishing normal relations with Baghdad and of enhancing regional stability and Western access to Persian Gulf oil. Toward this goal, NSD-26 called for Washington to "propose economic and political incentives for Iraq to moderate its behavior and to increase our influence with Iraq." Furthermore, the United States "should pursue, and seek to facilitate, opportunities for U.S. firms to participate in the reconstruction of the Iraqi economy, particularly in the energy area." At the same time, NSD-26 noted that Iraq had to be warned that any use of illegal chemical weapons or meddling in the affairs of other states could lead to a rupture in relations and economic and political sanctions.[2]

This concern over potential meddling was actually heightened by the end of the Cold War. While acknowledging that nations such as Iraq could no longer depend on support from the Soviet Union in a conflict with the United States, Scowcroft worried that some former client states would be more willing to take risks to achieve their goals without the restraining influence of the Kremlin. States with regional influence that possessed a large military and expansionist goals could continue to threaten American interests and become emboldened by the post–Cold War environment. As the Bush administration's March 1990 "National Security Strategy of the United States" noted, "highly destructive regional wars will remain a danger, made even greater by the expansion of armed forces of regional powers and the proliferation of advanced weaponry." This was particularly a concern in the Middle East, where either religious fanaticism or states such as Iraq with aspirations of regional dominance could threaten the energy sources on which the West depended.[3]

The Iraq strategy envisioned diplomacy rather than deterrence to contain Baghdad's potential threat to the region. Washington's Arab allies, particularly Egypt and Saudi Arabia, urged a conciliatory approach, claiming that a confrontational posture would be counterproductive in terms of both the response from Saddam Hussein and America's image in the region. In the wake of the overthrow of the Shah and the debacle in Lebanon, restoring U.S. credibility in the Arab world was a high priority for Scowcroft and was seen as essential to creating regional support for American policies. The Bush administration, therefore, adopted the approach of offering good relations while warning against actions that would disrupt the status quo.

Saddam Hussein showed little interest in improved relations with the United States as he became more antagonistic toward the West and his neighbors. In particular, he turned his ire toward Kuwait as the source of many of his problems. Iraq had borrowed over $30 billion from Kuwait during its war with Iran, and Saddam was furious that the Kuwaitis would not forgive the debt from a war that he claimed Iraq had fought to defend all Arabs from Iran. To pressure Kuwait, Baghdad inflamed ongoing border disputes over the area of the Rumaila oil field and the island of Būbiyān which controlled access to Iraq's major port. Kuwait had allowed Iraq to use the island during the Iraq-Iran War, and now Saddam wanted to retain control over it.

By July, tensions had reached the point that conflict appeared imminent. Saddam Hussein charged that Kuwait and the United Arab Emirates were exceeding OPEC production limits and in the process were driving down the price of oil in a manner particularly harmful to Iraq. He threatened to correct this situation and moved troops toward the Iraq border with Kuwait. Kuwait's unwillingness to forgive Iraq's debt, its failure to resolve the border disputes, and its alleged theft of oil from the disputed border region were all portrayed as attacks on Iraq. An American ambassador to Iraq, April Glaspie, was asked to secure clarification from Saddam Hussein on his intentions while making clear that the United States was "determined to ensure the free flow of oil through the Strait of Hormuz" and was "committed to supporting the individual and collective self-defense of our friends in the Gulf with whom we have deep and longstanding ties." Although directed by the State Department to state that officially the United States took "no position" on the border disputes in the region, Glaspie was to characterize Iraq's threats to use force to resolve the issues as "disturbing."[4]

Glaspie met with Saddam Hussein on July 25 for two hours and was assured by the Iraqi dictator that he did not want a conflict with the United States and that he was willing to settle the disputes through negotiations with other Arab leaders. The ambassador reported that Saddam was worried about American opposition and that "he does not want to further antagonize us. . . . We have fully caught his attention, and that is good." She advised the State Department to curtail public criticism of Iraq and wait on the negotiations before taking any further steps.[5] While the ambassador did tell the Iraqi dictator that President Bush sought better relations with Iraq, the charge that Glaspie somehow gave Saddam Hussein the impression that the United States would accept his conquest of Kuwait is spurious. The ambassador made clear Washington's desire for peace and stability in the region, but she also expressed concern over Iraq's portrayal of Kuwait's actions as "the equivalent of military aggression" and over Saddam's sending troops to the border. Moreover, she left no doubt that the United States would act to protect its interests in the region.[6] Even so, President Bush's cable to Saddam three days later was unambiguous regarding the American position. The United States, Bush stated, was encouraged by the ongoing diplomacy concerning the Iraq-

Kuwait dispute, but it still had "fundamental concerns about certain Iraqi policies and activities" and would "continue to support our other friends in the region."[7]

The administration's warnings were all for naught. On August 2, Iraq invaded Kuwait, creating the first post–Cold War international crisis. Initially, information was hard to obtain, but Scowcroft immediately decided that the United States had to take strong economic, diplomatic, and military measures in opposition to Iraq's action. Bush agreed to move warships toward the Persian Gulf, to freeze Iraqi and Kuwaiti assets in the United States, and to endorse U.N. Security Council Resolution 660, which condemned the invasion and called for an immediate removal of Iraq's forces from Kuwait and the restoration of its government. Scowcroft was, however, "frankly appalled" by that morning's National Security Council meeting to discuss the American response. The approach of many of the participants "suggested resignation to the invasion and even adaptation to a *fait accompli*." This left a large gap between Scowcroft, who saw invasion as a defining moment for the post–Cold War world and "as the major crisis of our time," and colleagues "who treated it as the crisis *du jour*."[8]

Scowcroft believed that others did not understand what was at stake for the United States and the precedent that would be set regarding aggression as the world moved beyond the Cold War international order. Squeezed together, knees to knees, on a C-20 Gulfstream flying to Aspen that morning to meet with British Prime Minister Margaret Thatcher and give a scheduled speech on foreign policy, Scowcroft convinced Bush that Iraq's conquest of Kuwait was a major crisis and that the president had to be willing to use force if necessary. The United States had to secure the withdrawal of Iraq's forces and the restoration of Kuwait's government. Anything short of this would be seen as weakness, would harm American credibility, and would provide a green light for aggression by other states. Scowcroft spent much of the flight revising Bush's speech while the president called congressional and foreign leaders to begin lining up international support for America's opposition to Iraq.

Prior to returning to Washington, D.C., from Colorado, Scowcroft spoke with Richard Haass and had him prepare a memo for distribution to all of the participants prior to the next NSC meeting. It set out both Scowcroft's analysis of the situation and the policy steps necessary to force Iraq's withdrawal from Kuwait. Its main premises were that the United States had to properly understand how Iraq fit into the larger context of American foreign policy, and that diplomacy and economic sanctions, while necessary steps, would most likely fail, leaving the use of military force as the only option for reversing the situation. Scowcroft was well aware of the risks involved with his recommendation, but an acceptance of the status quo would come with even higher costs: "We would be setting a terrible precedent—one that would only accelerate violent centrifugal tendencies—in this emerging 'post Cold War' era. We would be encouraging a dangerous adversary in the Gulf at a time when the United States has provided a de facto commitment to Gulf stability—a commitment reinforced by our statements and military movements—that also raises the issue of US reliability in a most serious way." In addition, it was necessary to "recognize too that Iraq has the capacity and the desire to complicate the peace process in the Middle East." A final decision was not immediately necessary, but preparation was essential. He concluded, "We don't need to decide where to draw any lines just yet, but we do need to take steps—moving forces, pressing allies and reluctant Arabs, etc.—that would at least give us a real choice if current efforts fall short."[9]

At the NSC meeting on August 3, Scowcroft broke from his normal role as discussion facilitator and proposed his own views at the outset. He voiced his concerns over the previous day's discussion and explained why U.S. vital interests demanded Washington's opposition to Iraq's action. In response to the sentiment that the United States might need to "acquiesce to an accommodation of the situation," he declared "that to accommodate Iraq should not be a policy option." There was "too much at stake" since it was "broadly viewed in the United States that a commitment to Kuwait is de facto based on our actions in the Gulf before." If the United States did not uphold its word, Iraq "would dominate OPEC politics, Palestinian politics and the PLO, and lead the Arab world to the detriment of the United States, and the great stakes we have in the Middle East." Therefore, the United States could not tolerate Iraqi control of Kuwait or the precedent it would set. By predesign, Deputy Secretary of State Lawrence Eagleburger spoke next to reinforce Scowcroft's points. He noted that "this is the first test of the post war system. As the bipolar contest is relaxed, it permits . . . giving people more flexibility because they are not worried about the involvement of the superpowers." If Iraq were successful, "others may try the same thing. It would be a bad lesson."[10]

The intelligence reports supported Scowcroft's position. The director of the CIA, William Webster, told the NSC that Saddam Hussein was consolidating Iraq's hold on Kuwait and that "all the intelligence shows he won't pull out. He will stay if not challenged within the next year. This will fundamentally alter the Persian Gulf region. He would be in an inequitable position, since he would control the second—and third—largest proven oil reserves with the fourth-largest army in the world." Saddam's power would also be enhanced by having "Kuwaiti assets, access to the Gulf, and the ability to pour money into his military. There is no apparent internal rival to Saddam. His ego cannot be satisfied; his ambition is to have ever more influence."[11] The focus of the rest of the meeting, and subsequent NSC meetings, became what Scowcroft wanted: the necessary steps—military, political, and economic—to oppose Iraq.

Scowcroft also feared an Arab solution to the problem. Egyptian President Hosni Mubarak wanted a two-day window to meet with Saudi King Fahd to work out a solution. The national security advisor feared a compromise solution that left Saddam in control of Kuwait, that alienated America's allies, and that made the United States look weak. It was vital, therefore, to get Saudi Arabia to oppose such an action and to request American forces for its defense. At the National Security Council meeting on August 4, Scowcroft told the principals that the first goal of the United States had to be getting Iraq out of Kuwait by imposing an embargo and sending a military force to Saudi Arabia. He knew from his conversations with them that the "Saudis are concerned about our seriousness," and "ground forces" would be the "best symbol of our commitment." King Fahd did not want to take the lead in opposing Saddam and be left vulnerable if the United States failed to act, yet Washington worried about the Arab nation's will to resist and willingness to accept American forces. Given this, Scowcroft was prepared to give Saudi Arabia his assurance that the United States would stand with Riyadh until the end.[12] As Scowcroft noted the next day, the United States had to be in position to deter Iraq from invading Saudi Arabia so that "when we begin to clamp down economically, Saddam has no military option."[13]

When Iraq invaded Kuwait, Secretary of State James Baker was in the Soviet Union meeting with his Russian counterpart. Baker and Soviet Foreign Minister Eduard Shevardnadze issued a joint statement condemning Iraq and endorsing the United Nations Resolution. This was a critical step, as it provided evidence that the Cold War was really over and that the former bitter adversaries could work together through the United Nations on common problems. Moreover, it made lining up support from other nations for U.S. policy much easier in the days ahead.

A strategy for implementing Scowcroft's policy was taking shape. The first step was to persuade the United Nations to back up its condemnation of Iraq's aggression by adopting economic sanctions, which was done on August 6 with the approval of Security Council Resolution 661. Second, the United States would lead an international force into Saudi Arabia to defend that nation and enforce the UN sanctions. The goal of both of these actions was to force the complete withdrawal of Iraq from Kuwait and to restore the legitimate government in Kuwait City. As President Bush told the press on August 5, he would not yet discuss specifics, but he took "very seriously our determination to reverse this awful aggression," and he would work with America's allies in a collective effort to bring about the withdrawal of Iraq's forces. "This will not stand, this aggression against Kuwait," Bush declared.[14]

The core of Scowcroft's analysis regarding why it was necessary for the United States to be prepared to take military action against Iraq rested on the internationalist positions that had guided his thinking throughout his career and most recently had led to success in Europe. These perspectives had shaped "long-held security and economic interests: preserving the balance of power in the Gulf, opposing unprovoked international aggression, and ensuring that no hostile regional power could hold hostage much of the world's oil supply." According to Scowcroft, another objective emerged early on and "grew in importance to us as we developed our response to the invasion. In the first days of the crisis we had started self-consciously to view our actions as setting a precedent for the approaching post–Cold War world. Soviet cooperation in condemning the attack provided the initial impetus for this line of thinking, inasmuch as it opened the way for the Security Council to operate as its founders had envisioned." Out of this developed his concept of a new world order. "From that point forward," Scowcroft wrote, "we tried to operate in a manner that would help establish a pattern for the future. Our foundation was the premise that the United States henceforth would be obligated to lead the world community to an unprecedented degree, as demonstrated by the Iraqi crisis, and that we should attempt to pursue our national interests, wherever possible, within a framework of concert with our friends and the international community."[15]

To Scowcroft's analysis, President Bush added a moral dimension and specific references to World War II. He saw the brutality of Iraq's attack on Kuwait as akin to Germany's invasion of Poland in 1939, and he saw the need to respond as necessary to avoid appeasement. At the time of Iraq's invasion of Kuwait, Bush was reading Martin Gilbert's history of the Second World War and a biography of Henry Stimson, one of the earliest critics of appeasement and an advocate of collective security against aggressor states. As Bush wrote, "I saw a direct analogy between what was occurring in Kuwait and what the Nazis had done. . . . I saw a chilling parallel with what the Iraqi occupiers were doing in Kuwait." This provided "a deep moral objection" to Iraq's invasion.[16]

The administration's final concern was the economic impact of Iraq's action on the United States and its allies. As noted in National Security Directive 45 (NSD-45), the United States had a vital interest in access to oil from the Persian Gulf. Given that the "United States now imports nearly half the oil it consumes and, as a result of the current crisis, could face a major threat to its economy," and given that America's main allies were "even more dependent on imported oil and more vulnerable to Iraqi threats," military forces were being deployed in conjunction with other nations to defend Saudi Arabia and enforce the UN-approved economic sanctions against Iraq.[17]

With Saudi approval for sending American troops to the kingdom obtained, Bush spoke to the American people on August 8 to explain American policy and its actions in response to the Iraqi occupation of Kuwait. The president began dramatically by stating that, "in the life of a nation, we're called upon to define who we are and what we believe." The current crisis demanded that the United States "stand up for what's right and condemn what's wrong, all in the cause of peace." Invoking images of World War II, Bush stated that "Iraq's tanks stormed in blitzkrieg fashion through Kuwait in a few short hours." It was in response to this aggression that he was acting by sending American forces to Saudi Arabia to defend that nation against Iraq in what became called Operation Desert Shield. "If history teaches us anything, it is that we must resist aggression or it will destroy our freedoms. Appeasement does not work. As was the case in the 1930's we see in Saddam Hussein an aggressive dictator threatening his neighbors." Since President Franklin D. Roosevelt was in office, Bush continued, the United States had been "committed to the security and stability of the Persian Gulf." America could not abandon its friends in this moment of need. Moreover, the nation was dependent on imported oil and "could face a major threat to its economic independence" if Iraq, with the world's fourth largest military, succeeded in gaining control over Kuwait's reserves. The independence of Saudi Arabia was a vital interest to the United States, and sending troops there would "preserve the integrity of Saudi Arabia and deter further Iraqi aggression." At a time when the world was "beginning a new era . . . an age of freedom," when the Cold War had come to an end in Europe because the United States and its allies had stood up for their values, it was essential that these same principles be upheld in the Middle East.[18]

On August 23, while fishing off the coast of Maine, Scowcroft and Bush had a long talk about the crisis in the Gulf and whether the United States could remove Saddam Hussein from Kuwait without force. After discussing the military situation, the strength of Iraq's forces, and the status of the international coalition, their thoughts turned to the level of force necessary, to comparisons with Vietnam, and to the larger meaning of American policy. Both men were well aware of the parallels that could be drawn to the Vietnam War and the shadow that conflict had cast over all American military actions. The Powell Doctrine shaped their thinking, and they were determined that, should the United States turn to a military solution to oust Saddam Hussein, the force employed would be overwhelming and the objective clear: freeing Kuwait and reestablishing its government. They believed that this course of action would elicit public support and that it would be a short war with a decisive ending. Scowcroft and Bush rejected the idea of expanding the conflict to the overthrow of Iraq's government, as they feared getting bogged down in an occupation of Iraq and an open-ended commitment to nation building.

Scowcroft turned the conversation toward making sure they "handled the crisis in a way which reflected the nature of the transformed world we would face in the future." Based on the changes taking place in Europe, they thought that the United States was "at a watershed of history." As Scowcroft observed, "The Soviet Union was standing alongside us, not only in the United Nations, but also in condemning and taking action against Iraqi aggression." With the two former adversaries now able to agree, "The Security Council could then perform the role envisioned for it by the UN framers. The United States and the Soviet Union could, in most cases, stand together against unprovoked interstate aggression." The term "new world order" was first used during this conversation to describe this possibility and the opportunity for using collective action against international aggression.[19]

These hopes were further buoyed during the president's meeting with Gorbachev in Helsinki on September 9. Having secured international condemnation of Iraq through the United Nations and put together a multinational military force in Saudi Arabia to enforce sanctions and defend the other Gulf states, it was essential to obtain Soviet understanding of the need to use force if the diplomatic and economic pressure being applied to Baghdad did not work. Bush told Gorbachev that he believed from the response to the crisis in the Gulf that there was an opportunity to create a new world order of collective security. "The bottom line for a new world order must be that Saddam Hussein cannot be allowed to profit from his aggression." The president stated that he was not sure Saddam understood how determined the United States was to removing him from Kuwait. "Sanctions are our preferred way of inducing him to withdraw and allow the return of Kuwait's leaders. . . . But if he does not withdraw, he must know that the status quo is unacceptable."[20]

The more the United States and the Soviet Union worked together on this, the quicker a solution to the present crisis would be found and the closer they would be to a new world order. "The world order I see coming out of this," Bush stated, "is a US and Soviet cooperation to solve not only this but other problems in the Middle East." Bush expressed the hope that he could tell the American people that with the two nations working together they could "close the book on the Cold War and offer them the vision of this new world order in which we will cooperate." Gorbachev provided the assurance Bush was seeking, stating that cooperation was essential. The Russian leader declared, "You should not doubt our position is [firm]. We have condemned Iraqi aggression and supported the UN. We are as one here."[21]

In order to build public support for American policies and introduce the idea of a new world order, Scowcroft, as the architect of American policy, appeared on numerous news programs in late August and in September. Speaking on CNN's *Newsmaker Saturday* on August 25, Scowcroft stipulated the coalition's demands for an to the crisis: the withdrawal of Iraq from Kuwait, the restoration of the legitimate government in Kuwait City, and the release of all foreigners being held by Iraqi forces. Washington would not negotiate on these points, and it was determined to succeed. Furthermore, Scowcroft noted that "one of the things which we're really seeing now is perhaps the emergence of a new world order. That's a strong term, but what we're seeing is the United Nations beginning to operate as it was foreseen to operate, when it was established in 1945–1946, prevented by the superpower conflict between the United States and the Soviet Union. Now we're seeing a Security Council beginning . . . to mobilize the civilized world community against aggression and against aggressors." The crisis was not just in the Gulf but had broader ramifications. If Iraq's aggression were allowed to stand, other dictators "may be emboldened by the way Saddam Hussein swept aside the rulers of a country." The United States was determined to send the signal that it "will not tolerate the kind of naked aggression that had been perpetrated by Iraq."[22]

The next day, Scowcroft was on *This Week with David Brinkley* setting out the same objectives and making the case that the administration was creating a new international system based on the principles of internationalism. The actions being taken in the Persian Gulf constituted "a case of collective action against an instance of naked aggression," Scowcroft opined. "And I think it shows that the United Nations and the world community perhaps now is prepared to operate the way it was envisioned when the U.N. Charter was adopted." The actual use of force was not necessary for this to happen. If the sanctions worked to compel Saddam Hussein to withdraw from Kuwait and he retained his power in Iraq, "there will still be a fundamentally different situation in that area, in that collective action will have been shown to work against a case of aggression; and, therefore, the situation will not be the same afterwards."[23]

Two weeks later, Scowcroft discussed the issue of U.S.-Soviet cooperation and the new world order on *Meet the Press*. The Bush-Gorbachev meeting in Helsinki was a historic moment, he said, because the United States obtained "nothing short of complete acceptance, implementation of the Security Council resolutions . . . and if steps taken so far do not do the job, then further steps will be considered." For the two former bitter enemies to reach an agreement on how to respond to aggression demonstrated how much had changed in the past year. The United States had worked very hard in the past to keep the Soviet Union out of the Middle East. Now, given "the change in character of U.S.-Soviet relations, the change of Soviet policy," and the "strong indications that they're playing a very responsible role in this crisis," it was possible to talk about a new era in international affairs.[24]

President Bush addressed a joint session of Congress on September 11 to explain the rationale for his policy toward Iraq, what was at stake in the decision to send troops to Saudi Arabia, and his vision for a new world order. Vital American interests were threatened by Iraq's aggression. "An Iraq permitted to swallow Kuwait would have the economic and military power, as well as the arrogance, to intimidate and coerce its neighbors—neighbors who control the lion's share of the world's remaining oil reserves. We cannot permit a resource so vital to be dominated by one so ruthless. And we won't." The United States sought the unconditional withdrawal of Iraqi forces from Kuwait and the restoration of the Kuwaiti government. "The security and stability of the Persian Gulf must be assured." The UN Security Council had endorsed U.S. policy through five separate resolutions, and most other nations in the world had condemned Iraq's invasion. "This is not, as Saddam Hussein would have it, the United States against Iraq. It is Iraq against the world." In addition, the United States and the Soviet Union agreed that Iraq's aggression could not be tolerated. "Clearly, no longer can a dictator count on East-West confrontation to stymie concerted United Nations action against aggression."[25]

This made the present a unique moment. Bush proclaimed that "the crisis in the Persian Gulf, as grave as it is, also offers a rare opportunity to move toward an historic period of cooperation. Out of these troubled times . . . a new world order—can emerge: a new era—freer from the threat of terror, stronger in the pursuit of justice, and more secure in the quest for peace." The president envisioned an international system based on the rule of law, collective security, respect for the rights of other nations, and a commitment to freedom and justice. How the current crisis in the Gulf was handled would shape the world for generations to come. "This is the first assault on the new world we seek, the first test of our mettle. Had we not responded to this first provocation with clarity of purpose, if we do not continue to demonstrate our determination, it would be a signal to actual and potential despots around the world. America and the world must defend common vital interests—and we will."[26]

Finally, the president declared that the events in the Gulf proved that "there is no substitute for American leadership. In the face of tyranny, let no one doubt American credibility and reliability. . . . We will stand by our friends." Bush would not put a timeline on how long it would take to liberate Kuwait. The sanctions imposed would take time to have their intended impact, and the situation could change. What was not in doubt, he declared, was that the United States would "not let this aggression stand."[27] The administration then turned to how it would force Iraq out of Kuwait.

THE GULF WAR

The coalition the administration assembled for Operation Desert Shield was impressive, with troops from twenty-nine countries that would total over 675,000 by the end of the year, 500,000 of them from the United States. In addition to the multinational force, over fifty nations had pledged more than $50 billion in assistance, with the largest amounts coming from Saudi Arabia, Kuwait, Japan, and Germany. By October, planning for the war began in earnest. Scowcroft and the core group of the NSC met on October 11 with military leaders to discuss strategy. General Powell presented a cautious plan that relied on airpower followed by a frontal assault on the Iraqi line of defense to secure the road to Kuwait City. The national security advisor was "appalled" by the plan, seeing it as an unenthusiastic effort "by people who didn't want to do the job." He expressed his displeasure and suggested an alternative plan of going around Iraq's forces to the west and trapping them in Kuwait.[28]

Scowcroft followed up on the meeting by writing a memo to Bush that called for a strong diplomatic push coupled with "accelerated preparations that provide a real alternative should diplomacy fail." He wanted another United Nations resolution that put a fixed date on Iraq's withdrawal and provided a clear signal that Iraqi refusal would be met by military action. His goal was to have this new Security Council resolution containing an ultimatum passed by the end of November to allow time for an additional military buildup and to prevent the charge that the administration did not allow sanctions and diplomacy to work. "I believe this general approach is preferable to sticking to sanctions," Scowcroft wrote to Bush. "It does not appear that sanctions alone will accomplish what we seek in the foreseeable future. Meanwhile, the hostages remain hostage and Kuwait is being destroyed." The longer the crisis dragged on, the harder it would be to maintain the coalition and the embargo. The time to take action was rapidly approaching.[29]

The National Security Council met again on October 30 to hear the military's revised plan for the liberation of Kuwait. President Bush, guided by Scowcroft's memo, opened the meeting by stating that it was time to decide if it was necessary to increase the pressure on Saddam Hussein by "pressing ahead on both the military and diplomatic tracks." He acknowledged that a decision to give Saddam a deadline was "in effect committing ourselves to war," but it might also increase the chances of a peaceful solution.[30] The decisions reached that day called for the United States to continue its military buildup in order to have the capacity to go on the offensive, and specified that January 15 should be the deadline set by the United Nations because it would take that long to get an American force of over 500,000 troops into place.

The president announced the further increase in American forces and the shift to an offensive strategy on November 8. He told the nation that prior to the invasion of Kuwait "we had succeeded in the struggle for freedom in Eastern Europe, and we'd hopefully begun a new era that offered the promise of peace." Since Iraq's attack on its neighbor, the United States had "made it clear that it would stand up to this aggression," consistent with the "policies it had adopted since World War II. To do this, Washington and its allies have forged a coalition of forces to put economic, political, and military pressure on Baghdad to force the unconditional withdrawal of its military from Kuwait." A total of 230,000 troops had been dispatched to Saudi Arabia, and the president was increasing the size of the American force "to ensure that the coalition has an adequate offensive military option should that be necessary to achieve our common goals."[31]

Throughout the fall, Bush and Scowcroft held a series of meetings with congressional leaders to discuss the crisis in the Persian Gulf and the proper American response. Many in Congress were concerned that the administration was moving toward the use of military force and in the process precluding options for a peaceful settlement. Democratic leaders George Mitchell, the Senate majority leader, and Tom Foley, speaker of the House, cautioned Bush that public support was based on backing sanctions and UN resolutions, not the prospect of fighting, and the president must seek a declaration of war before proceeding with an offensive strategy. The critics' common concern was that the administration was not giving the embargo a fair chance to work. A letter signed by eighty-one congressional Democrats expressed the worry that the consequences of using military force to resolve the crisis "would be catastrophic—resulting in the massive loss of lives, including 10,000–50,000 Americans."[32] Congressional unease was based on the lessons of the Vietnam War. Many members of Congress feared a long, drawn-out conflict, with American forces mired in an Iraqi quagmire. This so-called Vietnam syndrome, a reluctance to use American troops abroad out of a fear of becoming entangled in a conflict that became a stalemate, led many in Congress to seek a means short of war to end the crisis.

Scowcroft understood the worries about another Vietnam, but he did not believe they should prevent the use of force. Rather, these fears dictated that clear war aims be established and the necessary means for accomplishing them be put into place. He believed that the vital American interests of opposing aggression, maintaining stability in the Middle East, and ensuring access to the region's oil demanded an American response. It was up to the United States to set the pattern for the post–Cold War world and to lead the world by following the tenets of international-ism and collective security for the establishment of a new world order. Scowcroft had already established a set of aims by the time of these meet-ings that met most of the concerns expressed by Congress. Force would be used for the limited goal of liberating Kuwait and destroying Iraq's capacity to wage war against its neighbors. Any action beyond that, he believed, was unwise.

It was apparent to Scowcroft that Congress had little will to back the use of force which the administration now deemed to be almost certainly necessary to drive Iraq out of Kuwait. A negative vote in Congress would bolster Saddam Hussein's position while damaging the strength of the coalition. Yet it was politically necessary to go to Congress and get a resolution authorizing force if the president wanted to proceed. The ad-ministration had to make a better case for strong action. The first step was to secure an authorization for the use of force from the United Nations.

The administration obtained the passage of UN Security Council Reso-lution 678 on November 29. This resolution permitted the "member states cooperating with the government of Kuwait" to use "all necessary means" to carry out the previous UN resolutions regarding Iraq's invasion of Kuwait. The resolution also provided Iraq "one final opportunity, as a pause of good will," to withdraw by January 15, 1991. After that date, the coalition would have United Nations support for using force to uphold the demand for an unconditional withdrawal of Iraq's forces.[33] President Bush declared the next day that the UN action demonstrated how great the stakes were for the United States and its allies. "We're in the Gulf be-cause the world must not and cannot reward aggression. And we're there because our vital interests are at stake." The United States faced "a dan-gerous dictator all too willing to use force . . . and who desires to control one of the world's key resources—all at a time in history when the rules of the post–Cold War world are being written." Thus, Washington held to its previously stated position that Iraq must unconditionally withdraw from Kuwait and release all hostages. In addition, Bush announced that he would send Secretary of State Baker to meet with Saddam Hussein prior to the UN deadline to impress upon Iraq the determination of the United States and to arrange for the withdrawal of its forces.[34]

Scowcroft again made the tour of the television news programs to pres-ent the necessity of the United Nations' action and the administration's case. Prior to the UN Security Council vote on Resolution 678, Scowcroft told David Brinkley that while no one wanted it to come to war, "neither

From the Oval Office study, President Bush notifies world leaders and Congress on January 16, 1991, of the imminent attack on Iraqi troops in Kuwait by U.S. forces while National Security Advisor Brent Scowcroft reviews briefing materials. Courtesy of the George H. W. Bush Presidential Library.

are they eager to have this drawn out over an indefinite period of time." It was his belief, and that of the coalition, that the occupation of Kuwait "needs to be brought to an end." Scowcroft added, "It is my judgment that the best chance to avoid war is to confront Saddam Hussein with the prospects of war." As to the matter of congressional authorization for war, Scowcroft replied that the president was in consultation with the leadership of Congress and would continue to work closely with them.[35]

Speaking on *Face the Nation* on December 2, Scowcroft presented UN Resolution 678 as "designed to show Saddam Hussein the strength of the world coalition against him, the fact that there's no temporizing, that there's no negotiating, that he has to get out." If the coalition employed only sanctions, Iraq would think it could delay until the rest of the world grew tired of the issue. Scowcroft's message was that Saddam could not adopt this strategy; rather, he had to withdraw or face the consequences. This was the crucial point. The United States was "setting the stage for a new world as we come out of the . . . post–Cold War world. We have former enemies, the Soviet Union, the People's Republic of China, we have the great powers as envisioned in the United Nations behind moving toward this new world." All the nations in the coalition agreed that aggression would not be tolerated and would be reversed.[36]

The next weekend, Scowcroft appeared on CNN's *Newsmaker Saturday* and NBC's *Meet the Press*. He declared that the goal of the UN Security Council was "to convince Saddam Hussein that he has two options. And that is to withdraw, to respond to the U.N. resolutions, or to face catastrophe." It was essential that "Saddam Hussein understand clearly that the world community is against him and that the United States is determined to enforce, with the coalition, those United Nations resolutions, and that his options are very limited." The Iraqi dictator had to understand that "there is no wiggle room—there are no negotiations. He's not going to split the coalition. He's not going to split the American people, that . . . . what he has to do is get out." It was never the administration's position, Scowcroft stated, that sanctions alone would work, and the UN authorization to use "all means necessary" to obtain Iraq's withdrawal from Kuwait if it did not leave by January 15, 1991, was another part of the overall pressure being brought to bear. "What we are trying to demonstrate right now to Saddam Hussein is that he is . . . at the moment of truth. The world community has spoken—he has to get out, and he has to get out by January 15. We're underscoring that by moving more forces in." The president, Scowcroft said, was doing everything he could to accomplish this short of using force, but he would act if necessary.[37]

The war aims, and limits on the use of military power, were in place before Christmas. American and coalition forces would be employed to drive Iraq out of Kuwait and to inflict enough damage on Saddam's forces that he could no longer threaten his neighbors. This would coincide with the UN mandates and promises made to America's coalition partners. The question of whether to remove Saddam Hussein from power was discussed and rejected. That would take a full-scale invasion and the overthrow of his government, leaving the United States "facing an indefinite occupation of a hostile state and some dubious 'nation-building.' Realistically, if Saddam fell, it would not be a democracy emerging. . . . The best solution was to do as much damage as we could to his military, and wait for the Ba'ath regime to collapse." The Arab states in the coalition believed that Saddam could not politically survive a military defeat and would face a coup by senior officers. It was decided that this was a better option than risking a military assault on Baghdad that would go beyond the UN mandate and politically break up the coalition.[38]

On January 2, 1991, Bush met with Scowcroft, Baker, and White House Chief of Staff John Sununu to discuss pursuing a final effort to get word to Saddam that time was running out and that he faced a determined coalition that was prepared to take action. The purpose was to leave no question that the president had given sanctions and diplomacy every chance. After consulting with key allies, Bush announced the next day his offer to send Baker to Geneva to talk with a representative of Iraq's government, a meeting that was arranged for January 9. In addition to sending Baker to Geneva, Bush wrote a personal letter to Saddam on January 5 that once again detailed the U.S. position and its determination to back UN Security Council Resolution 678 with force should the January 15 deadline pass without a withdrawal from Kuwait. The Iraqi foreign minister, meeting with Baker in Geneva, and the Iraqi ambassador in Washington refused to deliver the letter to the Iraqi dictator.[39]

On January 3, the president met with congressional leaders seeking a demonstration of unity to show Saddam that the United States had the resolve to fight. Foley told Bush that a resolution authorizing the use of force would pass, but it would be a close vote. Scowcroft suggested that it would be best to hold the vote after Baker's trip to Geneva, when it was clear that diplomacy would never work. On January 8, Bush wrote to congressional leaders of both parties in the Senate and House asking for an endorsement of the "use of all necessary means to implement UN Security Council Resolution 678. Such action would send the clearest possible message to Saddam Hussein that he must withdraw without condition or delay from Kuwait. Anything less would only encourage Iraqi intransigence; anything less would risk detracting from the international coalition arrayed against Iraq's aggression."[40]

President Bush at his desk in the Oval Office study with National Security Advisor Scowcroft and Chief of Staff John Sununu. Courtesy of the George H. W. Bush Presidential Library.

Congressional debate began on January 10. Scowcroft and other senior officials, including the president, lobbied hard to obtain a favorable vote, working with allies on Capitol Hill to ensure that the House voted first to build pressure on a more reluctant Senate. Opponents of authorizing the use of force had a variety of arguments and claims. The most prevalent point was that the United States could prevail without war by letting the sanctions continue until they forced Iraq out of Kuwait. Others expressed concerns about the number of potential casualties, and that a fight for oil was not worth the deaths of thousands of Americans. Some saw the issue as a local fight between different despots that should not involve the United States. Finally, there were those who believed that the president, through his rhetoric and steps taken, had painted himself into a corner where his only option now appeared to be the use of force. It was up to Congress, they argued, to save him from this decision.

Supporters of the administration countered that peace could only be secured through the collective action of the multinational coalition, not through a policy of appeasement that rewarded aggression. If the United States did not lead the fight against Saddam Hussein, it would lose the position it had achieved in the wake of the end of the Cold War and its credibility with other nations. A sign of weakness would fracture the coalition and destroy a unique opportunity for forging a new world order in the post–Cold War world.

In a highly unusual move designed to prove that he had gone the extra mile for peace, on January 12, the same day that Congress was to vote, President Bush released his letter to Saddam Hussein to the press. Bush began his letter by noting that the crisis had started with Iraq's invasion of its neighbor and that war could only be avoided by an unconditional acceptance of Security Council Resolution 678. The president stated that he was writing Saddam directly "because what is at stake demands that no opportunity be lost to avoid what would be a certain calamity for the people of Iraq." He also noted that he was sending the letter "because it is said by some that you do not understand just how isolated Iraq is and what Iraq faces as a result." Bush sought to eliminate any doubt about what he was prepared to undertake to compel compliance with the UN resolutions. The United States preferred that Iraq heed the wishes of the international community and withdraw peacefully as called for by the United Nations. But anything short of full compliance was unacceptable, and there could be "no reward for aggression. Nor will there be any negotiations. Principle cannot be compromised."[41]

Bush plainly cataloged the potential costs of war to Iraq. "You will lose more than Kuwait. What is at issue here is not the future of Kuwait—it will be free, its government will be restored—but rather the future of Iraq." Iraq was already suffering from the sanctions imposed by the

United Nations and upheld by over one hundred nations. "Should war come, it will be a far greater tragedy for you and your country." The U.S.-led international coalition was prepared to do what was necessary to enforce the UN resolutions. "You may be tempted to find solace in the diversity of opinion that is American democracy," Bush noted. "You should resist any such temptation. Diversity ought not to be confused with division. Nor should you underestimate . . . America's will." The decision for war, Bush concluded, was in Iraq's hands.[42]

It is unclear if the letter changed any votes in Congress, but it did neutralize charges that Bush was rushing into war or had not tried to end the crisis peacefully. That evening, the House voted 250 to 183 in support of the resolution authorizing the president to use force after the UN deadline passed. In the Senate, ten Democrats joined the 52-47 majority that provided congressional approval for military action if the president found it necessary. Bush had secured crucial congressional approval for war.

On January 15, Bush signed National Security Directive 54, which authorized the use of military action against Iraq to force its removal from Kuwait and restore the pre-occupation government. The economic sanctions were deemed unable to accomplish "the intended objective of ending Iraq's occupation of Kuwait," and there was "no persuasive evidence that they will do so in a timely manner." Immediate action was necessary because "prolonging the current situation would be detrimental to the United States in that it would increase the costs of eventual military action, threaten the political cohesion of the coalition of countries arrayed against Iraq, allow for continued brutalization of the Kuwaiti people and destruction of their country, and cause added damage to the U.S. and world economies."[43] With this final piece, the steps toward war were complete.

On January 16, Bush announced to the nation that the United States and its coalition partners had begun Operation Desert Storm by launching air strikes against Iraq to dislodge its forces from Kuwait. Declaring that "we will not fail," the president stated that sanctions alone were insufficient and that he had exhausted all diplomatic options. Any further delay would cause greater damage to the world's economy and would only reward aggression. He promised that the conflict would not be "another Vietnam." He would provide the American forces with all the support they needed, and "they will not be asked to fight with one hand tied behind their back." Bush reiterated his main justification for the war, calling it "an historic moment." In the past year, the Cold War had come to an end, and set before the nation was the "opportunity to forge for ourselves and for future generations a new world order—a world where the rule of law, not the law of the jungle, governs the conduct of nations." Success would make credible the United Nations' role as a peacekeeper in line with the vision of its founders and the ability of the world to engage in collective security against aggression.[44]

The president returned again to this theme at the outset of his State of the Union speech on January 29. He cast the American war in the Persian Gulf as part of the historic mission of the United States. "We are Americans, part of something larger than ourselves. For two centuries, we've done the hard work of freedom. And tonight, we lead the world in facing down a threat to decency and humanity." The stakes went well beyond Iraq to "a big idea: a new world order" that brings together the nations of the world in collective security, freedom, rule of law, and the quest for peace. The world rejected the appeasement of aggression and sought to build upon the successful end of the Cold War that America's resolute stand for freedom had brought about. The United States had achieved its goal of "a Europe whole and free," and the "triumph of democratic ideas" was spreading from Eastern Europe to all parts of the world. For the new world order to come to fruition, "American leadership is indispensible." It had to continue to serve "as an inspiring example of freedom and democracy." Leadership comes with burdens and costs, "but we also know why the hopes of humanity turn to us. We are Americans: we have a unique responsibility to do the hard work of freedom. And when we do, freedom works." The nation was on the verge of "the next American century."[45]

Scowcroft has acknowledged that by the beginning of February he and the president were "impatient to begin the ground campaign." After three weeks, the United States had conducted over forty-four thousand air sorties over Iraq, about one every minute after the bombing began, and had fired hundreds of missiles from naval vessels in the Persian Gulf. The attacks had successfully nullified the Iraqi navy and air force and had caused significant damage to military and communication targets throughout the nation. Still, the national security advisor "never seriously entertained the idea that air power alone could do the job," noting that its advocates had overestimated the decisive impact it could have partly due to wishful thinking and the lower casualty rates it promised. Ground troops would be needed to drive Iraq out of Kuwait and to destroy the Iraqi army's offensive capabilities. It was not possible to bomb Iraqi forces in Kuwait without endangering Kuwaiti civilians and infrastructure. Yet the military continued to push back the date for the ground war, much to Scowcroft's dismay.[46]

President Bush visited three military bases on the first day of February to deliver the same message he had featured in his State of the Union message: the war with Iraq was necessary to preserve freedom, to stand up to international aggression, to move beyond the Vietnam syndrome, and to create a new world order. As he stated at Fort Stewart, Georgia, the American cause was just, and because it was, the United States would prevail. "And when we win—and we will—we will have taught a dangerous dictator and any tyrant tempted to follow in his footsteps that the U.S. has a new credibility, and that what we say goes, and that there is no place for lawless aggression in the Persian Gulf and in this new world order that we seek to create."[47] Four days later, Bush returned to the theme of Vietnam in response to a question from Helen Thomas of United Press International. Talking about how long the war would take, Bush said it "will not be a Vietnam. I don't believe it's going to be long and drawn-out."[48]

Yet Scowcroft and Bush knew that for it not to become another Vietnam, they had to keep America's goals limited and avoid sending troops into Iraq itself with a mission of overthrowing Saddam Hussein and engaging in nation building. The two men very much wanted to see Saddam removed from power, but they wanted it done by the Iraqis, which they believed would happen once he was defeated in Kuwait. As Bush stated on February 15, the war would end when Iraq complied with the coalition's demands and with UN Resolution 678, and he signaled that he would welcome a coup as an alternative ending to the war. "There's another way for the bloodshed to stop," the president stated, "and that is for the Iraqi military and the Iraqi people to take matters into their own hands—to force Saddam Hussein, the dictator, to step aside."[49]

Bush recalled his thinking prior to the land war in his memoir: "I firmly believed that we should not march into Baghdad. Our stated mission, as codified in UN resolutions, was a simple one—end the aggression, knock Iraq's forces out of Kuwait, and restore Kuwait's leaders. To occupy Iraq would instantly shatter our coalition, turning the whole Arab world against us, and make a broken tyrant into a latter-day Arab hero." This would have undone all efforts to restore stability in the region and create an American-led new world order. Furthermore, an occupation of Iraq "would have taken us beyond the imprimatur of international law bestowed by the resolutions of the Security Council, assigning young soldiers to a fruitless hunt for a securely entrenched dictator and condemning them to fight in what would be an unwinnable urban guerrilla war. It could only plunge that part of the world into even greater instability and destroy the credibility we were working so hard to reestablish."[50]

On February 22, Bush issued his final ultimatum to Saddam Hussein. Iraq had until twelve noon New York time the next day to begin an unconditional withdrawal from Kuwait, or it would face a land attack by coalition forces. Soon after the announcement, Bush met with Scowcroft, Powell, and Secretary of Defense Dick Cheney to discuss what the next few days would look like and what to expect. Powell stated that the

Iraqi army was beginning to crack and that it was still possible to delay the ground campaign a day at a time to see what developed. He said he "would rather see the Iraqis walk out than be driven out." Moreover, the costs to the United States of fighting would be high. "We will lose soldiers in substantial numbers at a time. It will be grisly." A ground engagement would destroy more of Iraq's military capabilities, "but the cost in lives and later problems is not worth it," Powell added. The president asked if he would prefer a negotiated end, to which the general responded, "If it met our conditions totally, yes. They will crack." Bush responded, "If they crack under force, it is better than withdrawal." "But at what cost?" Powell wanted to know.[51]

"This was a telling exchange," Scowcroft observed. He understood Powell's legitimate concerns, but he sided with the president who "saw the dangers of an Iraqi withdrawal before its army had been destroyed." If that were to occur, Iraq would remain a threat to its neighbors, and the opportunity to punish Baghdad's aggression would be lost. There was no prospect that Saudi Arabia would allow the large U.S. force to remain in its territory to contain Saddam. Scowcroft believed that "we had to act now while we were mobilized and in place."[52] More was at stake than just

President Bush examines papers with National Security Advisor Brent Scowcroft and Secretary of Defense Dick Cheney in the Oval Office of the White House. Courtesy of the George H. W. Bush Presidential Library.

freeing Kuwait. Due to the buildup of forces, the creation of an international coalition, and the justification of actions already taken, American credibility and the vision of a new world order were on the line as well. If the post–Cold War period was to be led by the United States and guided by the tenets of internationalism, the use of force was now required. In this sense, congressional critics who argued that the president had boxed himself in were correct. The assumptions on which Scowcroft had based American policy back in August had led logically to this point.

The president announced on February 23 that he had given the command to use all forces, including ground troops, to expel Iraqi forces, and that the "liberation of Kuwait has now entered a final phase." By the morning of February 27, a sense of victory pervaded a meeting in the Oval Office. The ground war had gone better than anyone had predicted in driving out Iraqi forces with minimal casualties. Scowcroft concluded that they had reached the end. Most of Iraq's army had been routed and were either in disarray or in a disorganized retreat. Others agreed that it was time to end the war; the United States had achieved its mission. A decision was reached to cease fighting at midnight Washington time, one hundred hours after the commencement of ground operations. A jubilant President Bush informed the nation that evening that Iraq's military forces were defeated and Kuwait was liberated. "Seven months ago, America and the world drew a line in the sand. We declared that the aggression against Kuwait would not stand. And tonight, America and the world have kept their word."[53]

On March 1, Bush provided an evaluation of the significance of the Gulf War, declaring that the end of the fighting was a proud day for America and that, "by God, we've kicked the Vietnam syndrome once and for all."[54] When asked later that day at a news conference if this statement, along with the talk of a new world order, meant a new period of using the American military around the world to resolve conflicts, he answered no; "because of what has happened, we won't have to use U.S. forces around the world." The United States had "a reestablished credibility" that was central to its ability to provide world leadership, collective security, and a peaceful international order.[55]

While the president's approval rating in the polls soared to over 90 percent in the immediate aftermath of the war, the extent of the U.S. victory was ambiguous. The administration had wisely limited the scope of the war to keep the coalition together and avoid getting bogged down in a long occupation of Iraq. Yet it lacked a plan for dealing with a defeated Iraq. After the war ended, there were uprisings by Kurds and Shiites against the Baath regime that were crushed by Saddam. Critics charged that Bush had incited the Iraqi people to rise up only to abandon them when a revolt no longer served the policy needs of the United States.

There is no doubt that Bush and Scowcroft sought the overthrow of Saddam and hoped that American military action would lead to a coup. Despite Bush's infelicitous words on February 15, they had always thought that it would be the Iraqi military that would topple Saddam and never sought a popular uprising that might lead in directions that were unpredictable. The indictment also credits too much power and influence to a statement by the president for the upheaval in Iraq. Those who lived under the rule of Saddam Hussein and saw him weakened by defeat had plenty of reasons of their own to take action, regardless of any statements from Washington.

What is fair to criticize was the decision to leave the Republican Guard intact and allow the Iraqi military to keep its helicopters and other weapons, which proved decisive in the subsequent crackdown by Saddam's regime that killed thousands in order to maintain Baath rule in Baghdad. Decisions that were supposed to allow for a stable, post-Saddam Iraq actually contributed to the dictator's ability to survive internally. The Bush administration did not want to see a disintegration of Iraq, and it feared Kurdish separatism as well as a Shiite Iraq aligned with Iran. In the aftermath of Saddam's killing of thousands of Kurds and Shiites, and the failure of a military coup to materialize, the Bush administration opted

General Scowcroft's briefing of President Bush on Iraq on August 26, 1990, at the dining room table at Walker's Point, Kennebunkport, Maine, is interrupted by the president's granddaughter Ellie LaBlond. Courtesy of the George H. W. Bush Presidential Library.

for a policy of containment against Iraq. Economic restrictions were kept in place, no-fly zones were established over the Kurdish north and the Shiite south, and diplomatic isolation continued as a means of weakening Saddam Hussein and preventing Iraq from threatening others. Scowcroft believed this preserved the gains from the war and demonstrated the viability of collective action to deter aggression and control states that threatened the international order.

At the end of the war, Scowcroft's critical role in shaping U.S. policy was acknowledged. The *New York Times* reported that Bush administration officials agreed that it was Scowcroft's "presentation at one of the meetings on August 3 . . . that made clear what the stakes were, crystallized people's thinking and galvanized support for a very strong response." It was also Scowcroft who was responsible for narrowly defining the war's aims, "especially the decision not to make the overthrow of Saddam Hussein a publicly stated objective," and who, in his discussion with Bush in Maine on August 23, 1990, crafted the outlines of the postwar objectives, "offering Mr. Bush the phrase that has become the White House slogan, 'new world order.'"[56] While all wars are ultimately the president's responsibility, Bush gave the lion's share of the credit to Scowcroft for conceiving the rationale for the war and carrying it forward. Writing about Scowcroft, Bush noted that he took a great deal of the "burden off the President, tasks the bureaucracy, sorts out the differences and never with credit for himself. He's always quiet but always there and always dependable."[57]

DEFENSE PLANNING GUIDANCE

With the Cold War over, the drafting of the biannual Defense Planning Guidance (DPG) in 1992 took on more than the normal importance of providing the parameters for future budgets. It was seen by many in the Department of Defense, who were dissatisfied with the outcome of the Gulf War, as providing a vehicle for establishing a different vision for the new world order than Scowcroft's. Neoconservatives such as Undersecretary of Defense for Policy Paul Wolfowitz disagreed with Bush's decision not to overthrow Saddam Hussein. Rather than overcoming the Vietnam syndrome, Wolfowitz and other like-minded officials believed that Bush and Scowcroft had succumbed to it in their fear of taking on the job of ousting Saddam and transforming Iraq, and had settled on a passive policy of containment that did not solve the fundamental problem America faced from the Baath regime. The 1992 Defense Planning Guidance was written under Wolfowitz's direction.

For Wolfowitz, the United States had missed an opportunity to abandon the caution of internationalism and use its influence to truly reshape the world. He was certain that the combination of American universal values and overwhelming military force was unbeatable. As the leading scholar on Wolfowitz's thinking has explained, his criticism of Bush and Scowcroft stemmed from Wolfowitz's "extraordinary certainty in the righteousness of American actions married to an extraordinary confidence in the efficacy of American arms."[58] The United States, therefore, should have supported the Shiites and the Kurds. Leaving the Iraqi despot in place was a sign of weakness, a lack of conviction in America's role in the world, and a form of appeasement. A tyrant such as Saddam "was in a class with few others—Stalin, Hitler, Kim Jong Il," Wolfowitz believed. "People of that order of evil . . . tend not to keep evil at home, they tend to export it in various ways and eventually it bites us."[59] Saddam would always threaten his neighbors and American interests.

The initial draft of the DPG noted that the nation faced a "fundamentally new situation which has been created by the collapse of the Soviet Union . . . and the discrediting of Communism as an ideology with global pretensions and influence." The most salient fact of the post–Cold War era was the triumph of the United States in the Gulf War over Iraq's aggression, "a defining event in US global leadership." Together, these American victories, along with the "integration of Germany and Japan into a US-led system of collective security have led to the creation of a democratic 'zone of peace.'" Maintaining this would take "ongoing U.S. leadership in global affairs." The purpose of the DPG was to define and provide clarity to the necessary requirements for the United States to defend its interests in a changed but still dangerous world.[60]

Two strategic objectives should guide American foreign policy. First, the United States had to take advantage of its current position as the sole superpower to "prevent the reemergence of a new rival . . . that poses a threat on the order of that posed formerly by the Soviet Union." That was the dominant concern, and it shaped the new "regional defense strategy," which was to "prevent any hostile power from dominating a region whose resources would . . . be sufficient to generate global power" and challenge the United States. To do so, Washington had to demonstrate the "leadership necessary to establish and protect a new order that holds the promise of convincing potential competitors that they need not aspire to a greater role or pursue a more aggressive posture to protect their legitimate interests." American policy should account for the "interest of the advanced industrial nations to discourage them from challenging our leadership or seeking to overturn the established political and economic order," and should deter other "potential competitors from even aspiring to a larger regional or global role." In brief, the goal was to assert and preserve American primacy in the world.[61]

While the post–Cold War world lacked a single adversary committed to the destruction of the United States, it presented Washington with a more unstable and therefore inherently dangerous world. In order to maintain its dominant position, the United States could not rely upon the assistance of others. Coalitions were always undependable beyond any immediate crisis they were put together to address, and challenges to American interests could not be forestalled by multilateral institutions, collective security, or greater economic interdependence. What would maintain order was American credibility—the understanding by other nations that the post–Cold War "world order is ultimately backed by the U.S." and that Washington was prepared to act unilaterally and preemptively to eliminate threats and protect its interests.[62] As Wolfowitz stated in 2000, the goal was "demonstrating that your friends will be protected and taken care of, that your enemies will be punished, and that those who refuse to support you will live to regret having done so."[63]

Using force to protect American interests and maintain stability was not the only goal. The second primary objective was to "address sources of regional conflict and instability in such a way as to promote increasing respect for international law . . . and encourage the spread of democratic forms of government and open economic systems." Although it was impossible for the United States to serve as the "world's 'policeman' by assuming responsibility for righting every wrong, we will retain preeminent responsibility for addressing selectively those wrongs which threaten not only our interests, but those of our allies and friends, or which could seriously unsettle international relations." The type of threats that could prompt preemptive action by the United States included the disruption of access to vital raw materials, particularly oil in the Persian Gulf; the development of weapons of mass destruction by rogue states; the use of terrorism; and potentially explosive regional conflicts.[64]

Therefore, the United States had to be willing to overthrow dictators such as Saddam Hussein and replace them with governments more in the image of the United States. Wolfowitz and other like-minded officials believed that the people in nations such as Iraq were yearning to be liberated from tyranny and to have their nations remade in the likeness of the United States. "I think democracy is a universal idea," Wolfowitz has stated. "And I think letting people rule themselves happens to be something that serves Americans and America's interests."[65] The relationship of the two strategic objectives was clear. Preemptive wars would eliminate evil rulers and threats to the United States while at the same time allowing the United States to transform countries and eventually regions into members of the ever-expanding democratic "zone of peace," led by the United States.

A redacted version of the DPG was leaked to the *New York Times* in March 1992, creating considerable discussion and criticism of the document. Commentators focused on the section that discussed how the United States should work to prevent the rise of any new power that would present a challenge to its dominance. Many suggested that the concern was with Japan and the newly reunited Germany. Both were seen as future economic competitors with the United States. There was especially talk in the early 1990s of Japan surpassing the United States and becoming the dominant economic force in the world, and books about an impending clash topped the best-seller list. Scowcroft did admit that he worried about keeping the alliance together and about increasing "West-West" conflict with Germany and Japan.[66]

The national security advisor was far more concerned about the new direction the DPG proposed for U.S. foreign policy, pulling it away from the tenets of internationalism and toward unilateralism as the best means for providing stability, protecting American interests, and exporting American values. While the actual writing of the DPG was done by Zalmay Khalilzad under the direction of I. Lewis "Scooter" Libby, Scowcroft saw it as the handiwork of Wolfowitz and as an indication of the divergent path he hoped to see the nation take. The differences might appear subtle to outsiders, but the distinction between American primacy versus American leadership was the essence of Scowcroft's and Wolfowitz's disagreement over policy. The focus of the draft DPG on potential threats, the emphasis on using force as an instrument of policy, and the discussion of preemptive wars while downplaying collective security, multilateral institutions, and cooperation with allies caused Scowcroft great discomfort and led him to intervene and demand changes. The final version reflected his and the president's internationalist orientation and policies.

Published in January 1993 with the title "Defense Strategy for the 1990s: The Regional Defense Strategy," the DPG had a very different orientation after most of the parts Scowcroft found objectionable had been removed. The basic premise was that the United States now found itself in a "new strategic era." The demise of the Soviet Union had altered the international challenges the nation faced, but it had not eliminated threats to the United States. The dramatic changes in Europe had "set the nation on a solid path to secure and extend the opportunities and hopes of this new era," as the "integration of the leading democracies into a U.S.-led system of collective security, and the prospects of expanding that system, significantly enhance our international position." This provided "an unprecedented opportunity to preserve with greater ease a security environment within which our democratic ideals can prosper." In order to secure that opening, U.S. foreign policy was moving "from Containment to the new Regional Defense Strategy."[67]

Instead of primacy and preemptive war, the document now emphasized a strategy based on collective security, multilateral institutions, and international cooperation. The fall of communism in Europe had eliminated the primary military threat to the United States and had provided it with a "marked lead in critical areas of warfare." Still, another great source of strength lay in the alliances developed during the Cold War. The "democratic 'zone of peace,' a community of democratic nations bound together by a web of political, economic, and security ties," embodied "a framework for security not through competitive rivalries in arms, but through cooperative approaches and collective security institutions. The combination of these trends has given our nation and our alliances great depth for our strategic position."[68]

The purpose of the regional defense strategy was "to enable the U.S. to lead in shaping an uncertain future so as to preserve and enhance this strategic depth won at such great pains." It would build on the successful approaches to the Cold War and "require us to strengthen our alliances and to extend the zone of peace to include the newly independent nations of Eastern Europe and the former Soviet Union" as they strove to build democratic, capitalist societies. Working with its allies, Washington needed to focus on regional threats and "preclude hostile nondemocratic powers from dominating regions critical to our interests and otherwise work to build an international environment conducive to our values." Thus, it was a primary strategic goal to "strengthen and extend the system of defense arrangements that binds democratic and like-minded nations together in common defense against aggression, builds habits of cooperation, [and] avoids the renationalization of security policies." This goal reflected "our preference for a collective response to preclude threats or, if necessary, to deal with them" and marked "a key feature of our Regional Defense Strategy." While the United States had to be prepared to act decisively if a timely collective response was not possible, maintaining the capability to act quickly should American interests be threatened did not undermine collective security. Rather, "history suggests that effective multilateral action is most likely to come about in response to U.S. leadership, not as an alternative to it."[69]

To construct the new world order, the United States had to remain mindful of what were seen by confirmed internationalists as strategic blunders that harmed the national interest. "At the end of World War I, and again to a lesser extent at the end of World War II, the United States as a nation made the mistake of believing that we had achieved a kind of permanent security, that a transformation of the security order achieved in substantial part through American sacrifice and leadership could be sustained without our leadership and significant American forces." The end of the Cold War presented the same danger of complacency. Any reduction of forces needed to be conducted carefully and in accordance with the security needs of the post–Cold War world. While the life-and-death threat of the contest with the Soviet Union had ended, "other threats endure, and new ones will arise." A sufficient force to carry out the regional defense strategy, the revised DPG concluded, would provide the United States "the means to lead common efforts to meet future challenges and to shape the future environment in ways that will give us greater security at lower cost."[70]

The neoconservative critique challenged the internationalist policies Scowcroft had worked so hard and long to reestablish and raised questions concerning what the Bush administration had accomplished. The Gulf War appeared to validate the tenets of internationalism, establishing the viability of collective security and the rule of law as the best means for achieving a peaceful international environment while discouraging and controlling potential and actual aggressors. In practical terms, however, it only safeguarded U.S. access to oil and established the containment of Saddam Hussein's power. The promise of a more stable world that secured U.S. interests remained unrealized, or at least dependent on the willingness of Washington to project its power. It had not transformed the region or ended other threats to American interests in the form of terrorism, civil wars, and the proliferation of weapons of mass destruction. This raised the question, in the wake of the liberation of Kuwait, of whether American power was more credible and hence a deterrent to threats, or whether that was a concept better suited for a Cold War–style confrontation with another superpower than for the type of challenges that now confronted the United States. If so, had Scowcroft oversold the benefits of internationalism, and was a different approach to the problems of the post–Cold War world called for? Well before September 11, 2001, the terms of what would become Scowcroft's disagreements over George W. Bush's policy toward Saddam Hussein and the ensuing Iraq War were already evident.

NOTES

1. George Bush and Brent Scowcroft, *A World Transformed* (New York: Vintage, 1998), xiv.

2. National Security Directive 26, "U.S. Policy toward the Persian Gulf," 2 October 1989, NSC: Richard Haass File, Iraq Pre 8/2/90, (hereafter Haass: Iraq Pre-War), GBPL.

3. "National Security Strategy of the United States," March 1990, 6, selected documents from the archives, GBPL; bushlibrary.tamu.edu/research.

4. Baker to Glaspie, "US Reaction to Iraqi Threats in the Gulf," 24 July 1990, Haass: Iraq Pre-War, GBPL.

5. Glaspie to Baker, "Ambassador's Meeting with Saddam Husayn," 25 July 1990, Haass: Iraq Pre-War, GBPL.

6. Glaspie to Baker, "Saddam's Message of Friendship to President Bush," 25 July 1990, Haass: Iraq Pre-War, GBPL.

7. Baker to Glaspie, "President's Response to Saddam Hussein's Message," 28 July 1990, Haass: Iraq Pre-War, GBPL.

8. Bush and Scowcroft, *A World Transformed*, 317.

9. Bush and Scowcroft, *A World Transformed*, 321–22.

10. National Security Council Meeting, 3 August 1990, NSC, Richard Haass File: Iraq-August 2, 1990–December 1990 (hereafter Haass: Iraq War), GBPL.

11. Bush and Scowcroft, *A World Transformed*, 322.

12. National Security Council Meeting, 4 August 1990, Haass: Iraq War, GBPL.

13. National Security Council Meeting, 5 August 1990, Haass: Iraq War, GBPL.

14. Bush and Scowcroft, *A World Transformed*, 333.

15. Bush and Scowcroft, *A World Transformed*, 399–400.

16. Bush and Scowcroft, *A World Transformed*, 375.

17. National Security Directive 45, "U.S. Policy in Response to the Iraqi Invasion of Kuwait," 20 August 1990, Haass: Iraq War, GBPL.

18. *Public Papers of the Presidents: George H. W. Bush, 1990* (Washington, DC: Government Printing Office, 1991), 2:1107–9.

19. Bush and Scowcroft, *A World Transformed*, 354–55.

20. Memorandum of Conversation between Bush and Gorbachev on 9 September 1990, Haass: Iraq War, GBPL.

21. Memorandum of Conversation between Bush and Gorbachev on 9 September 1990, Haass: Iraq War, GBPL.

22. *Newsmaker Saturday*, transcript, 25 August 1990, Counsel's Office: WH; William Otis File, Iraq/Desert Storm: Press Releases and Media Coverage, Box 5 (hereafter Otis File), GBPL.

23. *This Week with David Brinkley*, transcript, 26 August 1990, Otis File, GBPL.

24. *Meet the Press*, transcript, 9 September 1990, Otis File, GBPL.

25. *Public Papers of the Presidents: Bush, 1990*, 2:1218–22.

26. *Public Papers of the Presidents: Bush, 1990*, 2:1218–22.

27. *Public Papers of the Presidents: Bush, 1990*, 2:1218–22.

28. Bush and Scowcroft, *A World Transformed*, 381.

29. Bush and Scowcroft, *A World Transformed*, 392.

30. Bush and Scowcroft, *A World Transformed*, 393.

31. *Public Papers of the Presidents: Bush, 1990*, 2:1580–81.

32. Bush and Scowcroft, *A World Transformed*, 389.

33. "The Gulf Crisis: UN Security Council Actions," Communications: White House Office of Paul McNeill, Persian Gulf Working Group, GBPL.

34. Communications: White House Office of Paul McNeill: Persian Gulf Working Group, Dave Demerest Notebooks (hereafter McNeill File), GBPL.

35. *This Week with David Brinkley*, transcript, 25 November 1990, Otis File, GBPL.

36. *Face the Nation with Lesley Stahl*, transcript, 2 December 1990, Otis File, GBPL.

37. *Newsmaker Saturday*, transcript, 8 December 1990; *Meet the Press*, transcript, 9 December 1990, Otis File, GBPL.

38. Bush and Scowcroft, *A World Transformed*, 433.

39. Department of State, "Crisis in the Gulf," McNeill File, GBPL.

40. *Public Papers of the Presidents: George H. W. Bush, 1991* (Washington, DC: Government Printing Office, 1992), 1:13–14.

41. Department of State, *Dispatch*, vol. 2, no. 2, 14 January 1991 (Washington, DC: Government Printing Office, 1991).

42. Department of State, *Dispatch*, vol. 2, no. 2, 14 January 1991.

43. National Security Directive 54, "Responding to Iraqi Aggression in the Gulf," 15 January 1991, Haass: Iraq War, GBPL.

44. *Public Papers of the Presidents: Bush, 1991*, 1:42–45.

45. *Public Papers of the Presidents: Bush, 1991*, 1:74–75.

46. White House Press Office, "Desert Storm Facts," 5 February 1991, White House Office of the Chief of Staff: John Sununu Files: Persian Gulf War 1991, GBPL; Bush and Scowcroft, *A World Transformed*, 462.

47. *Public Papers of the Presidents: Bush, 1991*, 1:95.

48. *Public Papers of the Presidents: Bush, 1991*, 1:105.

49. *Public Papers of the Presidents: Bush, 1991*, 1:145.

50. Bush and Scowcroft, *A World Transformed*, 464.

51. Bush and Scowcroft, *A World Transformed*, 477.

52. Bush and Scowcroft, *A World Transformed*, 477–78.

53. *Public Papers of the Presidents: Bush, 1991*, 1:187–88.

54. *Public Papers of the Presidents: Bush, 1991*, 1:197.

55. *Public Papers of the Presidents: Bush, 1991*, 1:200–201.

56. "War in the Gulf," *New York Times*, 21 February 1991.

57. Bush and Scowcroft, *A World Transformed*, 487.

58. Andrew Bacevich, quoted in Thomas Ricks, *Fiasco* (Penguin: New York, 2006), 8.

59. Ricks, *Fiasco*, 16.

60. National Security Archive, *The Nuclear Vault*, "Prevent the Reemergence of a New Rival," Document 3: "FY 94–99 Defense Planning Guidance Sections for Comment," 18 February 1992, www.gwu.edu/~nsarchiv/nukevault/ebb245/index.htm (accessed 7 June 2010).

61. National Security Archive, "FY 94–99 Defense Planning," 18 February 1992.

62. National Security Archive, "FY 94–99 Defense Planning," 18 February 1992.

63. Ricks, *Fiasco*, 17.

64. National Security Archive, "FY 94–99 Defense Planning," 18 February 1992.

65. Ricks, *Fiasco*, 17.

66. James Mann, *Rise of the Vulcans: The History of Bush's War Cabinet* (New York: Penguin Books, 2004), 211.

67. National Security Archive, *The Nuclear Vault*, "Prevent the Reemergence of a New Rival," Document 15, "Defense Strategy for the 1990s: The Regional

Defense Strategy," January 1993, www.gwu.edu/~nsarchiv/nukevault/ebb245/index.htm (accessed 7 June 2010).

  68. National Security Archive, "Defense Strategy for the 1990s," January 1993.
  69. National Security Archive, "Defense Strategy for the 1990s," January 1993.
  70. National Security Archive, "Defense Strategy for the 1990s," January 1993.

6

⚜

Elder Statesman

Victory in the Gulf War failed to propel President Bush to a second term in office. The end of the war and the final demise of the Soviet Union led to a lessening of public concern over foreign affairs at the same time that domestic economic problems elicited displeasure with the administration's policies and calls for an economic peace dividend through cuts in defense spending. For the second time, Scowcroft was in an administration voted out of office and was unable to build upon the foreign policy achievements of the previous four years. Scowcroft hoped that the new administration would follow his and Bush's policies and approach to the world and create the promised new world order, but he was worried about the direction American foreign policy would take under President Bill Clinton. His greatest concern was that without the threat of the Soviet Union, and with public attention turning away from international affairs, the Clinton administration would be inattentive to foreign policy issues, leading to a drift in policy and a lack of purpose. At the same time, the former national security advisor was alarmed by the post–Cold War triumphalism that was taking hold in the nation, fueling both neoconservative thinking and a growing hubris about America and its position in the world.

Scowcroft stayed in Washington where in 1994 he founded an international business advisory firm, the Scowcroft Group, for corporations seeking knowledge and advice on doing business in different parts of the world. It provided evaluations of the political, economic, and business environment in specific nations and an understanding of the various factors that affected international investment and business. Except

171

for one *New York Times* op-ed piece in 1993, he stayed out of the public eye and foreign policy debates to allow Clinton to establish his policies without undue partisan rancor. In 1998, with the publication of his joint memoir with President Bush, *A World Transformed*, Scowcroft returned to the public arena. The work focused exclusively on the transformation of Eastern Europe, the end of the Cold War, German unification, China relations, and the Gulf War and provided a resounding defense of the Bush administration's foreign policy and commitment to post–World War II internationalism. Bush and Scowcroft emphasized the necessity of restraint in following a foreign policy of collective security and cooperation with allies while still providing leadership and a willingness to protect American and Western interests with force if necessary.

For Scowcroft, the basic tenets of internationalism remained viable in the post–Cold War world and necessary for addressing the challenges presented by globalization and the rising threat of terrorism. It was, he believed, a new era defined by the United States as the only superpower, with an opportunity to build on the achievements of the Bush years to further international cooperation, strengthen the Atlantic alliance, and establish a new world order conducive to American interests and values. To his dismay, the former national security advisor observed an emerging national arrogance derived from the assumption that the United States' disproportionate power could enable Washington to have its way internationally without regard for the opinions of others. "Not since at least the Roman Empire," Scowcroft opined, "had anyone had this much disparity in power. That was pretty heady stuff."[1] It led policy makers to forget the patient, multilateral, internationalist policies that had brought about this success and how the successful policies of the Cold War could be employed in the face of the new forces at work in the world.

The Clinton administration, Scowcroft believed, demonstrated signs of triumphalist thinking but was confused and befuddled by the end of the Cold War and the new threats that were emerging. Given the unparalleled power of the United States, leaders saw globalization as a force for spreading American values and institutions, without sensing the "politicization of the world's people" and the growing anti-West reaction. In a world "without the existential threat of the cold war," the United States seemed to confront only "one hundred pinprick problems." Rather than focusing on the danger presented by Moscow, Scowcroft believed, Washington was confronting a "myriad of little problems." This meant "there was no great urge to develop a strategy in the nineties"; first, "it would've been very hard" to formulate in the face of rapid change, and second, the Clinton administration did not "think we really needed one."[2]

The election of George W. Bush and the September 11 terrorist attack brought the triumphalist view to the fore as part of the neoconservative understanding that shaped the younger Bush's policies. There was bipartisan agreement on the need to combat terrorist groups, but disagreement over how that could be accomplished. Scowcroft believed that it would be best achieved by adhering to the tenets of internationalism and the approaches employed during the Cold War. His determination to make this case and influence the direction of American foreign policy led him to publicly oppose the Bush administration's policies and to assume the role of the leading critic of the run-up to the Iraq War. He saw the shifting of American focus, forces, and resources away from fighting al Qaeda and finding Osama bin Laden and toward the overthrow of Saddam Hussein and the occupation of Iraq as a tragic mistake that would harm long-term American interests. His disagreements with the neoconservative's policies were the culmination of his effort to maintain conservative internationalism as the predominant approach to foreign policy that dated back to the last years of the Vietnam War.

COLD WAR TRIUMPHALISM

"For the first time since the Hitler era," Brent Scowcroft wrote on July 2, 1993, "no would-be global dictator is working to overthrow the established order." This provided the United States with the "opportunity to mold an international system more compatible with the values we have held for two centuries." Bush and Scowcroft, however, no longer had their hands on the tiller of the ship of state, and the former national security advisor worried that the victories in the Cold War and the Gulf War had led to a false sense of security in the nation and a turning inward that was causing this "chance [to] pass through our fingers." There were calls for a peace dividend and greater attention to domestic matters amidst claims that the United States had "carried the weight of world leadership long enough" and that a large military was no longer necessary. Scowcroft saw these as understandable but "misguided" sentiments that neglected not only the responsibility of power, but practical, and "even selfish," national interests.[3]

In Scowcroft's view, the United States faced a choice in the post–Cold War world. It could continue its role as world leader and fashion a stable world order that would benefit American interests, or it could "turn inward as we did after World War I, until another mortal threat reminds us that our fate depends on the world in which we live." Choosing between domestic affairs and foreign policy was a false dichotomy because the United States could not "prosper amid chaos and conflict, economic isolation or hostile trading blocs. Foreign policy and domestic policy have become two sides of the same coin." Due to globalization, the United

States was more dependent upon the outer world than ever before, and free trade was vital to prosperity. During the Bush administration, Scowcroft noted, 70 percent of American economic growth came from exports, and export-related jobs increased by 42 percent. Similarly, threats to the United States, in the form of terrorism, drug traffickers, and environmental dangers, were issues that did not respect national boundaries.[4]

Moreover, there was no other nation to assume the role of world leadership. Without strong and enlightened leadership setting the course, "history will sooner or later serve up another nasty surprise." Scowcroft emphasized that he was not calling for the United States to become the world's police or to act unilaterally. Rather, he was asking for a continuation of internationalist policies, specifically collective action for deterrence against potential threats. "We should never forget," Scowcroft declared, "that while the context may have changed, the principle remains valid." It was unfortunate but true, Scowcroft concluded, that the United States did not "have the luxury of putting our leadership on hold until we get our domestic house in order," as there was "no holiday from history."[5]

In the wake of the Cold War, a triumphal interpretation of the American "victory" took hold. The United States was victorious, according to those who held this understanding, because of its values, its steadfast defense of liberalism, and its promotion of democracy. Popular magazines, op-ed pages, and bookshelves were filled with works by proponents of the view that the outcome of the Cold War was a vindication of building American strength to confront the Soviet Union, particularly under Ronald Reagan, and a validation of the superiority of American values and institutions. Francis Fukuyama, in his 1992 book *The End of History and the Last Man,* went so far as to claim that the U.S. victory over the Soviet Union in the Cold War marked the climax of a historical process, the "end of history," with the triumph of democracy and capitalism over fascism and communism in the twentieth century. With no viable ideologies left as alternatives, liberalism would expand to all parts of the world as a universal way to organize societies.[6]

Two years later, Tony Smith published an overview of American foreign policy from President William McKinley to the present that claimed that the promotion of democracy was the "central ambition of American foreign policy during the twentieth century," and that due to this unwavering commitment to free government, "by 1992 democracy stood unchallenged as the only form of mass politics that offered itself as a model worldwide." For Smith, the policy implications were evident. The active promotion of democracy abroad promised stability and prosperity and was the "product of an American conviction that if democracy were to spread, America's place in the world would be more secure."[7]

This line of thinking influenced the Clinton administration's policies. Clinton and his advisors came to depend on the forces of globalization, rather than on an overarching principle, to guide foreign policy and further American interests. Following the Cold War, the administration went in a variety of directions simultaneously. Clinton sought to garner a peace dividend by slowing the growth of defense spending and concentrating on domestic affairs, economic growth, and balancing the federal budget, and he relied on the promotion of globalization and free trade as the best means for advancing American values and fostering peace and prosperity. At the same time, Clinton sent American forces into Haiti and Kosovo to quell violence and change governments, and he continued the Bush administration's policy of containment in Iraq. The no-fly zones over the north and south were maintained, weapons inspections were carried out to enforce disarmament, and sanctions on military purchases and other economic activities were continued. During his term, Clinton ordered three separate air strikes against Iraqi military targets in an effort to enforce sanctions and compel compliance with inspectors. In 1998, after Saddam Hussein demanded an end to surprise inspections of weapons sites and announced that Iraq would no longer cooperate with the UN, the administration adopted a policy of "containment-plus," which increased military pressure, toughened the enforcement of the no-fly zones, provided almost $100 million for opposition forces committed to ousting Saddam Hussein from power, and tightened the economic sanctions against Iraq.

Meanwhile, terrorist attacks against the United States and its allies increased throughout the 1990s. In February 1993, a bomb was set off in the parking garage of the World Trade Center, killing six people and injuring over a thousand. In June 1996, the American air base in Dhahran was bombed, with nineteen dead and hundreds injured. When the U.S. embassies in Nairobi, Kenya, and Dar es Salaam, Tanzania, were blown up in 1998, with 257 dead, including 12 Americans, and over 5,000 hurt, Clinton ordered attacks against suspected terrorist locations in the Sudan and Afghanistan. The final terrorist attack of the decade came in October 2000, when seventeen sailors were killed aboard the USS *Cole*. The problems were compounded when the Taliban, an Islamic fundamentalist group, took power in Afghanistan in 1996. It provided a safe haven for the terrorist organization al Qaeda and its leader Osama bin Laden, a wealthy Saudi who opposed the government in Riyadh, who sought to establish traditional Islamic rule throughout the region, and who aimed to drive the United States and the West out of the Middle East. While there was no link between Iraq and the growing number of terrorist attacks by radical groups in the Middle East, the calls for stronger action against Saddam Hussein became a consistent part of U.S. foreign policy discussions.

Neoconservatives seized upon the increasing tensions with Iraq and the rising number of terrorist incidents to call for more aggressive action against Saddam Hussein. Disagreements over the Defense Planning Guidance proved to be a harbinger of a growing rift within the Republican Party over foreign policy. After leaving office, Bush and Scowcroft continued to defend their decisions concerning Iraq from a rising chorus of neoconservative critics. As Bush and Scowcroft wrote in their 1998 memoir, they were "disappointed that Saddam's defeat did not break his hold on power, as many of our Arab allies had predicted and we had come to expect." The uprisings by the Kurds and the Shiites were uncoordinated, and the military remained loyal to the dictator. Given that, they still did not doubt the wisdom of the decision to end the fighting with the liberation of Kuwait. "Trying to eliminate Saddam, extending the ground war into an occupation of Iraq, would have violated our guideline about not changing objectives in midstream, engaging in 'mission creep,' and would have incurred incalculable human and political costs. . . . We would have been forced to occupy Baghdad and, in effect, rule Iraq. The coalition would instantly have collapsed, the Arabs deserting it in anger and other allies pulling out as well. Under those circumstances, there was no viable 'exit strategy' we could see, violating another of our principles." This would have created another Vietnam-type war and undone their efforts at creating a new world order. As they further noted, "We had been self-consciously trying to set a pattern for handling aggression in the post–Cold War world. Going in and occupying Iraq, thus unilaterally exceeding the United Nations' mandate, would have destroyed the precedent of international response to aggression that we hoped to establish. Had we gone the invasion route, the United States could conceivably still be an occupying power in a bitterly hostile land."[8]

Leading neoconservatives disagreed. Fear of intervention and worrying about the response of allies had marred the conclusion of the Gulf War. In 1997, Robert Kagan and William Kristol founded the Project for the New American Century (PNAC) to "rally support for American global leadership." The group's name evoked publisher Henry Luce's famous 1941 essay, "The American Century," which argued that the failure of the United States to take up the responsibility of world leadership after World War I led directly to the Great Depression and World War II. The organization's "Statement of Principles" asserted that the United States had to "accept responsibility for America's unique role in preserving and extending an international order friendly to our security, our prosperity, and our principles." Having won the Cold War, PNAC feared that the nation had lost its will to lead and confront the challenges that lay ahead. The group asserted that the United States should be ready to use force preemptively to prevent any challenges to American hegemony. "The history of the 20th century should have taught us that it is important to shape circumstances before crises emerge, and to meet threats before they become dire. The history of this century should have taught us to embrace the cause of American leadership." Therefore, the United States had to be prepared "to challenge regimes hostile to our interests and values."[9]

Writing the year before in the journal *Foreign Affairs*, Kagan and Kristol outlined the vision of American leadership that PNAC would promote. "What should the U.S. role be? Benevolent global hegemony. Having defeated the 'evil empire,' the United States enjoys strategic and ideological predominance." Washington needed to enhance that position while promoting American interests and values. Echoing Luce, they argued that "in a world in which peace and American security depend on American power and the will to use it, the main threat the United States faces now and in the future is its own weakness." Relying on multilateral institutions and collective security, or lacking the will to act, preemptively if necessary, would bring about disaster. "American hegemony is the only reliable defense against a breakdown of peace and international order. The appropriate goal of American foreign policy, therefore, is to preserve that hegemony as far into the future as possible. To achieve this goal, the United States needs a neo-Reaganite foreign policy of military supremacy and moral confidence."[10]

Of particular concern to PNAC were Iraq and what the neoconservatives perceived as the failure of the Bush administration to remove Saddam Hussein from power. On January 26, 1998, the Project for the New American Century sent an open letter to President Clinton calling for a policy aimed "at the removal of Saddam Hussein's regime from power." Signed by eighteen people, including Robert Kagan, Zalmay Khalilzad, William Kristol, Donald Rumsfeld, and Paul Wolfowitz, it argued that the policy of containment was failing and that the United States "may soon face a threat in the Middle East more serious than any we have known since the end of the Cold War." Collective security and sanctions, the PNAC asserted, had failed, and it appeared that Saddam was now in the process of acquiring weapons of mass destruction. "The only acceptable strategy is one that eliminates the possibility that Iraq will be able to use or threaten to use weapons of mass destruction. . . . This means a willingness to undertake military action as diplomacy is clearly failing."[11] It was a bold call for preemptive war, regime change, and nation building in Iraq.

Saddam's defiance of UN weapons inspectors and the pressure from neoconservatives pushed Iraq to the forefront of political discussions and prompted the Clinton administration to take a harder line against Iraq. In 1998, the adoption of the containment-plus policy was matched with a more bellicose and triumphalist rhetoric that escalated the conflict between Washington and Baghdad. Speaking at Ohio State University on February 18, Secretary of State Madeleine Albright summarized the reason for containment-plus. She labeled Iraq "a rogue state that will use nuclear, chemical or biological weapons against us or our allies" and which presented the "greatest security threat" the United States faced. While many of Iraq's weapons had been destroyed since the end of the Gulf War, there was evidence "that Iraq continues to hide prohibited weapons and materials." Only by gaining UN inspectors unconditional access to all facilities and documents could the status of these weapons be determined. The United States had to be "prepared to use military force" to ensure this outcome.[12]

The next day on NBC's *Today Show*, Albright assured listeners that the United States sought a peaceful solution to the standoff with Iraq but was prepared to strike if necessary to ensure that Iraq did not acquire weapons of mass destruction. Containment, she asserted, had been successful for the past seven years, and that remained the goal. Air strikes were part of that policy and would be used if necessary to uphold it. "But if we have to use force, it is because we are America; we are the indispensible nation. We stand tall and we see further than other countries into the future, and we see the danger here to all of us."[13]

In December, the administration launched Operation Desert Fox, a four-day bombing campaign against Iraq that was the largest military campaign since the end of the Gulf War. Over four hundred cruise missiles, B-52 bombers, and the new B-1 swing-wing supersonic bombers were used to strike ninety-seven target sites used for the production of weapons, command-and-control operations, and intelligence headquarters. Evidence gathered at the time indicated that the strikes were effective in damaging Iraqi military capacity and destabilizing Saddam's regime. David Kay, who led the Iraq Survey Group, the George W. Bush administration's team that searched for weapons of mass destruction after the fall of Baghdad, concluded that the 1998 bombings had a devastating impact and that with the exception of missile building, Iraq's weapons programs "withered away, and never got momentum again." As Marine Brigadier General Anthony Zinni, who oversaw American operations, concluded, containment worked. Iraq's military was cut in half, and its weapons production was destroyed. Saddam "didn't threaten anyone in the region. He was contained."[14]

The immediate crisis passed, but Scowcroft grew increasingly alarmed about the Clinton administration's approach to foreign policy and the hubristic attitudes it displayed. Scowcroft set out the broad range of his concerns in his commencement speech on May 14, 2000, at the College of William and Mary. Noting that the United States found itself in a new era of international relations since the end of the Cold War, one where there was no mortal danger to the nation or overarching national security threat, he feared that the country was "becoming complacent" and failing to see the problems looming on the horizon. Freed of the danger of nuclear war and living in a time of great prosperity, a time when "serious scholars proclaim the end of history," Americans were confident that the world was moving closer to its values and institutions, and that any serious threats were rapidly receding in the rearview mirror of time. Scowcroft told the graduates that giving in to this way of thinking "would be worse than folly. . . . History has not and will not end," and new crises were sure to emerge. Failure to heed this warning had proved costly in the past. "For example, we quickly forgot the lessons of World War I— and had to relive them through World War II. Now we may already be forgetting the lessons of the Cold War."[15]

Success came from constant vigilance and conscious policy decisions that created the proper international environment for U.S. institutions and values to flourish; containment, collective security, cooperation with allies, and standing up to aggression had characterized U.S. Cold War foreign policy. The result was the favorable position the United States was now experiencing of prosperity, peace, and power. Indeed, "not since the Roman Empire had any nation dominated so much of the globe." Given this power, Scowcroft asked, "What should be America's role in this new world?" Of particular concern was the increasing globalization and interdependency of the world that was creating new and different threats. Greater international trading and capital flows, new information and communication technology, and the more rapid movement of people and ideas were providing greater prosperity but also unforeseen threats. Concomitant with globalization was the emergence of political forces "producing an ever more exclusive—and intolerant—particularism, based on ethnic, religious, cultural or other criteria, which are fractionating political entities and pulling them farther apart. These are all potentially revolutionary forces."[16]

The United States was, in Scowcroft's estimation, in an enviable position to meet these challenges. It had great power and was the "source of the political principles to which most of mankind aspires." Yet, this very source of strength was beginning to become a negative as a hubristic understanding of the United States and its role in the world was taking hold. Cold War triumphalism and talk of being an indispensable nation were dangerous shifts in attitude. American leaders had "come to be preaching—rather than teaching" American values around the world, and "then grading countries on the degree to which they approach the standards we have set." For other nations, globalization had become equated with American imperialism and domination. The United States was "increasingly seen as arrogant, unilateral, and indifferent to the views and

concerns of others. This seems to be becoming—unconsciously—a habit,"
and if it continued the United States "will eventually pay a heavy price."
The nation had to ask, "Are we ourselves really that flawless?" Scowcroft believed the United States had to provide world leadership, as only
Washington could "mobilize the international community to the tasks
which need to be accomplished." If America refused to lead, "nothing
will be done." But leadership entailed cooperation and "working with
others, rather than preaching at others." It was time for the country to
rededicate itself to the legacy and policies of those who "won World War
II and the Cold War" that placed the nation in the powerful and prosperous position it now enjoyed.[17]

The increasing threat of terrorism from nonstate actors in the Middle
East was a growing concern for Scowcroft by the end of the century, and
he thought it could be best met by sticking with the tenets of internationalism. The former national security advisor believed that only through
cooperation with other nations, good intelligence, and a sustained effort
to contain terrorist activities could the United States and its allies succeed in neutralizing this sinister and deadly threat to Western interests.
In August 2000, responding to the Clinton administration's National
Commission on Terrorism report, "Countering the Changing Threat of
International Terrorism," Scowcroft stipulated what he saw as necessary
to combat this increasing danger to the United States. The commission's
most important recommendation, Scowcroft believed, was the conclusion
"that good intelligence is the best anti-terrorist weapon." The fight against
terrorism could not be won "by building Jersey walls around our public
buildings and official residences, or by turning American embassies into
structures resembling strong points on the Maginot Line." Likewise, sporadic bombing strikes against terrorists camps were "fruitless—by and
large, terrorists don't care how many get killed," and they have few fixed
assets than can be destroyed. Defense was prudent and necessary, but
it would not effectively address the problem, and the image of America
cowering "behind concrete redoubts and concertina wire" was not one
that served the nation well.[18]

"Prevention," Scowcroft declared, "must be at the heart of our strategy." Central to an offensive strategy was "human intelligence operations
of a high order." Terrorists counted on surprise and fear of the unknown
to achieve their goals. They "live in a world in which the rules, mores, and
other trappings of civilization are almost entirely absent." This made the
United States ill equipped to combat the threat with traditional means,
and it placed the emphasis on creating intelligence capabilities that could
penetrate terrorist organizations and the areas of the world they inhabit,
and on working with people "who move freely in this nether world." The
ability to anticipate moves and disrupt operations would allow the United

States to "almost always keep them off balance, and often . . . thwart their nefarious activities," and the knowledge of terrorist networks and operations enabled "sealing off the funding which provides them equipment and movement" and attacked "them through their chief vulnerability."[19]

No approach would stop all threats, but prevention through human intelligence would provide the most effective means of protection. "Even imperfect success in such counter-terrorism intelligence practices would be effective. Instilling in the terrorists a fear that their organizations and operations have been penetrated would sow suspicion and dissension in their ranks and greatly reduce their effectiveness of operation."[20] All of this depended on the quality of intelligence gathered. Besides a policy commitment, good intelligence depended on cooperation with other like-minded nations. Without international cooperation, it would be impossible to infiltrate terrorist organizations or interfere with their receipt of capital.

Given his concern with terrorism, and knowing the predisposition toward unilateralism of some key members of George W. Bush's incoming foreign policy team, Scowcroft urged the new administration to improve relations with America's European allies. The euphoria after the victory in the Cold War that led to Clinton's sporadic focus on foreign policy issues, Scowcroft declared, had taken its toll on the Atlantic alliance and hampered Washington's ability to address foreign policy problems such as terrorism. Although there was no crisis at hand, the neglect over time was corrosive, and if it continued unchecked, "the slide toward estrangement could result in the relationship becoming one of the most serious in a series of troublesome issues confronting the United States." Most notably, there were tensions over the military role of NATO, trade relations with the European Union, and Western relations with Russia. The decision to expand NATO by admitting nations from Eastern Europe was perceived in Moscow as a hostile act and was damaging the West's ability to cooperate with the Kremlin on vital matters such as nuclear proliferation and terrorist activities. These problems "combine to threaten the unity of the Atlantic Community, a unity which has preserved Western values in the face of a forty-year assault by a hostile ideology."[21]

For the "United States to continue to thrive in the 21st century," Scowcroft wrote, the United States and Europe must cooperate closely. "The Atlantic Community is a central repository of the values most of the world seeks, and the economic and military power on which global stability and prosperity rest." Cooperation and progress, however, could not be taken for granted. Washington needed to reach out to its European allies and Russia, to build on past achievements, and to focus more on the areas of agreement and compatible interests in the face of shared threats from states and groups that promoted values antithetical to the West and sought to disrupt the world order. "The primary objective" of the new administration "must be to reverse trends now operating before they permanently disrupt what is still the world's most important relationship."[22]

SEPTEMBER 11, 2001

While Scowcroft had foreseen the danger of terrorism and spent almost two years warning about the threat it posed to the United States, he was just as shocked as everyone else by the events of September 11, 2001. The al Qaeda attack against the World Trade Center in New York and the Pentagon propelled fighting terrorism to the top of the nation's priorities. Overnight, a sense of national unity as well as international support emerged, and the second Bush administration vowed to bring those responsible to justice. As the administration sought the proper response, connections between Saddam Hussein and Osama bin Laden were discussed, since, for many, the problems presented by Iraq and al Qaeda merged together into one threat to the United States. In an address to a joint session of Congress on September 20, President George W. Bush declared war on terrorism. He told the nation that the reason al Qaeda attacked the United States, as it had previously attacked American embassies in Africa and the USS *Cole*, was because terrorist groups "hate our freedoms—our freedom of religion, our freedom of speech, our freedom to vote and assemble and disagree with each other." He bluntly declared to the world, "Either you are with us, or you are with the terrorists. . . . Any nation that continues to harbor or support terrorism will be regarded by the United States as a hostile regime." Bush linked the war on terror to previous American conflicts in the twentieth century, claiming that in their radical visions and quest for power, terrorists "follow in the path of fascism, and Nazism, and totalitarianism."[23]

   After September 11, Scowcroft's opinions were widely sought, and he returned to the themes he had been discussing over the past two years in a series of articles and interviews on how best to respond to al Qaeda's attack on the United States. The former national security advisor knew that the tragedy in New York and at the Pentagon provided neoconservatives with the opportunity to implement their policies, and he set out to prevent that as best he could. To successfully respond to and defeat terrorism, Scowcroft argued, the United States had to clearly define its objectives, differentiate between the threat presented by al Qaeda and a state like Iraq, develop better intelligence, work closely with its European allies, and cooperate with a coalition of nations in the Middle East. The immediate enemy was al Qaeda, and to successfully attack it and eliminate Osama bin Laden meant working with Pakistan and other nations that faced their own threats from terrorists and the Taliban. The United States had to act swiftly, with force, and with the determination to see the fight through over the long run. As he told Brit Hume of *Fox News Special Report with Brit Hume* on September 17, the administration should be looking toward a special-forces operation. This would be "pretty hard," given the difficult geography of Afghanistan, and would demand cooperation from Pakistan. "This is not an easy job, even if you can find him." The nation also had to realize that the struggle with terrorist groups would "take time and it will take patience." Isolated bombing of terrorists' camps was ineffective and made the United States look weak. Any response had to have a set objective and be carried out with "our friends and allies with us, supporting us with their own intelligence, with people who are willing to help."[24]

For many commentators, the threat the United States faced was reminiscent of events ten years earlier in the Persian Gulf. As speculation concerning links between Iraq and al Qaeda emerged, it also raised the question of whether the United States had made a mistake by not removing Saddam Hussein from power in 1991. Scowcroft was skeptical of any connection between Saddam and Osama bin Laden. It could be a marriage of convenience, he told Bryant Gumbel of the CBS *Early Show* on September 19, given that both hated the United States, but they were not "natural allies because bin Laden's people are really super-religious fanatics, and Saddam Hussein is head of the Ba'athist Party in Iraq, which is a socialist, anti-religious party." Even if there proved to be some links, Scowcroft opposed automatically including Iraq on a list of nations the United States should attack. "If it looks like we're using this terrible tragedy simply as an excuse to take another run at our old enemy, we'll lose a lot of support in the region, which we really need in order to have a comprehensive assault on terrorism." When Gumbel asked the general if he had any second thoughts about leaving Saddam in power, he replied that he had thought about it often and always reached the same conclusion. "If we had gone on and tried to take out Saddam, we would have been occupying an Arab land. We would have probably three times as many bin Ladens as we have now going after us." Moreover, he rejected the idea that the need to fight terrorism now was an extension of the Gulf War. The terrorist threat came from those who oppose American policies in the Middle East and "who resent who we are, the worst aspects in their mind of anti-religious modernism," and those were the groups the United States had to fight. The only way that the current crisis was the same as ten years earlier was in the need to build a coalition of nations to succeed. Effective coalitions are difficult because nations join with "very different perceptions of the problem and different objectives," but fighting terrorism is a difficult proposition, making the need for a multilateral approach "very important . . . to smoke these people out."[25]

The next month, Scowcroft used the op-ed page of the *Washington Post* to address these points and emphasize the need for a coalition. There was little that the present crisis and the Gulf War had in common, he wrote, "other than the surprising manner in which both presented themselves. The crisis in the Persian Gulf . . . appears more straightforward and traditional." The enemy was in a fixed location and the challenge was to overcome its military with a superior force. In retrospect, many wondered if the objective had been too limited, and if the United States could have avoided the current problem if Saddam Hussein had been removed from power. It was necessary to remember, Scowcroft responded, that America's Arab allies, "refusing to countenance an invasion of an Arab colleague, would have deserted" the United States. The level of hostility in the region would have been greater than at present, and an occupation "might well have spawned scores of Osama bin Ladens."[26]

Scowcroft reiterated the need for a coalition to achieve U.S. goals, which was the one similarity to the first Gulf War. "The liberation of Kuwait wouldn't have been possible," Scowcroft wrote, "without the development of a strong coalition of countries," and he was convinced that in the war on terrorism, Washington would be "even more dependent on coalition-building" than it was during the Gulf War. "To succeed in the present conflict, it is essential that we repeat the coalition-building of the Gulf conflict," even though it would be more difficult, as "potential members are even more disparate, the goals more nebulous, the means less obvious and the time frame indefinite." Understandably, given the shock of September 11, there were already those saying that Washington should not depend on a multilateral approach or wait on others. Partners would just make the effort more difficult and hold up action. "The United States knows what needs to be done, these voices say, and we should just go ahead and do it."[27]

The same laments were expressed in 1990, the former national security advisor reminded readers, and the critics today were just as wrong as they were a decade ago. A unilateral approach would fail. If the United States was to win the present campaign, "intelligence will be a key factor. The cooperation of the intelligence services of every friend and ally we can muster will greatly magnify our strength." Terrorists had to communicate to plan and coordinate their attacks, and they needed money to fund their operations. The communication lines and funding were the two most vulnerable points of their organizations and were the places where good intelligence work would make the difference between another 9/11 and a foiled plot. To attack these networks was "clearly impossible without widespread and determined international cooperation." Finally, it was essential that the United States infiltrate terrorist groups, a job "that can be done far more effectively" by foreign nationals. If done correctly, America could "master the terrorist menace."[28]

In Scowcroft's opinion, "no amount of homeland security" would compensate for good intelligence. "Success means a coalition, a broad coalition, a willing and enthusiastic coalition." The United States had done this before, in World War II, during the Cold War, and in the Gulf War, and it could do it again. There would be other benefits for the nation beyond the immediate purpose of defeating terrorist organizations. Building a viable, multilateral group of nations would "help erase the reputation the United States has been developing of being unilateral and indifferent, if not arrogant, to others"; it would help build bridges to nations where relations are currently strained, such as China, Iran, Pakistan, and Russia; and it would "provide the opportunity to reestablish the kind of cooperative warmth that used to characterize" relations with Europe. To effectively overcome the challenge posed by terrorism would take "wisdom and perseverance," and it was not something that could be done alone.[29]

As calls for attacks against Afghanistan and Iraq mounted, Scowcroft urged that a distinction be made between the danger posed by al Qaeda and Osama bin Laden and that presented by Saddam Hussein, and that priorities be established. Speaking on PBS's *Frontline*, he again defended the decision not to oust Saddam in 1991 and cautioned against using the current crisis as an excuse to remove the Iraqi dictator. Iraq had been successfully contained and greatly weakened over the past decade. While Saddam could become a threat again, he was currently only an irritant. Moreover, who was going to replace Saddam, keep the nation together, and rule Iraq? Certainly not the Iraqi National Congress that many neoconservatives were promoting. "It is weak, disparate, riven with disputes," Scowcroft opined, and "unattractive to almost anyone inside or out" of Iraq.[30]

The United States had to focus on the number-one target, al Qaeda. "We need to prosecute the Afghan/Osama bin Laden part of this whole thing in a way which will demonstrate that we know what we're doing, that we do it carefully, not wildly." Attacking Iraq would undermine those efforts. "We need to use scalpels, not sledgehammers," in going against the global terrorist networks and disrupting their ability to harm the United States and its allies. This was why coalitions and intelligence were so important to track the flow of money, get inside organizations, and monitor communications. Already, Germany had shown what could be gained through greater cooperation. In recent days, Berlin "revealed the background of a whole lot of the September 11 terrorists who were holed up in Germany—some of them for years." If the United States acted unilaterally without that type of information and help, "we're not going to win."[31]

He added, in talking with Chris Matthews on MSNBC's *Hardball* at the end of the month, a coalition would mean working with some unpleasant governments, such as Pakistan's, because the United States needed

"people in the region who know the region, who speak the language."
Washington had to admit what it did not know and find people with different perspectives to assist it. Americans had to realize that al Qaeda was
holed up in a difficult area with "a lot of nasty people," and if the United
States tried to "play by Marquis of Queensbury rules," it would get its
"clock cleaned" and end up with more terrorist states.[32]

The administration indicated soon after the September 11 attack that
Iraq would be at the center of its efforts in the war against terrorism.
On September 15, the Department of Defense announced three primary
targets: the Taliban, al Qaeda, and Iraq. There was much talk about the
lessons of Munich and not appeasing an aggressor any longer as the
administration worked on how to respond to 9/11. The logic of senior
officials was that if U.S. intelligence had missed the warning signs of September 11, then what was being missed about Iraq and its intentions? To
those pushing for an attack on Baghdad, Iraq presented a much greater
danger. Saddam Hussein, unlike Osama bin Laden, had billions of dollars
to spend on his military, an infrastructure and industry to produce weapons of mass destruction, and just as deep a hatred of the United States and
its allies as any terrorist group. In addition, he had a record of using poison gas on his citizens, aggression against his neighbors, defiance of the
international community, and unwillingness to cooperate with weapons
inspectors. Saddam Hussein could not be trusted.

THE IRAQ WAR

In his January 29, 2002, State of the Union address, President Bush went
public with the logic that was pushing him toward war with Iraq. The war
on terrorism had begun well, but the overthrow of the Taliban and the
pursuit of al Qaeda in Afghanistan was not the end, only the beginning.
The United States would continue its efforts to destroy terrorist camps,
disrupt terrorist organizations, and foil terrorist plots. A second goal was
"to prevent regimes that sponsor terror from threatening America or our
friends and allies with weapons of mass destruction." He identified North
Korea, Iran, and Iraq as an "axis of evil, arming to threaten the peace of
the world." If they obtained weapons of mass destruction, they could
threaten their neighbors or supply terrorist groups with new means to
harm others. All nations, Bush proclaimed, must know that "America will
do what is necessary to ensure our Nation's security." Time was not on
the side of the United States as terrorist groups and their state sponsors
plotted attacks. "I will not wait on events while dangers gather," Bush
declared. "I will not stand by as peril draws closer and closer. The United

States of America will not permit the world's most dangerous regimes to threaten us with the world's most destructive weapons."[33]

Iraq was singled out as a threat. The president stated that Iraq continued "to flaunt its hostility toward America and to support terror." Baghdad had sought "to develop anthrax and nerve gas and nuclear weapons for over a decade." Saddam Hussein had murdered thousands of his own citizens with poison gas, had expelled weapons inspectors from his country despite international agreements, and had waged war on neighboring states. "This is a regime," Bush claimed, "that has something to hide from the civilized world." The president vowed to defeat states and terrorist organizations that threatened the United States. "History has called America and our allies to action, and it is both our responsibility and our privilege to fight freedom's fight."[34] Bush had presented all of the components that would make up the case for war the next year: Iraq had weapons of mass destruction, it was led by an irrational and evil dictator, it supported terrorism, and it had to be stopped before it could cause harm.

Bush spent much of 2002 making the case for a new doctrine of preemptive war and overthrowing Saddam Hussein. His speech at West Point's graduation on June 1 previewed what would be called the Bush Doctrine and was representative of the logic and rationale for attacking Iraq. "For much of the last century, America's defense relied on the cold war doctrines of deterrence and containment," the president stated. New threats, however, required new approaches. Deterrence "means nothing against shadowy terrorist networks with no nation or citizens to defend. Containment is not possible when unbalanced dictators with weapons of mass destruction can deliver those weapons on missiles or secretly provide them to terrorist allies." Old thinking needed to be revised. "If we wait for threats to fully materialize, we will have waited too long." It was imperative to take the fight to the enemy and "confront the worst threats before they emerge." The nation had to be prepared "for preemptive action when necessary to defend our liberty and to defend our lives." It could not leave its safety or world peace "at the mercy of a few mad terrorists and tyrants."[35]

The United States fought for a good cause. Bush declared, "Our Nation's cause has always been larger than our Nation's defense. We fight, as we always fight, for a just peace, a peace that favors human liberty." The United States now found itself "in a conflict between good and evil," and "moral clarity was essential" for victory. "Some worry that it is somehow undiplomatic or impolite to speak the language of right and wrong," the president acknowledged. "I disagree. Different circumstances require different methods but not different moralities. Moral truth is the same in every culture, in every time, and in every place." Invoking the triumphal interpretation of the recent past, Bush stated that the twentieth century "ended with a single surviving model of human progress": Western liberalism. It was the goal of the United States to "work for a just and peaceful world beyond the war on terror" by spreading democracy and freedom.[36]

Scowcroft made headlines in August when he publicly criticized the Bush administration's talk of war against Iraq and regime change in Baghdad. Frustrated by the direction in which he saw Bush taking American foreign policy and his inability to convince the White House to reconsider its views, he again asserted his case for setting priorities concerning the threats the United States faced and for distinguishing between the immediate danger posed by terrorist groups and the irritation presented by Saddam Hussein. Appearing on CBS's *Face the Nation* on August 4, Scowcroft warned that a war against Iraq would pull American resources and attention away from the fight against terror, would alienate America's allies in the Middle East, and could potentially "turn the whole region into a cauldron, and thus destroy the war on terrorism."[37] Saddam was a problem for the United States, but not because of any ties to terrorism.

Scowcroft further developed his thoughts in an op-ed piece, "Don't Attack Saddam," in the *Wall Street Journal* on August 15, 2002. All could agree, Scowcroft opined, that Saddam Hussein was a brutal dictator who retained the ambition of dominating the Persian Gulf and the region's oil, and that the United States would be "better off when he is gone." Still, this did not justify waging war against Baghdad, and such an action would damage larger American objectives. The question was how to deal with the menace Saddam presented in the context of a more pressing American policy priority—the war on terrorism.[38]

Despite the appeal of getting rid of Saddam Hussein, Scowcroft argued, the case for war was weak. First, there was "scant evidence to tie Saddam to terrorist organizations, and even less to the Sept. 11 attacks. Indeed, Saddam's goals have little in common with the terrorists who threaten us, and there is little incentive for him to make common cause with them." Second, Iraq presented no danger to the United States, and its threat to the region was successfully contained. A decade of war followed by a decade of sanctions had weakened the Baath regime and left it seeking "weapons of mass destruction not to arm terrorists, but to deter us from intervening to block his aggressive designs." If a new threat from Baghdad did materialize, it could be dealt with at the proper time. At the moment, the "pre-eminent security priority" was the war on terrorism. "An attack on Iraq at this time would seriously jeopardize, if not destroy, the global counter-terrorist campaign" the United States was waging in Afghanistan and elsewhere.[39]

An attack on Iraq and the overthrow of Saddam's regime would lead to a protracted and costly occupation of Iraq that would drain resources and isolate the United States internationally at a time when it most needed to work with other nations. "Ignoring that clear sentiment would result in a serious degradation in international cooperation with us against terrorism. And make no mistake, we simply cannot win that war without enthusiastic international cooperation, especially on intelligence." The "most dire consequence" would be the "explosion of outrage against" the United States in the region, which would "stifle any cooperation on terrorism, and could even swell the ranks of the terrorists." Moreover, "a military campaign very likely would have to be followed by a large-scale, long-term military occupation." For Scowcroft, the focus of the United States had to remain on the war on terrorism. "Keeping counter-terrorism as our foremost priority" would ensure "success across the entire range of our security interests—including Iraq." But if the administration rejected an integrated approach in favor of war and regime change, it would "put at risk" the "campaign against terrorism as well as stability and security in a vital region of the world."[40]

National Security Advisor Condoleezza Rice called Scowcroft to complain that the *Wall Street Journal* article hurt the administration and made it appear as if the president's father disapproved of the administration's policy. She asked why he did not express his concerns in private. Scowcroft noted that he did not say anything different in the piece than he had said on CBS or had been saying since September 11. The problem was that no one in the administration would listen to him; so he concluded he had to state his views in public. It was an angry exchange, and it convinced Scowcroft that the administration was not interested in hearing divergent views or questioning its predetermined assumptions, and that the neoconservative ideology was overriding the evidence at hand.

The next month, Scowcroft gave the keynote speech at a U.S. Institute of Peace Conference on America's Challenges in a Changed World. During the 1990s, Scowcroft asserted, American foreign policy lacked focus, as the nation no longer faced the "awesome pressure of nuclear holocaust." The sense of relief this brought meant that foreign policy "drifted without any deep inquisition" into changes taking place in the world. The Clinton administration focused on the positive aspects of globalization as the means for bringing progress and prosperity to an integrating world, seemingly convinced of Fukuyama's claim in *The End of History* that the "triumph of liberal democracy, market economy and the absence of conflict" were inevitable.[41]

What was missed, according to the former national security advisor, were the negative reactions to globalization and the new challenges to the nation-state. The more rapid communication, easier flow of international capital, and greater mobility of people was resented by many in the poorer and weaker nations who saw globalization as an "onslaught of a bewildering mélange of forces disrupting their lives, their culture, their values," and the ability of their governments to provide services or protect them. Greater international integration was equated with political, economic, and cultural imperialism at the same time that the political tendency in the world was toward societies dividing "into ever smaller, more homogenous, more intolerant political entities." This development, Scowcroft believed, was the breeding ground for a terrorism that represented both specific grievances and an "existential" response to changes in the world.[42]

Understanding this new international context was necessary for formulating the correct policies to defeat terrorism. Scowcroft reiterated his arguments from his recent op-ed piece on the need for a coalition to fight and win this war, a war that was "going to be primarily a war of intelligence" and, ironically, a high-tech fight in terms of tracing money, intercepting communications, and challenging the ideology of groups fighting against the encroachment of modern ways. "Whenever terrorists talk, whenever they move, whenever they spend money, whenever they get money, they leave traces," and the United States had to be able to pick up those trails.[43]

Scowcroft saw a number of problems arising in the war on terrorism. The administration was moving away from cooperation with allies toward a unilateral approach that reflected an attitude that somehow America could win all by itself. Scowcroft noted a recent cartoon that captured the danger that other issues were "interfering with the concentration on the war on al Qaeda." It showed a billboard with the caption "America's Most Wanted," and a workman pasting a portrait of Saddam Hussein over one of Osama bin Laden. It was imperative, Scowcroft warned, that the United States keep its focus on the primary threat it faced, global terrorist networks, and not allow policy to be derailed.[44] What Scowcroft said was not new. He had made all of the same points for the past two years. But with the administration now pressing toward war, it elicited a sharp response from the White House.

Scowcroft was talking a different language from the neoconservatives who now had control over American foreign policy. While the former national security advisor invoked the lessons of the Cold War, the need for stability, deterrence, containment, and coalitions, the administration wanted a foreign policy designed to change the politics and realities of the Middle East. Preemptive war, unilateralism, democratic change, liberation, and freedom were the new goals in a quest to alter governments in the region so that they would no longer harbor terrorists or threaten the United States. Vice President Dick Cheney delivered the first rejoinder in a monthlong public relations blitz to justify war against Iraq. Speaking to the national convention of the Veterans of Foreign Wars on August

26, Cheney branded Iraq a threat to the United States and called for war to remove Saddam Hussein from power. "Simply stated," the vice president asserted, "there is no doubt that Saddam Hussein now has weapons of mass destruction. There is no doubt that he is amassing them to use against our friends, against our allies, and against us." Containment had been a viable strategy during the Cold War, but it was "not possible when dictators obtain weapons of mass destruction and are prepared to share them with terrorists who intend to inflict catastrophic casualties on the United States." A new approach was necessary, and time was not on the side of the United States. "The risks of inaction are far greater than the risks of action," he asserted. "We realize wars are never won on the defensive." The United States had to take the fight to the source of the problem. Two weeks later on *Meet the Press*, he dismissed critics when he told Tim Russert that they had not "seen all the intelligence that we have seen." Echoing these themes, National Security Advisor Condoleezza Rice told CNN on September 8 that the United States could not wait to see what Saddam Hussein would do before acting, as "we don't want the smoking gun to be a mushroom cloud."[45]

On September 17, the White House released the new "National Security Strategy of the United States," which set forth the Bush Doctrine of preemptive war that the president had outlined in his speech at the U.S. Military Academy. There were three components to the strategy: preserve the United States' position as the lone superpower in the world, take the offensive in the war on terrorism by using preemptive attacks before the threat was fully realized, and promote democracy and expand freedom in the world. The centerpiece was the rationale for shifting away from the precepts of internationalism to a policy based on preemptive action. The post–Cold War threat to the nation came from rogue states and their terrorist allies who sought weapons of mass destruction to advance their aggressive plans and destroy freedom. The United States, the National Security Strategy stated, "must be prepared to stop rogue states and their terrorist clients before they are able to threaten or use weapons of mass destruction." This threat demanded action. "To forestall or prevent such hostile acts by our adversaries, the United States will, if necessary, act preemptively."[46]

Scowcroft did not back down. Appearing on news shows in September, he continued to argue that waging war against Iraq would "damage our effectiveness in the war on terrorism." Containment had worked, and Saddam's regime was weak. It was necessary to put the threat he presented in perspective. The top priority of the nation had to be the war on terrorism, and "the cockpit of the war on terrorism is the Middle East and we've got to have the support of nations there, if we are to win." Going to war against Iraq would alienate much of that necessary support in the

Middle East and in Europe. Saddam was a problem, but he was "not a problem because of terrorism." There still was no solid evidence to link him to September 11 or al Qaeda. Therefore, the two problems were distinct and had to be treated that way.[47]

Speaking in Cincinnati on October 7, prior to the congressional vote to authorize the use of American force in Iraq, President Bush made his most pointed comments on the need for war. The United States faced a direct threat from Iraq due to "its history of aggression and its drive toward an arsenal of terror." The president asserted that Iraq possessed chemical and biological weapons and was actively working to obtain nuclear weapons, and that it "has given shelter and support to terrorism and practices terror against its own people." He linked that danger to the vulnerability America felt on September 11 and proclaimed his resolve "to confront every threat, from any source, that could bring sudden terror and suffering to America." All agreed that the "Iraqi dictator must not be permitted to threaten America and the world with horrible poisons and diseases and gases and atomic weapons." The president further averred that there were links between Baghdad and al Qaeda, and that "Iraq could decide on any given day to provide a biological or chemical weapon to a terrorist group or individual terrorists. Alliance with terrorists could allow the Iraqi regime to attack America without leaving any fingerprints."[48]

Directly taking up Scowcroft's criticisms, Bush dismissed the idea that attacking Iraq would detract from the war on terror. "To the contrary, confronting the threat posed by Iraq is crucial to winning the war on terror." The threat was real. "Saddam Hussein is harboring terrorists and the instruments of terror, the instruments of mass death and destruction. . . . The risk is simply too great that he will use them or provide them to a terror network." Containment had not worked; Saddam still had weapons of mass destruction and still sought to increase his supply. To delay action was too risky as there could be "no peace if our security depends on the will and whims of a ruthless and aggressive dictator," Bush asserted. "I'm not willing to stake one American life on trusting Saddam Hussein." Failure by the United States to act "would embolden other tyrants, allow terrorists access to new weapons and new resources," and reward aggression. "Knowing these realities," Bush claimed, "America must not ignore the threat gathering against us. Facing clear evidence of peril, we cannot wait for the final proof, the smoking gun, that could come in the form of a mushroom cloud." Finally, he rejected the argument that regime change in Iraq would create instability. "The situation could hardly get worse for world security." Rather, the liberation of Iraq would bring freedom to that nation and hope for its future. "If military action is necessary, the United States . . . will help the Iraqi people rebuild their economy and create the institutions of liberty in a unified Iraq at peace with its neighbors."[49]

The case for war—Iraq was led by a brutal dictator who possessed weapons of mass destruction, Baghdad had links to terrorism which compounded the threat to the United States, and regime change would bring freedom to Iraq and begin the transformation of the region—was a compelling case to many a little over a year after the September 11 attacks, and the administration appeared to have evidence to support its claims. On October 16, Congress authorized the use of America's military against Iraq, 77 for in the Senate and 296 in the House. What had not been addressed was Scowcroft's ultimate question about the war: once Saddam Hussein was overthrown, what was the next step? Few were as prescient as the former national security advisor in recognizing that Washington could win the war and occupy Baghdad but still lose the peace that followed.

The Bush administration went to war optimistic that it would quickly overthrow Saddam Hussein's regime and bring freedom to Iraq. The "shock and awe" strategy of using a small force of 145,000 troops in conjunction with technological superiority to provide speed and overwhelming firepower would deliver a quick knockout blow, and American forces would be greeted as liberators, with people pouring into the streets cheering for them. A free Iraq would emerge after the Baathist Party was driven from power, while oil revenues would cover the costs of establishing a new government. The Department of Defense was contemptuous of critics who suggested that it would take hundreds of thousands of troops to bring stability to postwar Iraq. Deputy Secretary of Defense Wolfowitz told Congress that it was "hard to conceive that it would take more forces to provide stability . . . than it would take to conduct the war itself and to secure the surrender of Saddam's security forces and his army—hard to imagine."[50]

Operation Iraqi Freedom was launched on March 20, 2003. By April 9, U.S. forces were in Baghdad, and on May 1, the president announced that major combat operations were over and, "in the battle of Iraq, the United States and our allies have prevailed." And so it appeared that spring, with Saddam Hussein in hiding, his army defeated, and the regime ousted from power. However, that optimistic view unraveled over the next two years. Soon after the American occupation began, instability yielded to an insurgency marked by attacks on U.S. forces and internecine fighting between religious and ethnic groups, and freedom did not come to Iraq or any other part of the region. Moreover, no weapons of mass destruction, the casus belli, were found in Iraq, leading to more questions about the administration's case for the war. By 2005, the majority of Americans had concluded that the war was a mistake. The problems that beset the American mission in Iraq bore out Scowcroft's criticisms and concerns.

The former national security advisor, however, did not seek to take credit for being correct. Moreover, he was sensitive to the perception that his criticisms of the president's policy were seen in some circles as representing Bush Senior. Scowcroft, therefore, refrained from commenting on the war for almost two years. When he did again speak out, starting in 2005, the retired lieutenant general was more interested in the issue of what the United States should do about the problem it had created in Iraq than in rehashing the debates over the policy decisions that had led Washington into Baghdad. He focused on how the war could be fought to create a lasting peace. "Such a review could usefully begin," Scowcroft wrote in January 2006 in the *Washington Post*, "by turning over to the historians questions about how and why we got into Iraq. Whatever questions remain, we are there in force, and the central issue that confronts us is how we move forward most effectively."[51] In many ways, Scowcroft's analysis of the Bush administration's methods of fighting and plans for Iraq after the overthrow of Saddam was as devastating as his critique of the logic and need for the war.

Scowcroft was appalled by how little thought the administration had given to postwar Iraq. Bush and his advisors had acted on the assumption that once Saddam was removed, a functioning bureaucracy and society would be in place that could quickly be transformed into a democratic state. Administration officials had overlooked the need to provide security and the danger of sectarian violence, and thus they were not prepared for the postwar chaos and fear that emerged. Without a plan, there was no chance to build a stable and functioning society. "I just don't know how you operate unless you continually challenge your own assumptions," Scowcroft said.[52] Yet he watched the administration stick to its beliefs, unwilling to rethink its policy as the situation in Iraq spiraled downward.

Teaming with another former national security advisor, Sandy Berger, who served under Bill Clinton, Scowcroft examined the postconflict capabilities of the United States for the Council on Foreign Relations.[53] In a summary of their findings which Scowcroft wrote for the *National Interest*, he criticized the Bush national security team for not giving as much attention to the "stabilization and reconstruction" phase of victory as it did fighting the war. Weak and failed states were a reality of the post–Cold War world and presented a challenge to the national security of the United States. "Failed states and nations emerging from conflict will remain a significant feature of the international landscape for the foreseeable future." American policy must focus on creating stability and then work to rebuild these countries. Due to the "complexity and the interagency nature of policy decisions associated with stabilization and reconstruction," Scowcroft advised that the National Security Council "should have responsibility for overarching policy in this area." Only "decisive leadership to direct the proper roles of the military and civilian agencies" would allow the United States to achieve any outcomes that could be termed successful. The current emphasis on military technology, high-intensity conflict, and winning quickly with few casualties "has had an unintended consequence. Rapid victory collapses the enemy but does not destroy it. Adversaries can go underground to wage guerilla warfare, creating a need for more troops for longer periods of time during the stabilization and reconstruction phases. This unintended consequence of military 'transformation'" had implications for policy making as well as fighting.[54]

Returning to one of his central themes, Scowcroft argued that nation building could only be done successfully through international coalitions, and "enhancing America's capability to conduct stabilization and reconstruction operations in cooperation with others should be a top foreign policy priority." In a succinct description of the current situation in Iraq, Scowcroft noted that economic and political improvements could not develop in states suffering from ongoing fighting or terrorist interference. "Where conflict has been followed by inattention and unmet promises, violence can reappear and spread, and military advantages can be lost in chaos and corruption." He concluded that the United States could no longer "afford to mount costly military actions and then treat the follow-on mission with anything less than the same seriousness of purpose."[55]

The stakes in the final outcome in Iraq, Scowcroft believed, were "enormous." It was in the center of a critical region, and "a failed Iraq could be a catastrophe for the Middle East and a calamity for the world."[56] For these reasons, the United States had to stay in Iraq and develop new policies that would lead to a peaceful, stable, and unified nation. Anything less would be a "strategic defeat" that would embolden America's enemies and demoralize its allies. "Our Arab friends would rightly feel we had abandoned them to face alone a radicalism that has been greatly inflamed by American actions in the region and which could pose a serious threat to their own governments." There was no easy solution, but to "avoid these dire consequences," Scowcroft again insisted that the United States had to "secure the support of the countries of the region" as well as its European allies. For these reasons, Scowcroft would support the "surge," the increase of American forces sent in 2007, because the increase in troops was "directed at accomplishing specific, defined missions." Iraq was "not just a troublesome issue from which we can walk away if it seems too costly to continue." The stability of the Middle East and the "global perception of the reliability of the United States as a partner in a deeply troubled world" were at stake.[57]

CONCLUSION

The Iraq War discredited most of the neoconservative's arguments about the benefits of preemptive war, regime change, and unilateral action, yet no new foreign policy consensus has emerged. In July 2007, in an essay entitled "The Dispensable Nation," which can be seen as a summation of Scowcroft's thoughts on the problems facing the United States, the former national security advisor reasserted his commitment to the tenets of internationalism while providing some guiding thoughts on how American power should be used. He addressed the central paradox concerning the question of when and how to use America's overwhelming power to protect the nation's interests and advance its values and institutions. The United States, Scowcroft believed, was "slow to recognize how revolutionary the changes sweeping the globe" were. The transformations being brought about by globalization were comparable to those unleashed by industrialization in the nineteenth century. In this new context, would the "United States remain the 'indispensible nation' in global affairs?"[58]

The dilemma, as Scowcroft saw it, was that "the world is not susceptible to U.S. domination—but without U.S. leadership not much can be achieved." Scowcroft did believe in American exceptionalism and that the nation could be "a different sort of great power than the others." He rejected, however, unilateralism and the neoconservative approach to foreign policy as a hubristic and flawed view of the nation and of the world. The United States was "not indispensable in the sense that those of us in Washington are the only ones who know what needs to be done for the good of the entire human race, and that the rest of the world can either join us or be against us." The post–Cold War euphoria made it appear that the "United States was now in such a unique position—having so much of the world's military and economic power at its disposal—that we had almost no choice but to take advantage of this power to transform the world along liberal and democratic lines." Many believed that the nation had to seize the moment, and that, "by acting unilaterally, we could achieve good results," thereby forcing others to recognize the correctness of the United States. This was not leadership, and it only bred anger, resentment, and resistance to what was perceived as a quest for an American empire. The only transformation achieved was in the reputation of the United States, where it was "more disliked around the world than at any point in history."[59]

Still, the United States was for Scowcroft the indispensable nation because no other power had the "ability to mobilize the world community to undertake the great projects of the day." The United States was a "catalyst" for action, able to mobilize "nations from different parts of the world and from both the developed and developing world to join truly multinational coalitions with global reach." In a time when it is more difficult for individual states "to cope with the threats" of the post–Cold War world—terrorism, pandemics, environmental change, mass migrations—nations need to cooperate in order to remedy these problems. The starting point for Washington had to be repairing the Atlantic alliance that had been frayed by the disagreements over Iraq. "A strengthened Atlantic community" would be "in a position to work with other major powers and regional blocs to advance an agenda for common action on such matters as the environment."[60]

It was necessary, Scowcroft believed, to return to traditional methods of diplomacy, such as forging coalitions and building international organizations, while at the same time recognizing that the "nature of power had been changing" in the post–Cold War world. Despite its immense military power, the United States found itself in a stalemate in Iraq against opponents "who are not even an organized state adversary" and who negate much of the nation's might. The current stresses on the international system were coming from globalization and the integration of vast populations in Africa, Asia, and Latin America into the global system. Conflict was emerging "within states—particularly as a state collapses—or between a state and non-state actors." In these circumstances, power "resides more in the collectivity of states rather than in the hands of any individual power."[61]

As he had done throughout his public life, Scowcroft continued to put service to the nation at the center of what has been a remarkable career. From the difficult last days of the Vietnam War to the tragedy in Iraq, he maintained his principles and commitment to a conservative internationalism that he was convinced would best serve the national interest. Scowcroft believed the United States had to act as a world leader to protect its interests and institutions. He sought continuity in policy making that focused on containment of aggression, stability, international cooperation, and collective security as the best means for protecting the nation. As his thinking and recommendations on policy for the post–Cold War world demonstrated, the tenets of internationalism were guiding principles, rather than rigid maxims, that Scowcroft adapted to an ever-changing world. For these reasons, Scowcroft had been at the center of debates over American foreign policy since the 1970s.

Scowcroft experienced success and failure in policy making and in his efforts to hold off what he saw as misguided new approaches to international relations. The Vietnam War convinced Scowcroft of the need to recognize the limits of American power and pursue détente to control the arms race, create stability, and contain the Soviet Union. The Ford administration was able to bring a final end to the Vietnam War without further recrimination, restore political stability and trust after Watergate, and use détente to bring about the Helsinki agreements that were so important to the collapse of communism in Europe. Yet the administration was unable to convince the nation of the correctness of this approach to foreign policy, was criticized from multiple perspectives, and lost the election to Jimmy Carter and his promise to pursue a more moral foreign policy.

Over the ensuing twelve years, American diplomacy swung like a pendulum from Carter's human rights policy to Ronald Reagan's hard-line Cold War views. When he was again at the helm of the National Security Council in 1989 under George H. W. Bush, Scowcroft was determined to stop the movement begun by the Reagan administration and anchor America's policy to the tenets of internationalism. The first Bush administration oversaw the most remarkable four years in American foreign policy since the 1940s. It successfully steered the nation's course through the collapse of communism in Eastern Europe to help bring about German unification and a peaceful end to the Cold War, it charted a middle course in response to the Chinese crackdown in Tiananmen Square which imposed sanctions but did not rupture relations, it built an international coalition that rebuffed Iraqi aggression in the Gulf War, and it sought to establish a new world order in the post–Cold War world based on American leadership of multilateral institutions and cooperative approaches to international problems.

Once again out of office after a defeat at the polls, Scowcroft watched the foreign policy pendulum again swing as a new post–Cold War hubris and neoconservative thinking took hold. In response to the terrorist attack on September 11, 2001, the younger Bush led the nation into a war in Iraq that violated all of Scowcroft's foreign policy precepts. The former national security advisor saw the momentum building toward a use of American power that had not been sufficiently thought through in terms of the consequences it would have on the region and the United States. The war raised again the thorny question of where to draw the line between world leadership and dictating to the world, and the dilemma of seeing the United States as essential to world peace and progress yet acknowledging the limits of its power. In his own rhetoric about creating a new world order, Scowcroft could be accused of exaggerating the importance of the United States and its ability to shape events. The United States had at times embraced collective security in the past when such actions functioned in accordance with American guidelines and in conjunction with American goals. But when its allies disagreed, as many did prior to the escalation of the Vietnam War and the Iraq War, the United States acted independently, sure of the correctness of its policy.

Many of the long-term issues that Scowcroft struggled with were not new in the making of American foreign policy. The nation has held the idea of its manifest destiny and its mission in the world since its founding. There were always two parts to the exceptionalists' credo that at times were at odds and led to different policies but stemmed from the same set of ideas. One was the need for intervention to protect American interests or to expand U.S. influence and shape the world. The other was that the

United States should be the exemplar nation to others, leading through its example, as a beacon of light and hope. Scowcroft's internationalist beliefs, as he readily acknowledged, were a variant of American exceptionalism, and his rhetoric, particularly when discussing a new world order, sounded exceedingly Wilsonian. Even as he recognized and acted to counter the arrogance, unilateralism, interventionism, and imperial behavior that often characterized American foreign policy, Scowcroft drew many of his own ideas and concepts from the same understanding of the necessity for America to act as a world leader.

Thus Scowcroft's efforts to stop the swings of the policy pendulum were dependent on the individuals holding office rather than on a distinct understanding of the nation's role in the world. Scowcroft has been an exemplar of a modest, bipartisan policy maker, a man who is able to foresee different contingencies and perspectives, to act with restraint, and to accept limits on American power. These traits and his historical understanding have led him to believe that an internationalist policy best serves the nation's interests. The first Bush administration built and worked with an international coalition and demonstrated the restraint necessary to keep it intact during the Gulf War. This effort to establish the viability of collective security, rule of law, and international cooperation turned in part on the personalities of the men in charge of policy and their approach to international relations. But it also turned on the fact that U.S. interests coincided with those of other members of the coalition.

The nation was at a crossroads when Scowcroft left office in 1993. Despite the significant accomplishments of successfully ending the Cold War and achieving victory in the Persian Gulf, no consensus emerged behind the Bush administration's internationalist policies, and Scowcroft was unable to institutionalize his views. Whether the United States would follow internationalist or unilateralist ideas emerged at the end of the Cold War at the heart of the question of the direction of American foreign policy. The point of departure was how to go about creating the new world order, spreading American values and institutions, and securing American interests. That his example and practice of policy making did not last should not detract from Scowcroft's considerable achievements while in office and the value of his cautious internationalist approach to foreign policy.

NOTES

1. Zbigniew Brzezinski and Brent Scowcroft, *America and the World: Conversations on the Future of American Foreign Policy*, moderated by David Ignatius (New York: Basic Books, 2008), 13–14.

2. Brzezinski and Scowcroft, *America and the World*, 3, 13–15.

3. Scowcroft, "Who Can Harness History? Only the U.S.," *New York Times*, 2 July 1993.

4. Scowcroft, "Who Can Harness History?"

5. Scowcroft, "Who Can Harness History?"

6. Francis Fukuyama, *The Last Man and the End of History* (New York: Free Press, 1992).

7. Tony Smith, *America's Mission* (Princeton, NJ: Princeton University Press, 1994), 3–4, 267, xiii.

8. George Bush and Brent Scowcroft, *A World Transformed* (New York: Vintage, 1998), 488–89.

9. Project for the New American Century, "Statement of Principles," 3 June 1997, www.newamericancentury.org/statementofprinciples.html (accessed 9 June 2010).

10. Robert Kagan and William Kristol. "Toward a Neo-Reaganite Foreign Policy." *Foreign Affairs* 75, no. 4 (July/August 1996): 18–32.

11. Project for the New American Century to William J. Clinton, 26 January 1998, in *The Iraq War Reader*, ed. Micah L. Sifry and Christopher Cerf (Touchstone Book: New York, 2003), 199–201.

12. United States Information Service, "Transcript: Town Hall Meeting on Iraq at Ohio State February 18," www.fas.org/news/iraq/1998/02/20/98022006_tpo.html (accessed 7 July 2010).

13. Secretary of State Madeleine K. Albright, interview, *Today Show*, 19 February 1998, http://secretary.state.gov/www/statements/1998/980219a.html (accessed 12 July 2010).

14. Thomas Ricks, *Fiasco* (Penguin: New York, 2006), 21–22.

15. Brent Scowcroft, Commencement Speech, 14 May 2000, The College of William and Mary, www.scowcroft.com/html/announcements/announce.html (accessed 14 July 2008).

16. Scowcroft, Commencement Speech.

17. Scowcroft, Commencement Speech.

18. Brent Scowcroft, "Confront Terrorism," *Issue Brief*, 9 August 2000, www.scowcroft.com/html/announcements/announce.html (accessed 14 July 2008).

19. Scowcroft, "Confront Terrorism."

20. Scowcroft, "Confront Terrorism."

21. Brent Scowcroft, "Wither the Atlantic Community," *Issue Brief*, 21 March 2001, www.scowcroft.com/html/announcements/announce.html (accessed 14 July 2008).

22. Scowcroft, "Wither the Atlantic Community."

23. *Public Papers of the Presidents: George W. Bush, 2001* (Washington, DC: Government Printing Office, 2002), 2:1140–44.

24. Brit Hume, "Interview with Brent Scowcroft," *Fox News: Special Report with Brit Hume*, 17 September 2001. www.scowcroft.com/html/announcements/announce.html (accessed 14 July 2008).

25. Bryant Gumbel, "Interview with Brent Scowcroft," *CBS News: The Early Show*, 19 September 2001. www.scowcroft.com/html/announcements/announce.html (accessed 14 July 2008).

26. Scowcroft, "Build a Coalition," *The Washington Post*, 16 October 2001.

27. Scowcroft, "Build a Coalition."

28. Scowcroft, "Build a Coalition."

29. Scowcroft, "Build a Coalition."

30. PBS *Frontline*, "Gunning for Saddam: Interviews: Brent Scowcroft," October 2001, www.pbs.org/wgbh/pages/frontline/shows/gunning/interviews/scowcroft.html (accessed 14 July 2008).

31. PBS *Frontline*, "Gunning for Saddam: Interviews: Brent Scowcroft."

32. Chris Matthews, "Interview with Brent Scowcroft," *MSNBC: Hardball with Chris Matthews*, 29 October 2001. www.scowcroft.com/html/announcements/announce.html (accessed 14 July 2008).

33. *Public Papers of the Presidents: George W. Bush, 2002* (Washington, DC: Government Printing Office, 2005), 1:129–33.

34. *Public Papers of the Presidents: Bush, 2002* (Washington, DC: Government Printing Office, 2005), 1:129–33.

35. *Public Papers of the Presidents: Bush*, 2002, 1:917–21.

36. *Public Papers of the Presidents: Bush*, 2002, 1:917–21.

37. Ricks, *Fiasco*, 47.

38. Brent Scowcroft, "Don't Attack Saddam," *Wall Street Journal*, 15 August 2002.

39. Scowcroft, "Don't Attack Saddam."

40. Scowcroft, "Don't Attack Saddam."

41. Brent Scowcroft, "America's Challenges in a Changed World," U.S. Institute of Peace Conference, 5 September 2002, www.scowcroft.com/html/announcements/announce.html (accessed 14 July 2008).

42. Scowcroft, "America's Challenges in a Changed World."

43. Scowcroft, "America's Challenges in a Changed World."

44. Scowcroft, "America's Challenges in a Changed World."

45. Quoted in Ricks, *Fiasco*, 49, 51, 58.

46. The White House, "National Security Strategy of the United States," 17 September 2002, http://georgewbush-whitehouse.archives.gov/nsc/nss/2002/index.html (accessed 16 April 2006).

47. Judy Woodruff, "Interview with Brent Scowcroft," *CNN: Inside Politics*, 9 September 2002; Tim Russert, "Interview with Brent Scowcroft," *NBC News: Meet the Press*, 15 September 2002, www.scowcroft.com/html/announcements/announce.html (accessed 14 July 2008).

48. *Public Papers of the Presidents: Bush*, 2002 (Washington, DC: Government Printing Office, 2005), 2:1751–56.

49. *Public Papers of the Presidents: Bush*, 2002, 1:1751–56.

50. Ricks, *Fiasco*, 96–98.

51. Brent Scowcroft, "Focusing on 'Success' in Iraq," *Washington Post*, 16 January 2007.

52. Quoted in Bob Woodward, *State of Denial* (New York: Simon & Schuster, 2006), 420.

53. Samuel Berger and Brent Scowcroft, *In the Wake of War: Improving U.S. Post-Conflict Capabilities: Report of an Independent Task Force Sponsored by the Council on Foreign Relations* (New York: Council on Foreign Relations Press, 2005).

54. Brent Scowcroft, "In the Wake of War: Getting Serious about Nation-Building," *The National Interest*, Fall 2005.

55. Scowcroft, "In the Wake of War."

56. Scowcroft, "Focusing on 'Success' in Iraq."

57. Brent Scowcroft, "Getting the Middle East Back on Our Side," *Washington Post*, 4 January 2007.

58. Brent Scowcroft, "The Dispensable Nation?" *The National Interest*, 1 July 2007, www.nationalinterest.org/Article.aspx?id=14778 (accessed 15 July 2010).

59. Scowcroft, "The Dispensable Nation?"

60. Scowcroft, "The Dispensable Nation?"

61. Scowcroft, "The Dispensable Nation?"

Bibliographic Essay

Brent Scowcroft's numerous publications are the essential starting place for understanding his career. The most important of these are "Congress and Foreign Policy: An Examination of Congressional Attitudes toward the Foreign Aid Programs to Spain and Yugoslavia" (Ph.D. dissertation, Columbia University, 1967); "Deterrence and Strategic Superiority," *Orbis* 13, no. 2 (1969): 435–54; "American Attitudes toward Foreign Policy," *Naval War College Review* 32, no. 2 (1979): 11–19; with John C. Campbell and Andrew Jackson Goodpaster, *Oil and Turmoil: Western Choices in the Middle East/The Atlantic Council's Special Working Group on the Middle East* (Boulder, CO: Westview Press, 1979); with Kenneth Rush and Joseph J. Wolf, *The Credibility of the NATO Deterrent: Bringing the NATO Deterrent up to Date/The Council's Working Group on the Credibility of the NATO Deterrent* (Washington, DC: Atlantic Council, 1981); *Military Service in the United States* (Englewood Cliffs, NJ: Prentice Hall, 1982); with Kenneth Rush and Joseph J. Wolf, *Strengthening Deterrence: NATO and the Credibility of Western Defense in the 1980s: The Atlantic Council's Working Group on the Credibility of the NATO Deterrent* (Boston: Ballinger Publishing, 1982); forward to *Presidential Control of Foreign Policy: Management or Mishap?* by Robert E. Hunter (New York: Praeger, 1982); *Report of the President's Commission on Strategic Forces (the Scowcroft Report)* (Washington, DC: Government Printing Office, 1983); with James R. Greene, *Western Interests and U.S. Policy Options in the Caribbean Basin: Report of the Atlantic Council's Working Group on the Caribbean Basin* (Boston: Oelgeschlager, Gunn & Hain, 1984); forward to *The Presidency and National Security Policy*, by R. Gordon Hoxie and Ryan J. Barilleaux (New York: Center

203

for the Study of the Presidency and Congress, 1984); with John Tower and Edmund S. Muskie, *The Tower Commission Report: The Full Text of the President's Special Review Board* (New York: Bantam, 1987); with James R. Woolsey and Thomas H. Etzold, *Defending Peace and Freedom: Toward Strategic Stability in the Year 2000* (Lanham, MD: University Press of America, 1988); with John H. McElroy, *A More Effective Civil Space Program: The Final Report of the CSIS Study of Civil Space Policy* (Washington, DC: Center for Strategic and International Studies, 1989); his memoir with George H. W. Bush *A World Transformed* (New York: Knopf, 1998); with Bob Graham and Michael Shifter, *Toward Greater Peace and Security in Colombia: Forging a Constructive U.S. Policy: Report of an Independent Task Force* (New York: Council on Foreign Relations Press, 2000); "Don't Attack Saddam," *Wall Street Journal*, 15 August 2002; with Samuel Berger, *In the Wake of War: Improving U.S. Post-Conflict Capabilities: Report of an Independent Task Force Sponsored by the Council on Foreign Relations* (New York: Council on Foreign Relations Press, 2005); "The Dispensable Nation?" *National Interest*, 1 July 2007. A joint interview of Scowcroft and Zbigniew Brzezinski by David Ignatius, *America and the World: Conversations on the Future of American Foreign Policy* (New York: Basic Books, 2008) is also valuable. In addition, see Scowcroft's opinion pieces and interviews cited in the endnotes.

Manuscript collections that contain significant amounts of material on Scowcroft are the Gerald R. Ford Presidential Library, Ann Arbor, Michigan, for his first term as national security advisor, and the George H. W. Bush Presidential Library, College Station, Texas, for his second term as national security advisor. The National Archives, College Park, Maryland, has the Richard Nixon Presidential Materials, National Security Council Files, for the National Security Council Records from Scowcroft's service as a military advisor to the NSC and deputy assistant to the president for national security affairs; the Chile Declassification Project Records regarding American policy toward Chile during the 1970s; and Record Group 273: Records of the National Security Council. The Jimmy Carter Presidential Library, Atlanta, Georgia, and the Ronald Reagan Presidential Library, Simi Valley, California, each have a small number of files on Scowcroft's service to the respective administrations.

There is no comprehensive study of Scowcroft's career. Bartholomew H. Sparrow, "Realism's Practitioner: Brent Scowcroft and the Making of the New World Order, 1989–1993," *Diplomatic History*, January 2010, 141–75, is a first-rate examination of his role as national security advisor to George H. W. Bush. Jeffrey Goldberg, "Breaking Ranks: What Turned Brent Scowcroft against the Bush Administration?" *New Yorker*, 31 October 2005, is insightful on Scowcroft's opposition to the Iraq War. Ivo Daalder and I. M. Destler, *In the Shadow of the Oval Office: Profiles of the National Security Advisers and the Presidents They Served—From JFK to George*

W. Bush (New York: Simon and Schuster, 2009); David Rothkopf, *Running the World: The Inside Story of the National Security Council and the Architects of American Power* (New York: Public Affairs, 2005); and Robert M. Gates, *From the Shadows: The Ultimate Insider's Story of Five Presidents and How They Won the Cold War* (New York: Simon and Schuster, 1996) compare Scowcroft favorably to others who served as national security advisors. Andrew Bacevich, *American Empire: The Realities and Consequences of U.S. Diplomacy* (Cambridge, MA: Harvard University Press, 2002) is highly critical of Scowcroft's policy toward China after Tiananmen Square. A good example of neoconservative criticism of the Gulf War can be found in Robert Kagan and William Kristol, "Toward a Neo-Reaganite Foreign Policy," *Foreign Affairs* 75, no. 4 (July/August 1996): 18–32.

For broader studies of the post–Vietnam War period, see James T. Patterson, *Restless Giant: The United States from Watergate to Bush v. Gore* (New York: Oxford University Press, 2005) and Sean Wilentz, *The Age of Reagan: A History, 1974–2008* (New York: HarperCollins, 2008). On the Ford years, Douglas Brinkley, *Gerald R. Ford* (New York: Times Books, 2007) and John R. Greene, *The Presidency of Gerald R. Ford* (Lawrence: University Press of Kansas, 1995) provide good introductions to the issues of the time. See Gerald R. Ford, *A Time to Heal* (New York: Harper and Row, 1979) for Scowcroft's crucial role in formulating the administration's foreign policy and the president's assessment of his national security advisor. William Bundy, *A Tangled Web: The Making of Foreign Policy in the Nixon Presidency* (New York: Hill and Wang, 1998) is a detailed critique of foreign policy under Nixon by a former State Department official, and James Reichley, *Conservatives in an Age of Change: The Nixon and Ford Administrations* (Washington, DC: Brookings Institution, 1981) provides valuable insights based on extensive interviews with officials in both the Nixon and Ford administrations. Raymond Garthoff, *Détente and Confrontation: American-Soviet Relations from Nixon to Reagan* (Washington, DC: Brookings Institution, 1985) is essential for understanding détente.

The best introductions to neoconservative thinking are John Ehrman, *The Rise of Neoconservatism: Intellectuals and Foreign Affairs, 1945–1994* (New Haven, CT: Yale University Press, 1995); Stefan Halper and Jonathan Clarke, *America Alone: The Neo-Conservatives and the Global Order* (New York: Cambridge University Press, 2004); James Mann, *Rise of the Vulcans: The History of Bush's War Cabinet* (New York: Penguin, 2004); and Jacob Heilbrunn, *They Knew They Were Right: The Rise of the Neocons* (New York: Doubleday, 2008). For examples of Cold War triumphalism, see Francis Fukuyama, *The End of History and the Last Man* (New York: Free Press, 1992) and Tony Smith, *America's Mission: The United States and the Worldwide Struggle for Democracy in the Twentieth Century* (Princeton, NJ: Princeton University Press, 1994). Chalmers Johnson's "Blowback

Trilogy," *Blowback: The Costs and Consequences of American Empire* (New York: Metropolitan Books, 2000); *The Sorrows of Empire: Militarism, Secrecy, and the End of the Republic* (New York: Metropolitan Books, 2004); and *Nemesis: The Last Days of the American Republic* (New York: Metropolitan Books, 2006), provides a devastating critique of the triumphalist understanding of recent American foreign policy.

Douglas Little, *American Orientalism: The United States and the Middle East since 1945* (Chapel Hill: University of North Carolina Press, 2002); Peter Hahn, *Crisis and Crossfire: the United States and the Middle East since 1945* (Washington, DC: Potomac Books, 2005); and Michael B. Oren, *Power, Faith, and Fantasy: America in the Middle East, 1776 to the Present* (New York: Norton, 2007) are excellent accounts of American foreign policy and the Middle East and provide a necessary context for understanding relations with Iraq.

John R. Greene, *The Presidency of George Bush* (Lawrence: University of Kansas Press, 2000) and Timothy Naftali, *George H. W. Bush* (New York: Times Books, 2007) provide valuable introductions to the forty-first president's tenure in office. On the end of the Cold War, Michael R. Beschloss and Strobe Talbott, *At the Highest Levels: The Inside Story of the End of the Cold War* (Boston: Little, Brown, 1994) remains a good place to start; Raymond Garthoff, *The Great Transition: American-Soviet Relations and the End of the Cold War* (Washington, DC: Brookings Institute, 1994) provides a wealth of detail; Don Oberdorfer, *From the Cold War to a New Era: The United States and the End of the Soviet Union, 1983–1991* (Baltimore, MD: Johns Hopkins University Press, 1998) is a valuable journalist analysis; Christopher Maynard, *Out of the Shadow: George H. W. Bush and the End of the Cold War* (College Station: Texas A&M Press, 2008) covers the key events in 1989; and Michael J. Hogan, ed., *The End of the Cold War: Its Meaning and Implications* (New York: Cambridge University Press, 1992) provides a range of valuable views. Two new books are essential: Mary Elise Sarotte, *1989: The Struggle to Create Post–Cold War Europe* (Princeton, NJ: Princeton University Press, 2009) examines the events from the perspective of various nations; and Jeffrey A. Engel, *The Fall of the Berlin Wall: The Revolutionary Legacy of 1989* (New York: Oxford University Press, 2009) is an excellent historical analysis twenty years after the events. James Mann, *About Face: A History of America's Curious Relationship with China from Nixon to Clinton* (New York: Knopf, 1999) provides valuable context for understanding American policy during the Tiananmen Square crisis.

David Halberstam, *War in a Time of Peace: Bush, Clinton, and the Generals* (New York: Scribner, 2001) and Derek Chollet and James Goldgeier, *America between the Wars: From 11/9 to 9/11* (New York: Public Affairs, 2008) cover foreign policy at the end of the George H. W. Bush administration and during the Clinton years. Concerning American policy toward terrorism prior to 9/11, see Richard A. Clarke, *Against All Enemies: Inside America's War on Terror* (New York: Free Press, 2004), the former coordinator for security, infrastructure protection, and counterterrorism's impassioned account of his efforts to alert the government to the threat posed by al Qaeda.

George Packer, *The Assassins' Gate: America in Iraq* (New York: Farrar, Straus and Giroux, 2005); Thomas Ricks, *Fiasco: The American Military Adventure in Iraq* (New York: Penguin, 2006); and Lloyd C. Gardner, *The Long Road to Baghdad: A History of U.S. Foreign Policy from the 1970s to the Present* (New York: New Press, 2008) are excellent studies of American policy and the Iraq War. Micah L. Sifry and Christopher Cerf, eds., *The Iraq War Reader* (New York: Touchstone, 2003) contains useful documents concerning Scowcroft's disagreement with the Bush administration's policy. Bob Woodward's four books on Bush's foreign policy, *Bush at War* (New York: Simon and Schuster, 2002); *Plan of Attack* (New York: Simon and Schuster, 2004); *State of Denial: Bush at War, Part III* (New York: Simon and Schuster, 2006); and *The War Within: A Secret White House History, 2006–2008* (New York: Simon and Schuster, 2008), provide a wealth of information on the Iraq War.

Index

About the Author

David F. Schmitz is the Robert Allen Skotheim Chair of History at Whitman College. He is the author of *The Triumph of Internationalism: Franklin D. Roosevelt and a World in Crisis, 1933–1941; The United States and Right-Wing Dictatorships, 1965–1989; Thank God They're on Our Side: The United States and Right-Wing Dictatorships, 1921–1965; Henry L. Stimson: The First Wise Man; The United States and Fascist Italy, 1922–1940; and The Tet Offensive: Politics, War, and Public Opinion,* and the coeditor of, with Richard D. Challener, *Appeasement in Europe: A Reassessment of U.S. Policies,* and with T. Christopher Jespersen, *Architects of the American Century: Individuals and Institutions in Twentieth-Century U.S. Foreign Policymaking.*